SUPER
PREDATOR

SUPER PREDATOR

BILL CLINTON'S USE AND ABUSE OF BLACK AMERICA

NATHAN J. ROBINSON

CA
PRESS

TO THE 800,000.
THEY WILL NEVER BE FORGOTTEN.

*"They are often the kinds of kids
that are called 'super-predators.'
No conscience, no empathy.
We can talk about why they ended up that way,
but first we have to bring them to heel."*

—HILLARY CLINTON,
Keene, New Hampshire, 1996.

Published by:
CURRENT AFFAIRS PRESS
P.O. Box 441394
W. Somerville, MA 02144
currentaffairs.org

First U.S. Edition

Distributed in Great Britain by
JASON D.D.M. PICCADILLY, LTD.
WATERS & SMITH

ISBN 978-0692736890

LIBRARY OF CONGRESS CATALOG-IN-PUBLICATION DATA
Robinson, Nathan J.
Superpredator:
Bill Clinton's use and abuse of black america / Nathan J. Robinson
p. cm
Includes bibliographical references and index
ISBN 978-0692736890
1. Clinton, William J. 2. Political science 3. Race relations
4. Criminal justice 1. Title

TABLE OF CONTENTS

SUPER PREDATOR

BILL CLINTON'S USE AND ABUSE OF BLACK AMERICA

NATHAN J. ROBINSON

CA
PRESS

Bill Clinton engages in constructive discourse with his critics.

INTRODUCTION
"They Need to Be Brought to Heel"

O N THE EVENING OF APRIL 7TH, 2016, AT A CAMPAIGN event in Philadelphia, Bill Clinton lost his temper. Clinton had found himself noisily confronted by members of the Black Lives Matter activist group, who repeatedly interrupted his speech to denounce him. The activists carried signs that read "Welfare reform increased poverty" and "Clinton crime bill destroyed our communities."

Bristling at the protesters' continual outbursts, Clinton began to raise his voice. He challenged the activists' portrayals of his record on welfare and crime. He insisted that thanks to his policies, poverty had decreased and our streets were safer. Clinton claimed that the protesters simply didn't want to know the facts, as evidenced by the vehemence of their clamor: "They won't hush. When someone won't hush and listen, that ain't democracy. They're afraid of the truth. Don't be afraid of the truth."[1] Of course, one could perhaps take issue with Clinton's equation of hushing and democracy ("Hush and Listen" sounding like the official slogan of a folksy police state run by bayou Stalinists). But the testiest part of the exchange, and the one that made the next morning's headlines, concerned the phrase "superpredator."

The seeds of the "superpredator" scuffle were sown many years earlier. At an event in New Hampshire in 1996, Hillary Clinton had been discussing the administration's "organized effort against gangs." She described gangs as a nationwide problem, one requiring a muscly policy response, with our generation having to face up to gangs "just as in a previous generation we had an organized effort against the mob." Gangs were a scourge, she suggested, and to deal with them we must exercise the full might of the law's brawny arm. "We need to take these people on," she declared.[2]

But it was a particular couple of sentences in Hillary Clinton's gang monologue that would haunt her, and would be the direct cause of Bill Clinton's news-making outburst 20 years later. Describing the type of juvenile gang members she was referring to, Hillary said:

> *They are not just gangs of kids anymore. They are often the kinds of kids that are called 'super-predators.' No conscience, no empathy. We can talk about why they ended up that way but first we have to bring them to heel.*[3]

Her words were not controversial at the time. But in the 2016 election, they proved a source of significant embarrassment. By that time, the "tough on crime" political rhetoric of the 1990's was under strong criticism. The Black Lives Matter movement arose as a reaction to decades of abusive policing practices and failed criminal justice policies. To a new generation of activists, Hillary's having called kids "superpredators" seemed perverse.

At first, Clinton seemed bewildered by the criticism. When a Black Lives Matter activist named Ashley Williams crashed a Clinton fundraiser holding a sign with the infamous quote, a tense exchange ensued:

HILLARY CLINTON: I think we've got somebody saying [something] here, have you? [reading sign] "Bring them to heel?"

ASHLEY WILLIAMS: We want you to apologize for mass incarceration. I'm not a superpredator, Hillary Clinton.

CLINTON: Okay fine, we'll talk about it.

WILLIAMS: Will you apologize to black people for mass incarceration?

CLINTON: Well, can I talk, and then maybe you can listen to what I say. Fine. Thank you very much. There are a lot of issues in this campaign. The very first speech that I gave back in April was about criminal justice reform.

WILLIAMS: You called black people "superpredators."

UNIDENTIFIED FUNDRAISER ATTENDEE: You're being inappropriate, that's rude.

WILLIAMS: She called black people "superpredators," *that* is rude.

CLINTON: Do you want to hear the facts or do you just want to talk?

WILLIAMS: I know that you called black people "superpredators" in 1994,[4] please explain it to us. You owe black people an apology.

CLINTON: If you give me a chance to talk, I'll come to your side... You know what! Nobody's ever asked me [this] before. You're the first person to ask me and I am happy to address it. But you are the first person to ask me.[5]

At that point, Clinton moved on, and Williams was escorted from the event by Secret Service. But faced with the prospect of continuing to be dogged by sign-wielding Black Lives Matter supporters, Clinton soon repudiated her use of the phrase in a conversation with *The Washington Post*'s Jonathan Capehart. "Looking back," she said, "I shouldn't have used those words, and I wouldn't use them today."[6] She emphasized her commitment to children, and mentioned the importance of ending the notorious "school-to-prison pipeline" that ensnares so many young African Americans.

Given that Hillary herself had just disowned the words and apologized for using them, one might therefore have expected Bill Clinton to display a similar contrition when confronted by the activists in Philadelphia. But when they mentioned the phrase "superpredator," he exploded in unqualified defense of the term:

> *I don't know how you would describe the gang leaders who got 13-year-olds hopped up on crack and sent them out in the streets to murder other African-American children! Maybe you thought they were good citizens, [Hillary] didn't. You are defending the people who kill the lives you say matter.*[7]

Clinton went on to defend every aspect of his criminal justice policy, chiding the activists by suggesting that they didn't care about victims. This was despite his having previously apologized to the NAACP for his role in expanding the prison system, saying "I signed a bill that made the problem worse... and I want to admit it."[8]

Clinton's acidic hectoring of the Philadelphia activists quickly made the news. Charles Pierce of *Esquire* accused Clinton of not having any idea what Black Lives Matter actually stands for.[9] Steven Thrasher of *The Guardian* said the incident was telling of Clinton's character, exposing "how ugly, racist and narcissistic he really is."[10] Michelle Goldberg of *Slate* said Bill Clinton had become a liability to Hillary's campaign and should be fired.[11] Goldberg said it was "baffling" that Bill Clinton, after previously disowning his crime policy, would go back to defending it. It seemed an insanity for Clinton to now justify such measures as being in the interest of black lives, and indeed Goldberg openly wondered whether he was "slipping, mentally."

Bill Clinton's words were certainly curious. A man who has always portrayed himself as a friend to black Americans, Clinton had seemed just as sincere in his apology for his actions as in his later defense of them. Which was the real Clinton: the one who apologized for his crime bill, or the one who snapped at people who criticized his crime bill? Was Clinton a good-hearted and progressive-minded criminal justice reformer, or an insensitive relic of the "tough on crime" era who still believed in conservative fables about roving sociopathic African American preteens? To many observers, the whole thing seemed paradoxical.

But for those acquainted with Clinton's political history, there was nothing especially "baffling" about his behavior in Philadelphia. His stance was not unpredictable or inscrutable, nor was it the product of some senile bewilderment. Rather, it was simply the most blatant expression of traits that have been present in Clinton's character since his early political career. From the very beginning, Clinton's political success has been built on his skillful maneuvering between different rhetorical stances, his "triangulation" between right and left.

Bill Clinton has always been a person who says one thing to the NAACP, and another to white audiences. What happened in Philadelphia may have startled the young black activists who sought to challenge Clinton, but it shouldn't have. For twenty years, Bill Clinton has shown a tendency to reverse himself on prior commitments, most especially those made to African American constituencies.

Perhaps the only surprising thing about this is that anybody is still surprised.

THE MYTH OF THE "SUPERPREDATOR" WOULD HAVE TERRIBLE consequences for American children. In the mid-1990s, fueled by alarmist pseudoscholarship by quack criminologists, a number of politicians sounded the alarm about a concerning new trend: the rise of a new breed of sociopathic juvenile delinquent, incapable of empathy and hell-bent on robbing, raping, and terrorizing every decent churchgoing Middle American community.

The 1980's and 1990's were a heyday for nationwide moral panics. The coming of the superpredators was just one of the paralyzing terrors of the period, which also included widespread fear of Satanic abuse at daycares and razorblades in Halloween candy. The superpredator legend, however, was more deeply insidious. The term was coined by John DiIulio, Jr., a professor at Princeton University. DiIulio interpreted rising juvenile crime statistics to mean that a "new breed" of juvenile offender had been born, one who was "stone cold,"[12] "fatherless, Godless, and jobless,"[13] and had "absolutely no respect for human life and no sense of the future."[14]

DiIulio and his coauthors elaborated that superpredators were:

> *Radically impulsive, brutally remorseless youngsters,*
> *including ever more preteenage boys, who murder,*
> *assault, rape, rob, burglarize, deal deadly drugs,*
> *join gun-toting gangs, and create serious communal*
> *disorders. They do not fear the stigma of arrest, the*
> *pains of imprisonment, or the pangs of conscience.*
> *They perceive hardly any relationship between*
> *doing right (or wrong) now and being rewarded*
> *(or punished) for it later. To these mean-street*
> *youngsters, the words "right" and "wrong" have no*
> *fixed moral meaning.*[15]

For devising this theory, DiIulio was rewarded with an invitation to the White House, where he and a group of other experts spent three-and-a-half hours with President Clinton, dining on "gourmet Szechwan wonton and lamb."[16]

Confirming DiIulio's analysis was James Q. Wilson, the conservative political scientist who had devised the theory of "broken windows" policing. The broken windows theory posited that minor crimes in a neighborhood (such as the breaking of windows) tended to lead to major ones, so police should harshly focus on rounding up petty criminals if they wanted to prevent major violent crimes. Put into practice, this amounted to the endless apprehension of fare jumpers and homeless squeegee people. It also created the intellectual justification for totalitarian "stop and frisk" policies that introduced an exasperating and often terrifying ordeal into nearly every young black New Yorker's life. "Broken windows" had very little academic support[17] (it hadn't been introduced in a peer-reviewed journal, but in a short article for *The Atlantic* magazine[18]), but Wilson still felt confident in pronouncing on the "superpredator" phenomenon. He predicted that by the year 2000, "there will be a million more people between the ages of 14 and 17 than there are now" and "six percent of them will become high rate, repeat offenders—thirty thousand more young muggers, killers and thieves than we have now."[19] DiIulio and Wilson said that it was past time to panic. "Get ready," warned Wilson.[20] Not only were the superpredators here, but a lethal tsunami of them was rising in the distance, preparing to engulf civilization.

As James C. Howell documents, just a year later, as crime rates continued to decrease, DiIulio "pushed the horizon back 10 years and raised the ante."[21] This time DiIulio projected that "by the year 2010, there will be approximately 270,000 more juvenile super-predators on the streets than there were in 1990."[22] Like a Baptist apocalypse forecaster, the moment the sky didn't fall according to prophecy, a new doomsday was announced, with just as much confidence as the last.

So despite all evidence to the contrary, segments of the right continued to anticipate "a bloodbath of teenager-perpetrated violence,"[23] perpetrated by "radically impulsive, brutally remorseless" "elementary school youngsters who pack guns instead of lunches" and "have absolutely no respect for human life."[24] The notion gained political cache, and was spoken of in Congress and on the national media. It even was even propagated, and given a major credibility boost, by one or two prominent liberals, perhaps the most prominent of whom was Hillary Rodham Clinton.

There was always a race element to the superpredator theory, which is why *The New Jim Crow* author and legal scholar Michelle Alexander says Clinton "used racially coded rhetoric to cast black children as animals."[25] It wasn't just subtext; DiIulio spoke in explicitly racial terms. "By simple math," he wrote, "in a decade today's 4-to-7-year-olds will become 14-to-17-year-olds. By 2005, the number of males in this age group will have risen about 25 percent overall *and 50 percent for blacks.* [emphasis added] To some extent, it's just that simple: More boys begets more bad boys…. [The additional boys will mean] more murderers, rapists and muggers on the streets than we have today."[26] DiIulio speculated that "the demographic bulge of the next 10 years will unleash an army of young male predatory street criminals who will make even the leaders of the Bloods and Crips—known as OGs, for 'original gangsters'—look tame by comparison…"[27] DiIulio explained that these boys traveled in "wolf packs," and that black violence "tended to be more serious" than white violence, "for example, aggravated assaults rather than simple assaults, and attacks involving guns rather than weaponless violence."[28] Michelle Alexander may therefore overstate the extent to which the superpredator language was "coded" in the first place; the theory's most prominent advocate was openly stating that the "wolves" in question were black. He could not really have been more explicit about his meaning if he had simply written the n-word over and over on the op-ed page of the *Wall Street Journal.*

In the years since, nearly everyone has abandoned the super-predator story, for the essential reason that it was, to put it simply, statistically illiterate race-baiting pseudoscience. As a group of criminologists explained in a brief to the Supreme Court, "the fear of an impending generation of superpredators proved to be unfounded. Empirical research that has analyzed the increase in violent crime during the early- to mid-1990s and its subsequent decline demonstrates that the juvenile superpredator was a myth and the predictions of future youth violence were baseless."[29] In fact, the criminologists had "been unable to identify any scholarly research published in the last decade that provides support for the notion of the juvenile superpredator."[30] Among the criminologists who filed the brief were John DiIulio and James Q. Wilson, who humbly conceded that their findings had been in error.

The harm done to young people, however, was incalculable. Having been scientifically diagnosed as remorseless and demonic, poor children accused of crimes were increasingly given the kind of harsh punishments previously reserved for adults. New York University criminologist Mark Kleiman says there was a direct link between that single "fallacious bit of science" and the expansion of the use of the adult justice system to prosecute children. "Based on [the superpredator theory]," Kleiman writes, "dozens of states passed laws allowing juveniles to be tried and sentenced as adults, with predictably disastrous results."[31] As the Equal Justice Initiative has observed, "the superpredator myth contributed to the dismantling of transfer restrictions, the lowering of the minimum age for adult prosecution of children, and it threw thousands of children into an ill-suited and excessive punishment regime."[32] In early 1996, the *Sunday Mail* described the panic that was overtaking Illinois:

> *'It's Lord of the Flies on a massive scale,' Chicago's Cook County State Attorney Jack O'Malley said... We've become a nation being terrorized by our children...' Already, the State of Illinois has introduced new laws to deal with this terrifying new 'crime bomb,' ruling that children as young as 10 will be sent to juvenile jails. The State is rushing construction of its first 'kiddie prison' to replace the traditional, less punitive 'youth detention facility' to enforce the get-tough policy of jail cells instead of cozy dormitories.*[33]

The shift to viewing kids as comparable to the worst adult offenders allowed all manner of abuses to be inflicted on young people for whom the effects are especially damaging. Juvenile solitary confinement has been routinely used in American prisons, despite having been recognized as a form of torture by United Nations Human Rights Committee.[34] Kids have been held in tiny cells for 23 hours per day, leading to madness and suicide. The practice produces stories such as that of Kalief Browder, who was sent to Rikers Island jail at the age of 16, spending two years in solitary confinement awaiting trial for stealing a backpack, and ultimately killing himself after finally being released and having the charges dropped.[35] A joint report by the ACLU and Human Rights Watch, which interviewed over 100 people who had been held in solitary confinement while under the age of 18, summarized some of the intense psychological torment inflicted:

> *Many of the young people interviewed spoke in harrowing detail about struggling with one or more of a range of serious mental health problems during their time in solitary. They talked about thoughts of suicide and self-harm; visual and auditory hallucinations; feelings of depression; acute anxiety;*

shifting sleep patterns; nightmares and traumatic memories; and uncontrollable anger or rage. Some young people, particularly those who reported having been identified as having a mental disability before entering solitary confinement, struggled more than others. Fifteen young people described cutting or harming themselves or thinking about or attempting suicide one or more times while in solitary confinement.[36]

Housing juveniles in adult facilities can be an equally inhumane practice in itself. As the weakest members of the population, juveniles housed in adult facilities are likely to be brutally raped by older inmates,[37] and are at an increased risk of suicide.[38] T.J. Parsell was sent to prison in Michigan at the age of 17 for robbing $53 from a one-hour photo store using a toy gun. He describes his arrival:

On my first day there—the same day that my classmates were getting ready for the prom—a group of older inmates spiked my drink, lured me down to a cell and raped me. And that was just the beginning. Laughing, they bragged about their conquest and flipped a coin to see which one of them got to keep me. For the remainder of my nearly five-year sentence, I was the property of another inmate.[39]

Teenagers like Parsell were being housed in adult facilities long before the "superpredator" horror stories. But the more young offenders are dehumanized, the more dilapidated becomes the thin barrier of empathy that keeps society from inflicting psychological, physical, and emotional torment on the weak. As criminal justice journalist Natasha Vargas-Cooper writes, while "the scourge of the super-predators never came to be…

the infrastructure for cruelty, torture, and life-long captivity of juvenile offenders was cemented."[40]

But to say the "superpredator" notion has been "discredited" is to overestimate the extent to which it was accepted in the first place, and risks exonerating those who recited the term during the mid-90s. The moment the "superpredator" concept was introduced, reputable criminologists stepped forward to rebut it. Few serious scholars gave the notion any credence, and they made their objections loudly known. "Everybody believes that just because it sounds good," the research director of the National Center for Juvenile Justice told the press in 1996.[41] Harvard government professor David Kennedy said that "What this whole super-predator argument misses is that [increasing teen violence] is not some inexorable natural progression" but rather the product of "very specific" social dynamics such as the easy availability of guns.[42] Other public policy experts called the idea "unduly alarmist" and said its proponents "lack a sense of history and comparative criminology."[43] DiIulio himself didn't try to persuade the rest of his field; *The Toronto Star* reported that "asked recently to cite research supporting his theory, DiIulio declined to be interviewed."[44])

The political conservatism of the theory was hardly smuggled in under cover of night. DiIulio's "Coming of the Super Predators" first appeared in William Kristol's conservative *Weekly Standard*,[45] and the handful of scholars who peddled the theory had strong, open ties to right-wing politics, so it was plainly partisan rather than scholastic. Even the language used by the professors, of "Godless" and "brutal" juveniles without "fixed values," was plainly the talk of Republican Party moralists, rather than dispassionate social scientists. Nobody in the professional circles of a "children's rights" liberal like Hillary Clinton would have given the "superpredator" concept a lick of intellectual credence, even when it was at the peak of its infamy.

It was therefore deeply wrong to spread the lie even when it was most popular. Yet to defend it in 2016 is on another level entirely. When Bill Clinton said in Philadelphia that he didn't know how else one would describe the kids who got "13 year olds hopped up on crack and sent them out to murder" other kids, he revived an ugly legend that led to the incarceration and rape of scores of young people.

Speaking this way can still have harmful ripple effects. When *Washington Post* writer Jonathan Capehart reported Hillary Clinton's apology for her remark, he implied that superpredators did exist, but that they didn't include upstanding young people like the Black Lives Matter activist who had challenged Clinton.[46] Old wives' tales are slow to die, and people's fear of teen superpredators is easily revived. It took years to debunk this folktale the first time around; once people believe that young people are potential superpredators, fear takes over their decision-making, and they become willing to impose truly barbaric punishments on kids who break the law. After all, if such offenders are not actually children, but superpredators, one need not empathize with them. One can talk in terms like "bring them to heel," which is the sort of thing one says about a dog.

IT MAY HAVE BEEN SURPRISING, GIVEN THAT HILLARY CLINTON has made a strong effort to connect with African American voters, that Bill Clinton would have revived a nasty racist cliché about animalistic juveniles. But in fact, this simultaneous maintenance of warmth toward individual African Americans and support for policies that hurt the African American community has been a consistent inconsistency throughout Bill Clinton's political career.

Bill Clinton has long been famous for his unusually congenial relationship with black people. Part of this comes from African Americans' respect for Clinton's rise from a humble Southern upbringing; Jesse Jackson, Jr. said that "African Americans iden-

tify with Bill Clinton's personal story and personal experience."[47]
But many who met Clinton were also impressed by how comfortable and natural he seemed when interacting with black people.
Unlike most white politicians, who even when well-intentioned
become clumsy and guilt-ridden in conversations with people
of other races, Bill Clinton seemed to legitimately enjoy spending time around African Americans. "He would throw his arm
around a black person and shoot the breeze," recounts former
Congressional Black Caucus leader Kweisi Mfume. "He had a way
of connecting with black folks that most presidents simply didn't
have."[48] Clinton golfed regularly with his black advisor and best
friend Vernon Jordan, and seemed to love attending black church
services and schmoozing with parishioners; for the President to
actually have preexisting close personal relationships with black
people was unprecedented. "He understands the black experience," says Harvard Law School professor Charles Ogletree.[49]

But Clinton's personal warmth toward African Americans did
not translate into policies that favored their interests. Throughout his presidency, Clinton's actual actions on issues relevant to
black Americans were at odds with his repeated rhetorical commitments to civil rights and racial equality. Clinton presided over
a massive continuing expansion of the American prison system,
escalated the War on Drugs, and made it easier to administer
the death penalty while opposing an effort by black legislators
to prohibit racially biased capital punishment. In social policy,
Clinton campaigned on a plan to end the welfare system, and
successfully did so, promoting, passing, and signing an act that
all but eliminated government financial support for poor families. And Clinton's deregulation of the financial system laid the
foundation for the disastrous economic crisis that would wipe
out black wealth a few years after he left office.[50]

In fact, when Bill Clinton's actions, rather than his words, are
scrutinized closely, they reveal a record far more damaging to

black interests than that of even many Republican presidents. George W. Bush, for all his atrocities abroad, never signed any law that inflicted the kind of harm that Clinton's crime and welfare policies did. As Michelle Alexander has observed, Clinton escalated the War on Drugs "beyond what many conservatives had imagined possible… ultimately doing more harm to black communities than Reagan ever did."[51] Historian Christopher Brian Booker refers to Clinton's "central role in the incarceration binge in the black community,"[52] and Charles Ogletree has called it "shocking and regrettable that more African Americans were incarcerated on Bill Clinton's watch than any other president's in the history of the United States."[53]

Yet despite the record of his presidency, Clinton always has managed to maintain a sense of goodwill among a large majority of African Americans. In 2002, he was inducted into the Arkansas Black Hall of Fame alongside Al Green, as the first white inductee in the Hall of Fame's 10-year existence.[54] Clinton's African American former Transportation Secretary Rodney Slater has called him a "soul brother" who "wanted our love and wanted to share his love with us."[55] And though the quote's original context became mangled over time, Toni Morrison's remark about Clinton as the "first black president" has stuck as a label for Clinton, with plenty of blacks acknowledging that, even if Clinton wasn't the first black president, he was certainly the first president that black people truly liked.

He therefore escaped serious blowback in the black community, even as the prisons became engorged with young black men and young black mothers were cast into low-paying jobs by Clinton's Dickensian "workfare" initiative. Because Clinton gave the appearance of caring, which no other president before him had done, he was cut a stunning amount of slack. As African American Arkansas newspaper columnist Deborah Mathis explained, "they made allowances for Bill Clinton because they thought that his heart was good and it didn't matter that some of his policies were lacking."[56] Clinton would always be sure to meet with and listen to black leaders before inevitably double-crossing them. The respect Clinton showed toward black advisors and congressmen (he never missed the annual dinner of the Congressional Black Caucus) went a long way to help him earn their forgiveness for his actual substantive decisions. Black Entertainment Television CEO Robert Johnson explained that by "[g]iving props to black folks for coming out and voting, going to churches saying 'you're the reason I'm here and I will always be there for you,' the guy could get away with anything."[57] Indeed, Clinton got away with nearly everything, earning very little flak from black voters even as he betrayed nearly every one of their policy priorities.

To suggest that this means black voters were somehow "fooled" by Clinton would be both demeaning and untrue. Certainly, it seems paradoxical that Clinton could remain beloved by a constituency on whom his policies inflicted terrible harm, and whose ideals he shamelessly betrayed over and over. But the explanation offered by Clinton's African American supporters, that it was simply *nice to actually be listened to for once,* is perfectly understandable. Clinton spoke to black voters like they mattered, and in a way that didn't seem patronizing or forced, and in doing so instantly differentiated himself from every single other white politician in the country.

But one doesn't have to imply that Clinton hoodwinked black voters in order to point out that this achievement, in itself, is not really an achievement at all. "Treating Black America like it exists" may have won Clinton first prize among white people, but it really shouldn't win anybody a prize at all. In reality, *not* treating Black America like it exists is an outrage, and what Clinton did should be the basic precondition of being a moral human being. It in no way delegitimizes the feelings of African Americans to argue that they had the right to expect more. Mere acknowledgment may be nice, but to put someone into the Black Hall of Fame because he was a non-patronizing Southerner sets a very low standard indeed. Naturally, black expectations for white politicians were never going to be very high. But if playing the saxophone and putting a black man in charge of the Transportation Department are sufficient actions to earn a pass for mass incarceration, politicians will feel little need to make an effort toward materially adjusting America's substantive racial inequities.

It's possible that, after examining the evidence, one could still think that Bill Clinton deserves the respect that black Americans have given him. But since the full facts are rarely assembled, it's not unreasonable to think that some of the positive judgments would change if they incorporated the history more fully. It is therefore worth going systematically through Bill Clinton's actions, distinguishing truths from impression, spin from substance.

In doing so, we can hopefully develop an informed evaluation of Clinton's record on race. It is possible that this will reaffirm the idea of Clinton as the nation's "first black president," a "soul brother" who fought great opposition to advance the cause of civil rights. But it's also possible that the record may show something different. When Clinton's actions are set against his words, and we try to fairly and carefully figure out what his motivation could possibly have been, the popularly received image of him cannot hold up. There are simply too many points at which a person who honestly cared about the wellbeing of the black community could not have acted in the way Clinton did. There are too many instances in which Clinton was vested with total discretion over his course of action, yet chose the course that would make African Americans worse off and Clinton himself better off.

Motivations are difficult things to analyze; people can only ever see one another from the outside, so all statements of others' intentions must necessarily be speculative. But if a person purports to hold certain essential beliefs, we can ask whether their actions are consistent with their beliefs, and whether someone with those beliefs would have taken those actions.

In the case of Bill Clinton, while he is plainly not a white supremacist, three competing perspectives on the evidence can be debated. Clinton is either (1) a person sincerely committed to racial justice, who tried his best to advance it given limited political constraints, (2) a person who wants to be politically successful and adored, and is committed to racial justice only to the extent that it goes toward bringing about political success and adoration, or (3) a person who is both committed to racial justice and intensely desirous of success and adoration.

In order to test which of these theories is true, it is necessary to see which of them explains all the known historical facts. The third theory, that Clinton is a complex mixture of both imperatives, may seem intuitively the most plausible. But the hypothesis of this book is as follows: Bill Clinton has never given any indication whatsoever that he is committed to racial justice, except to the extent that it serves his personal interests. While Bill Clinton has offered a great deal of lip service to wanting to end American racism, in *every single* instance in which he was challenged to make his actions conform with his belief in the principle, he did not. Whenever Clinton was asked to "put his money where his mouth was," he refused. This means that there is no evidence to conclude that Clinton was a "mixture" of good intention and political calculation; at no point did Clinton make a non-calculated decision.

The key question here concerns *sacrifice*: if a person truly believes that racial equality is a principle worth fighting for, she would be willing to give something up in order to achieve it. Clinton's principles, by contrast, ceased to exist the moment they came at even a small personal or political cost, meaning that they couldn't have existed at all.

Let us imagine two business owners in early 1960's Alabama. They are both proprietors of lunch counters, and both have decided to integrate and begin serving black patrons. But only one of them has decided to integrate because he detests racism. The other has decided to integrate because he has come to believe that segregation is unprofitable; black diners comprise a whole new untapped customer base. Both of these people's *actions* are the same, but one of them believes in fighting racism, and one of them believes in making money. If the two outcomes look the same, how can we tell who cares about racism and who cares only about his own bottom line?

The test comes when having an integrated lunch counter becomes *unprofitable.* If someone is committed to integration as a principle, then if integration comes at a cost, it will not change that person's commitment. But if someone is committed to integration simply because discrimination means excluding potential customers, then if white customers started offering huge premiums for segregated dining experiences, a pure profiteer would reverse course. Adjust the financial incentives, and you'll find out who is committed to what for which reasons and to what degree.

The point here is this: nobody is a "good" person if she takes morally right actions only when they benefit her personally. For this means she is perfectly willing to take morally wrong actions, *at the right price.* She may go through life looking like a benevolent angel, because the right thing and the profitable thing happen to have frequently coincided. But the test of whether she *is* an angel will come when she is asked to make a sacrifice. If someone truly cares about justice, as opposed to caring mostly about "being liked by black people," then they would be willing to risk their popularity if it meant advancing justice. How do you know whether someone is committed to justice or merely self-interest? Watch what happens when that person is forced to choose between the two.

Bill Clinton took many progressive steps on race; he appointed an unprecedented number of black officials and gave black leaders a "seat at the table" politically. But *taking progressive steps on race does not make one a racial progressive.* It may mean one is not a *racist,* but like the business owner who cares about African Americans solely to the extent that they buy milkshakes at his lunch counter, it doesn't mean one has anything that can be called a "good heart." A good-hearted person will stand up for you when things get tough; an egotist will be your best friend until the moment he's asked to give something up, at which point he'll swiftly vamoose. If all the paeans and patronage that Clinton gave to African Americans were simply to garner black loyalty and to flatter his own self-conception, then there is nothing to be admired. A person who is not racist, but is amorally committed to political advancement, will nevertheless end up perpetrating racist acts. After all, if he is happy to serve any dominant political interest, then he will happily serve the interests of white supremacists, should those interests happen to predominate or serve his success.

The facts should thus be examined carefully in order to determine whether Clinton was truly an amoral politico or a constrained progressive. And ultimately, as will be seen, the characterization of Clinton as a flawed but sincere friend to black America is impossible to square with those facts. A friend is someone who will lift a finger to help you; Clinton would quite literally not even do that.

Bill Clinton is not a sinister man. He doesn't go through the world *desiring* to inflict pain. But the extremity of his narcissism, and his negligible commitment to his stated values, make him something that is ultimately equally toxic. For Clinton doesn't *care* whether he inflicts pain. He is an affable but ruthless opportunist, one who ended up treating black people with an unparalleled cruelty and cynicism, and whose progressive racial rhetoric masked a willingness to devastatingly harm black communities in the service of self-interested political ends.

As a matter of fact, when we examine the record closely, we may find a certain familiar kind of character emerging, one we've heard of somewhere before: an individual who is "stone cold," thinking only of himself and his own gratification, willing to harm anyone who gets in his way. An individual "brutal" and "without fixed values," and with little regard for the boundaries of right and wrong. Not your typical *predator*, but perhaps something far worse, and ultimately far more dangerous…

Thus while it may have turned out that there were no hordes of superpredators lurking in the dingy shadows of our metropolises, such creatures do exist. As for "no conscience, no empathy," when it comes to black lives, a certain former President closely matches the suspect's description.

But while we can talk about how he ended up that way, it may be too late to bring him to heel.

Clinton is applauded for Making America Safer.

CHAPTER ONE
Tough on Crime

O N THANKSGIVING EVENING IN 1915, WILLIAM J. Simmons gathered fifteen men, and ascended the windy summit of Georgia's imposing Stone Mountain, just outside of Atlanta. Atop the mountain, they built an altar of sixteen boulders, upon which they placed an American flag, a copy of the Holy Bible, and an unsheathed sword. Then, standing in the moonlight, they raised an enormous wooden cross, and set it alight. With "the angels" watching over them "shout[ing] hosannas," Simmons and his men pronounced the Ku Klux Klan newly reborn, and inaugurated a new and terrible phase for an organization that had lain dormant for several decades.[58] This was the beginning, they declared, of a new Imperial Empire.

1915 was the year of D.W. Griffith's notorious Klan-glorifying blockbuster *Birth of a Nation*, which romanticized the role of terrorist posses in the post-Civil War South and created a nationwide burst of nostalgia for the great halcyon years of white supremacy.

1915 was also the year of the Leo Frank lynching. Frank, the director of an Atlanta pencil factory, had been wrongfully convicted of strangling a 13-year-old employee at the factory, Mary Phagan. When Frank's death sentence was commuted to life imprisonment, a mob of local worthies (including an ex-Governor and the future president of the State Senate) tore him from his prison cell and hanged him from a tree in Marietta.[59]

It was in the fervor of white bloodlust emerging from the Frank killing and the Griffith film that William J. Simmons and his band of enthusiastic bigots ascended Stone Mountain. They would initiate what is known as the "Second Klan," which eagerly and viciously picked up where the first left off. The organization's original anti-black mission statement expanded to encompass all-new violent intolerances, such as anti-Catholicism, anti-Semitism, and xenophobia.

In the years following the Klan's resurrection ceremony, Stone Mountain became an iconic site for American white supremacists. The group held regular events there, having been granted a special easement by the mountain's owners. In the 1920s, they began fundraising with the United Daughters of the Confederacy,[60] for the purposes of erecting an enormous monument to the Confederacy on the mountain's face. Over the next 50 years, dedicated Georgians gradually managed to commission the largest bas-relief sculpture in the world: a breathtakingly imposing carving towering 400 feet above the ground and measuring 1.5 square acres, depicting Jefferson Davis, Stonewall Jackson, and Robert E. Lee astride charging stallions. The initial sculpting of the stunning monument was by a Klansman named Gutzon Borglum, who would become well-known for his work on what is perhaps the only more physically impressive monument in America: Mount Rushmore.[61]

With its supersized granite tribute to the heroes of the Old South, Stone Mountain Park became a gathering spot for America's un-Reconstructed neo-Confederates. For most of the 20th century it held the Klan's annual Labor Day cross-burning,[62] and well into the 1990's it was hosting an "antebellum jubilee," "complete with hoop skirts and a decked-out pre-Civil War plan-tation."[63] The streets around the park were (and still are) named for Davis, Jackson, and Lee, and the summertime laser-shows it projected onto the mountainside had a elaborate final sequence featuring an enormous Confederate flag and a recording of Elvis singing "Dixie." (Black laser enthusiasts would occasionally boo at the grotesque finale.[64]) All of this made the mountain a site of deep contention over racial symbolism, in fact "one of the most sensitive locations in Georgia."[65] Georgia Congressman and civil rights legend John Lewis said that when he first moved to the Atlanta area, "we didn't dare go to Stone Mountain because that's where the Klan had rallies."[66]

The rallies persisted until 1991.[67] A speaker at the 1985 event called for a new wave of "white vigilantes" across the country. "Death to the race mixers," he said, forecasting that "when the hour of retribution strikes, there will be 10 million dead ones in America."[68] A firsthand report from another 1980's event described the surreal sight of "kiosks selling popcorn, soft drinks, and KKK T-shirts."[69] (Several concessions to modernization had been made, namely the presence of a few Klansmen in business suits and the fact that organizers insisted the event was to be called a "cross lighting" rather than a "cross burning."[70])

The town of Stone Mountain itself also became a "white supremacist mecca,"[71] sitting as it did in the shadow of the "shrine of the Ku Klux Klan."[72] In 1988, it voted to name a park after the notorious Imperial Wizard who had been instrumental in building the monument, and who had also designed the Klan's second-generation robes.[73] (After controversy, the decision was rescinded. Instead, he got an official plaque in the park and had a small lake named after him.[74])

There was a reason, then, that in Dr. Martin Luther King's "I Have a Dream Speech," he made sure to single out a specific plea: "let freedom ring from Stone Mountain of

Georgia."[75] A dream that freedom could ring from Stone Mountain was ambitious indeed; perhaps no other location in the country has remained so closely associated with white supremacy for so long.

BILL CLINTON WAS A NEW DEMOCRAT. AND NEW DEMOCRATS, unlike the old Roosevelt liberals, were tough on crime. With the Democratic Party having lost three Presidential elections in a row, Clinton argued that political success required the jettisoning of many of the left's most cherished tenets. In particular, Clinton aimed to woo the so-called "Reagan Democrats," the somewhat socially conservative white voters who had fled the party during the 1960s and 1970s. And doing this, in part, required what Michelle Alexander calls "signaling to poor and working-class whites that he was willing to be tougher on black communities than Republicans had been."[76]

Crime was a key issue on which Clinton tried to distinguish himself in this respect. In 1988, Michael Dukakis had been relentlessly and effectively criticized by Republicans as "soft on crime." Dukakis was dogged by a Republican televised advertisement showing a hairy, menacing black inmate who had raped a woman while free on a furlough scheme that Dukakis had approved as governor.[77] Bill Clinton was determined not to suffer the same kind of attacks; nobody would accuse him of coddling "inner city" criminals. "I can be nicked on a lot," he said, "but no one can say I'm soft on crime."[78]

So he shed his platform of any soft liberal pity for the rights of criminal defendants, and brought his anti-crime rhetoric in line with that of the Republicans. He even made sure to take a detour from the campaign trail and return to Arkansas to preside over an execution. (See Chapter Six.) Clinton was concerned, first and foremost, with sending a carefully tailored message to white America. And one of the most effective deliveries of that message came in the form of a press conference held at one of the most infamous sites in the South: Stone Mountain.

In the early 1990s, though it was a town with a population of less than 6,000, Stone Mountain was home to a small state correctional facility. It was not among the state's more consequential prisons, holding only a few hundred people. Prisoners were given "boot camp" style routines and discipline, and were put to work maintaining the grounds of the monument.[79]

The complex was nestled directly at the Mountain's foot, at the outer edge of the park, just off Robert E. Lee Boulevard. It was located at 5500 Venable Street, a road named after the same legendary local Klan leader, James Venable, who ran the rallies and designed the uniforms and nearly got a park dedicated to him.[80] (The prison might as well have been at 5500 Ku Klux Klan Avenue.)

It was here that Clinton's campaign arranged an astute campaign photo opportunity, just before Super Tuesday. Clinton traveled to the out-of-the-way facility alongside other prominent conservative Southern Democrats. These included Georgia's governor, Zell Miller (later known for splashily ditching the Democratic party with a bombastic speech at the 2004 Republican National Convention, before co-chairing Newt Gingrich's 2012 bellyflop of a presidential campaign) and Senator Sam Nunn (notorious in Congress for firing staff members if he found out they were gay,[81] and for launching a relentless public crusade against the scourge of homosexualism in the American military). Tagging along with Nunn, Miller, and Clinton was Congressman Ben Jones, previously best remembered for his supporting role as "Cooter" on the *Dukes of Hazzard*[82] and more recently becoming a prominent advocate for the public display of the Confederate Flag. (According to Jones, it represents "courage and family and good times."[83])

At the Stone Mountain Correctional Institution, the four men gave a press conference, of little apparent purpose except to show them standing in front of a phalanx of dour jump-suited inmates, all but a sprinkling of whom were black. The resulting photograph, printed in the next day's newspapers (and visible on this book's cover), sent an unmistakable message. If President Clinton wanted to "signal to poor and working-class whites that he was willing to be tougher on black communities than Republicans had been," he could hardly have done better than to stand in front of a shackled mass of black men at the base of Stone Mountain.

There is little question that Clinton knew what he was doing in going to Stone Mountain. As Christopher Petrella explained in a recent *Boston Review* article about the incident, the site was too consequential and notorious, and the photo-op too perfectly aligned with Clinton's open goal of reassuring the white populace, for it to have been anything but completely deliberate:

> It is hard to imagine the DLC would not have been aware of Stone Mountain's significance as a theater of white supremacy when it staged Clinton's campaign event at the prison there. In fact, the choice of that particular place as a campaign stop—arranging white political leaders in business suits in front of subjugated black male prisoners in jumpsuits—is illegible except in light of this history.[84]

By picking such an allusive location, Clinton managed to quietly convey to the right parties that, even though he might be no white supremacist, he was not the sort of Democrat to go ripping the Stars and Bars off every last Dixie flagpole, nor one who would let members of the more troublesome races go swarming freely across the land.

Nobody mistook the message at the time. Clinton was instantly criticized by his opponents for the repugnant racial undercurrents of the event. Iowa Senator Tom Harkin said the Stone Mountain photo offered an ugly depiction of the Democratic party's priorities: "What this picture demonstrates is an insensitivity... A picture is worth a thousand words, and we can't afford to have pictures like this going around America in major newspapers because it sends the wrong message about what we want to be as Americans."[85] California governor Jerry Brown was even more forthright, saying that Clinton and the other politicians looked "like colonial masters" trying to tell white voters "Don't worry, we'll keep them in their place."[86] Brown said the implication was clear: "Two white men and forty black prisoners, what's he saying? He's saying we got 'em under control, folks."

Defending himself, Clinton accused his opponents of playing "racial politics," and insisted that the facility was for "youths" who were "get[ing] their lives back together."[87] (It is mysterious why Clinton thought it made it better rather than worse that the inmates were youths.) Clinton spokesman George Stephanopoulos called Harkin's criticism "the act of a desperate man."[88]

But the event doesn't look any better with hindsight than it did on the campaign trail. Re-examining the visual record, Tom Harkin seems less desperate than accurate: after all, the photo shows a buoyant Clinton standing in front of black kids stored in a pen at the base of an infamous Confederate monument and pilgrimage site, only a year after its Klan picnics had finally stopped. For a clutch of white politicians to pose in front of black inmates would be mildly nauseating in the most innocuous of locales; that Clinton did it with a pair of open bigots at the entrance to the "Confederate Rushmore"[89] should violently churn the stomach.

From the beginning, though, Bill Clinton had made a priority of appealing to the Reagan Democrats, that highly sought-after group of white "Middle American" voters whose support the Democrats had steadily lost during the McGovern-Carter-Mondale-Dukakis years. Clinton solidified the political cliché of targeting "the forgotten middle class," what he referred to as "the people who used to vote for us."[90]

This required subtly assuaging the fears of white voters in particular. As Democratic strategist Ted Van Dyk phrased it, Clinton's New Democratic politics were intended to signal to "Reagan Democrats that it is safe to come home to their party because poor, black, Hispanic, urban, homeless, hungry, and other people and problems out of favor in Middle America will no longer get the favored treatment they got from mushy 1960s and 1970s Democratic liberals."[91] Clinton pollster Stanley Greenberg, in an article that *The American Prospect*'s editors called "widely recognized for its influence on Bill Clinton's presidential campaign,"[92] wrote that the Democratic Party had become "too identified with minorities and special interests to speak for average Americans."[93] Clinton thus called himself "a different kind of Democrat," which observers interpreted to mean that he was "a centrist candidate more attuned than his predecessors to the concerns and values of the white, middle-class voters who had deserted the party."[94]

Clinton thus intentionally avoided paying any attention to racial injustice. In their 1992 campaign book, *Putting People First*, Clinton and Al Gore included only one mention of race: a criticism of racial quotas.[95] They did feature a chapter on civil rights, but this was "mostly about people with disabilities."[96] As political scientist Corey Robin writes, Clinton intended to "win over white voters by declaring to the American electorate: We are not the Party of Jesse Jackson, we are not the Rainbow Coalition."[97] The cynical reasoning was that since black voters were hardly likely to vote Republican, but white voters were, Democrats' political platforms should focus on issues that matter to white people. Because black voters were reliably loyal to the party (their only alternative being the party of Trent Lott, Jesse Helms, and Strom Thurmond), there was nothing to gain electorally from the pursuit of racial equality. The irony, of course, is that this meant selling out the party's strongest supporters precisely because of the strength of their support.

A major part of the new white-focused agenda involved prioritizing the issue of crime. The crime rate in the 1980s and early 1990s was especially high,[98] and with the devastating attack on Dukakis, Republicans had shown they could successfully capitalize on the widespread fear of crime in order to achieve political success. Clinton and the New Democrats believed that Democrats should never again cede this issue to the conservatives who had traditionally parlayed it into electoral success.

But while getting tough on inner-city criminals had always been a favorite mantra of the Right, it had also always been met with charges that by "inner city criminals," Republicans just meant "poor blacks." When Richard Nixon accepted the Republican nomination in 1968, his "law and order" policies were so widely seen as a euphemism for ending civil rights gains that in his convention speech he felt the need to specifically address "those who say that law and order is the code word for racism."[99] (Confirming nearly every word of his critics' charges, the defense Nixon gave of "law and order" in his speech largely involved denouncing "government programs for the unemployed" and "programs for the poor."[100])

Clinton's embrace of Republican anti-crime rhetoric was therefore unprecedented, and "signaled a dramatic shift in Democratic priorities.[101] Previously, many Democrats had resisted pressure to placate white fears with "get tough" rhetoric. During a 1988 debate, Dukakis was asked whether he would support the death penalty even if his wife Kitty was raped and murdered. "No, I don't," Dukakis replied. "I think you know that I've opposed the death penalty during all of my life. I don't see any evidence that it's a deterrent and I think there are better and more effective ways to deal with violent crime."[102] Dukakis received intense criticism for the response, for reasons he professed himself unable to fathom.[103] This generation of national liberal politicians had been unwilling to surrender their ideological commitment to compassion, even as they paid a strong electoral price for it. The 1992 Clinton campaign jettisoned that commitment, reasoning that winning elections was more important than maintaining purity of principle.

Some of this, however, was not simply the politically expedient discarding of liberal sympathies, but reflected longstanding conservative commitments on Clinton's part. Capital punishment in particular was not a "compromise" with the electorate, Clinton having consistently supported the death penalty throughout his career in politics. Clinton had never commuted a death sentence while serving as Arkansas' governor, and "from 1983 to 1993, he repeatedly ordered the Arkansas Department of Corrections to schedule execution dates for Arkansas Death Row inmates."[104] On *Saturday Night Live*, Phil Hartman's impersonation of Clinton caricatured the governor's over-the-top punitive stance, with Hartman's Clinton bragging that "no state is tougher on crime. Last year we passed Florida to become #2 in executions by lethal injection, and first in crushed by heavy stones."[105]

The newer, tougher Clinton stance caused other Democrats to follow suit, since as Daryl Carter explains, "Clinton actually sat at the head of the Democratic Party, thereby forcing Democrats to place crime prevention at the top of their domestic agenda."[106] Along with his other more conservative "New Democrat" proposals (such as ending welfare), Clinton's raising of the crime issue would help build a Democratic/Republican consensus around a number of ideas that had previously been the sole provenance of the right. And the strategy worked, insofar as it successfully kept Clinton from being painted as a bleeding-heart during the 1992 election. As University of Texas criminologist Mark Warr noted, by positioning himself as harsher than the Republicans, Clinton "neutralized that issue in a way no Democrat has been able to do for 30 years." After that, it simply "becomes a macho competition: Who hates criminals more?"[107]

Upon taking office in 1993, Bill Clinton seemed determined not to let the Republicans win that competition. Once Clinton became president, passing a "crime bill" became a major Democratic priority. Clinton's senior advisor Rahm Emanuel said in a memo that the bill would be "a vehicle to communicate to the public a set of strongly-held values that the President embraces, as well as the President's tough stance on crime and criminals."[108]

The resulting bill, the Violent Crime Control and Law Enforcement Act, signed by Clinton in 1994, was perhaps one of the harshest laws in the history of the country. But the New Democrats embraced it as being representative of their new face. Senate majority leader George Mitchell proudly claimed the crime bill for his party. "This is a Democratic bill," Mitchell declared. "The author of the bill is a Democrat. The principal supporter for this bill is a Democratic president."[109]

The crime bill overflowed with new provisions and programs. It allocated nearly $10 billion for the construction of new prisons,[110] expanded the number of death-penalty eligible federal crimes from two to fifty-eight, eliminated a statute that prohibited the execution of mentally incapacitated defendants, created special deportation courts for noncitizens accused of "engaging in terrorist activity," added new mechanisms for tracking sex offenders after they had served their sentences, introduced a "three strikes" law that gave mandatory life sentences for third offenses, gave $10.8 billion dollars to local police departments to hire 100,000 new officers, introduced "truth in sentencing" requirements and allowed children as young as thirteen to be tried as adults.[111]

"Truth in sentencing" (TIS) was a delicate political euphemism for "no more parole." Previously, it had been customary to grant a prisoner's release long before the end of his sentence. By the time of the crime bill, on average, people convicted of violent crimes served 55% of the sentences that they had been given on paper. In the new era of limitless toughness, the idea of letting murderers and members of juvenile wolfpacks out of prison early was politically toxic. The crime bill therefore required states to enact "truth in sentencing" laws if they wanted to receive a portion of the billions earmarked for prison construction. (Evidently, states lobbied Congress heavily against the truth-in-sentencing requirement, fearing that incarcerating people for longer stretches would mean "a huge increase in the number of people in state prisons, and a huge cost in prison construction programs."[112])

The degree to which the federal TIS provisions actually ended up prodding the states to become more punitive is still debated, though the Annenberg Public Policy Center concluded that the crime bill "did create incentives for states to build prisons and increase sentences, and thereby contributed to increased incarceration."[113] In the aftermath of the bill, parole in the country continued to rapidly disappear. As the Equal Justice Initiative (EJI) explains, by 1999, 29 states had removed discretionary parole and adopted the 85 percent criterion specified by the crime bill.[114] Eight states eliminated parole altogether the same year as the Crime Act (and by 2001, eight more had done so). As the EJI documents "[i]n return, the federal government awarded states $2.7 billion in grants to construct, expand, or renovate correctional facilities between 1996 and 2001... And the tough sentencing laws states enacted in order to get those federal dollars continue to keep people in prison today."[115]

The Crime Control Act also took college funding away from inmates. Previously, prisoners had been able to apply for federal Pell Grants in order to cover the cost of pursuing a college degree. Clinton's bill made prisoners ineligible for the grants, a policy that remained in place for 20 years until Barack Obama began to reverse it.

Cutting the grants was not exactly a consensus policy. Of all people, conservative *Washington Post* columnist George Will publicly urged caution in removing prisoner Pell Grants. Calling out "Sherriff Clinton" and a Congress full of "would-be Wyatt Earps" and their "fight-to-the-finish against crime," Will sympathetically profiled a Maryland prisoner nicknamed Peanut who was using a Pell Grant to educate himself:

> *Peanut's given name is Eugene Taylor. He has spent about half of his 42 years situated as he now is, behind bars and barbed wire, sentenced to life plus 25 years for murder and armed robbery. He dropped out of school in the 9th grade. The school, he indicates, had no strong objection. Sentimentalists who think there is no such thing as a bad boy never met Peanut in his misspent youth.... In his well-spent years in prison he has passed the eight-hour examination for a high school equivalency certification, and using Pell grants he has taken enough courses for a community college degree. But a provision of the crime bill the Senate has passed would make prisoners ineligible for such grants, which subsidize post-secondary education for low- and moderate-income students.*[116]

Will concluded by suggesting that "Congress should consider the fact that Peanut may be at large in a few years, at which time Baltimore's streets, which he left long ago, may be a bit safer than they would be if he had not acquired some social skills with the help of his Pell grant." Another *Post* writer, liberal columnist Colman McCarthy, wrote that "[i]f calls from

the Justice Department were as loud for 100,000 prison teachers as they are for 100,000 more police, a decrease in crime
would be in sight."[117]

Even the man from whom the Pell Grant takes its name,
Senator Claiborne Pell of Rhode Island, entered his vociferous
objection into the Congressional Record. "We must maintain
our commitment to corrections education," Pell said. "Criminals should be sentenced and incarcerated, but let us also be
concerned with their rehabilitation so that prison does not
remain a revolving door."[118]

As the proposed cut was under discussion, a prison English
instructor published an op-ed in the *Baltimore Sun* entitled "Cutting prison Pell Grants would be a crime":

> *I teach freshman English in Essex Community
> College's prison program at the Maryland House
> of Correction in Jessup, a medium-security prison
> where some 156 student-inmates are enrolled
> in college programs out of a prison population of
> 1,400. Some 75 percent of the inmates lack a high
> school diploma, and many are functionally illiterate.
> Without Pell Grants to pay for student tuition and
> books, our two-year degree program most likely will
> shut down. That would leave the state's general
> equivalency diploma program as the only real
> rehabilitation service at the overcrowded prison,
> known by staff and inmates as 'The Cut.'...*[119]

The instructor quoted letters his students had written to President
Clinton. One said: "what society fails to comprehend is that prison
is a college within itself, and ignorance needs no textbooks or
formal teachers to promote criminal mentality." Another inmate-
student, John Sipes, said: "Without college, I would be entering
the city streets with no job skills, and having served 10 years in

prison for narcotics violations, I would be at a loss. I feel I can do things on my own for the first time . . . I have gained self-respect."

The inmates' letters to Clinton did nothing. The President remained silent on the subject of the Pell Grant elimination, quietly signing it into law without a hint of opposition or reluctance. Their primary source of funding gone, many prison college programs quickly folded. In 1994, 71% of prisons had offered associate's degree programs, while by 1998 only 37% did. Likewise with bachelor's programs, which dropped from 48% of prisons in 1994 to 20% in 1998. Altogether, over 350 prison college programs disappeared in just a few years.[120]

Among the 1994 crime bill's many heartless initiatives, the prisoner Pell Grant elimination is perhaps comparatively among the less significant. But it stands out for its sheer pointless mean-spiritedness. A large body of evidence shows that correctional education is not simply a handout to prisoners; because prisoners who receive education while in prison are less likely to re-offend, giving high school and college courses ultimately saves money for the state. An obsessively comprehensive 2014 meta-analysis from the RAND Corporation, which reviewed nearly every single study on correctional education and its effects, concluded that "we no longer need to debate whether correctional education works."[121] Investing in prisoner education yields considerable returns.

From a moral perspective, whether or not to distribute education should not strictly depend on whether doing so saves the government a few dollars on something else. And speaking of the "returns" and "yields" of an "investment" in prisoners implies that they are a form of capital to be maximized, rather than human beings with basic entitlements. Making pure "cost-saving" arguments can be dangerous, because often the humane option and the cheap option are not the same. The theory of liberal arts education, to the extent that one can be discerned, is that the "life of the mind" is self-justifying, that learning should not be nakedly oriented toward preparing students to take up their place in a job market. So it may be that a program is good and necessary even though it doesn't produce much as far as the spreadsheets are concerned.

But in this particular case, every last nickel spent on the program was likely reaping benefits in reducing crime, which usefully demonstrates that Pell Grant elimination was solely about vengefulness. Here was an efficient policy, one that even George Will recognized as being pragmatic and sensible. There was no evidence of abuse or fraud in the program. Yet "tough on crime" politicians took it away, denying prisoners the ability to rehabilitate themselves, and deliberately starving their minds for no good reason.

Today, the correctional education system is a flimsy patchwork, and for many, attaining meaningful qualifications while in prison is impossible. With a decentralized network of fifty state corrections departments, each with their own varying degree of enthusiasm for rehabilitative philosophies and practices, plus an opaque and sprawling federal system, the level of education offered is both inconsistent and arbitrary. Jeff Smith, a former Missouri state senator who wrote a memoir after a campaign finance violation landed him in federal prison, recalls that the only actual class offered in his facility was "hydroponics."[122] Those inmates who had no use for learning how to "grow tomatoes in water" were left without additional options.

The elimination of prisoner Pell Grants is only a partial cause of the present state of affairs. But it did destroy a number of successful programs. With a stroke of Bill Clinton's pen, tens of thousands of prisoners were kept from bettering themselves.

BILL CLINTON NEVER TREATED THESE MEASURES AS SOME SORT of morally queasy compromise with Republicans; he advocated them himself and was unequivocal in his defense of them, treating them as a positive good rather than a necessary evil. As a British newspaper observed at the time: "Mr. Clinton is couching his defense of the bill in punitive terms, praising its extensions of the death penalty, and its funds to increase prisons and police numbers by 20 per cent, and mandatory life sentences for a third felony conviction."[123] His support was not qualified by any serious doubts; he emphatically stated that the crime bill reflected the country's "values." At his signing ceremony, Clinton announced that in passing the bill, "[w]e together are taking a big step toward bringing the laws of our land in line with the values of our people."[124]

But as criminal justice journalist Natasha Vargas-Cooper observes, "those values would come to define the current morass of mass incarceration: punitive, arbitrary, and fear-based."[125] Clinton's crime bill "is now widely seen as contributing to the human catastrophe of mass incarceration,"[126] with Clinton overseeing the largest increase prison inmates of any American president, including Ronald Reagan. Throughout the 1990's, the prison population continued to rapidly expand, until millions were housed in U.S. jails and prisons. (See Figure 1A, next page.)

The statistics are by now depressingly familiar. The prison boom had especially harsh consequences for African Americans. Soon, 1 in every 15 black men would be in jail or prison, with 1/3 being incarcerated in their lifetimes. Prison sentences of black men were nearly 20% longer than those of white men for similar crimes.[127] More black men are under correctional control than were enslaved in 1850,[128] and a black child whose father didn't complete high school has a 50% chance of seeing him incarcerated by the time she reaches the age of fourteen.[129]

Mass incarceration ripped black communities apart, taking parents away from children and husbands away from wives.

FIGURE 1A

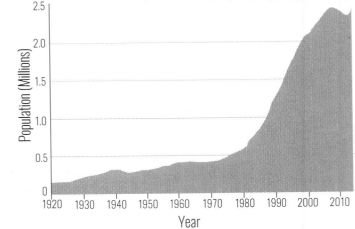

U.S. Incarcerated Population 1920-2014

Source: Bureau of Justice Statistics, Correctional Population Trends, 1980-2009, Correctional Populations In The United States, 2014, Historical Corrections Statistics in the United States, 1850-1984.

Sociologists Bruce Western and Becky Pettit write about the prison "poverty trap," whereby those released from prison are stuck in a neverending cycle of joblessness and despair, with prison compounding preexisting disadvantages and steadily eroding social institutions. Those released from prison have a hard time finding jobs, and "workers with prison records experience significant declines in earnings and employment."[130] Western and Pettit also document the effects of prisons on families. Not only does it take parents away from children by locking up fathers, but "parents in prison are likely to divorce or separate, and through the contagious effects of the institution, their children are in some degree 'prisonized,' exposed to the routines of prison life through visitation and the parole supervision of their parents."[131]

The Violent Crime Control Act was the apotheosis of late-20th Century American draconianism. When the bill was finally signed into law, Jesse Jackson called it a "criminal act," invoking Jim Crow and lambasting Clinton. In his remarks, Jackson said:

> *The civil rights struggle, the racial justice struggle, the gender equality struggle continues. In Biblical terms, there was a great celebration when David slew Goliath. But they didn't celebrate too long, because while they were glad that David beat Goliath, Goliath had sons. And the giants kept coming. So the day we beat Jim Crow in the South, "Jim Crow, Esquire" keeps coming. And when Jim Crow was a wolf wearing wolf's clothes, we were psychologically positioned to fight Jim Crow. But when Jim Crow goes to Yale or someplace, and disguises his wolf instinct in sheep's clothing... The Bible reminds us that when wolves come in sheep's clothing, they're more deceptive. So if Bush says 'fast-track jobs to Mexico' we say 'No! We've got to fight for our jobs' but if Clinton says 'NAFTA' we say 'Well, NAFTA, that's a little different.' It's the same thing. If Reagan had proposed a Howard Johnson 'sixty new flavors of killing' plan, if Reagan had proposed ten billion dollars in new prison construction, while school systems in D.C. close because of lack of capital improvement, and others should be closed for the same reason, there'd have been massive demonstrations. Reagan could not have put through this crime bill. Bush could not have put through this crime bill. It's a combination of Kool-Aid and cyanide.*[132]

But the 1994 crime bill was only the beginning of Clinton's implementation of "get tough" policymaking. Those attempting to excuse Clinton for the crime bill have argued that it was a reasonable response to the excessive crime rates of the period.[133] Yet even as people were noting declines in criminal violence later on, during the mid-1990s, Clinton was still attempting to seem tougher on crime than Republicans. In 1996, under the headline "While Crime Has Declined, The Campaign Rhetoric Hasn't," the *Philadelphia Inquirer* took note of the strange contradiction between the reality of the crime statistics and the overheated political rhetoric about crime coming from both Clinton and Dole.[134]

While Americans became steadily safer, Bill Clinton continued to propose extreme new initiatives on crime control. Clinton advocated strict curfews for juveniles, a policy almost certain to lead to the racially disproportionate hassling of African American young people, and difficulties for teens who worked late at jobs.[135] He promoted and signed legislation cutting school funding from states that did not adopt "zero tolerance" expulsion policies for a child that brought a gun to school.[136] (Hillary Clinton brags proudly of this policy, and several of the other crime control initiatives, in her memoir.[137]) Clinton also supported amending the Constitution to add a "crime victims' rights" provision.[138]

Clinton also took a number of executive steps to advance and expand the reach of the Drug War. Clinton "greatly expand[ed] the scope of routine drug testing" in the federal prison system, by requiring that every person arrested be given a drug test, instead of the previous policy of testing at random.[139] Not only that, but Clinton pressured state governments to adopt the same policy, vowing "to take all appropriate steps to encourage the states to adopt and implement the same policies that we are initiating at the federal level."[140] Clinton was also strongly insistent on strict drug-testing for all parolees, saying: "It's time to say to parolees, if you go back on drugs, you'll go back to jail."[141]

Clinton even tried to insinuate his drug testing programs into unprecedented realms. He proposed, for example, that every teenager should be required to take a drug test before being issued a driver's license. Speaking in favor of his initiative, Clinton said:

I believe we should use the privilege of a driver's license to demand responsible behavior by young people when it comes to drugs, too… We're already saying to teens if you drink you aren't allowed to drive. Now we should say that teens should pass a drug test as a condition of getting a driver's license. Our message should be simple: No drugs or no driver's license.[142]

When Clinton released this plan, the legal director of the ACLU called it "this drug mania gone crazy."[143] The ACLU pointed out that the idea was downright foolish from a social policy perspective, since "depriving somebody of the ability to drive may mean depriving them of the ability to go to school, get a job, support their families or do the kinds of things that prevent them from doing drugs."[144]

PERHAPS ONE OF CLINTON'S MOST SHAMEFUL DRUG WAR ignominies was the issue of the crack cocaine sentencing disparity. Here, Clinton not only knowingly and materially furthered the enactment of a racist policy, but he misled black leaders about his role in doing so.

Civil rights groups had long objected to a major injustice in cocaine sentencing policy. While those convicted of possessing powdered cocaine faced a one-year prison sentence, crack possessors received a mandatory five years. And for dealers, trafficking in five grams of crack was treated with the same severity as tracking in 500 grams of powder cocaine, a 100-1 disparity. As everyone knew, crack cocaine users were far more likely to be black than powder cocaine users; the vast majority of those prosecuted federally on crack charges were black or Latino.[145]

The end result was that black cocaine addicts and dealers were given far higher prison sentences than their white counterparts, even when they had handled precisely the same amount of cocaine. As Representative Melvin Watt explained, "[i]f somebody is convicted of selling $225 worth of crack cocaine, they get the same penalty as somebody who sells $50,000 worth of powder cocaine… Poor young kids who can afford only crack go to jail. Rich young kids who can afford powder go home and sleep in their own beds."[146]

Activists and black leaders had long fought to have crack and powder cocaine sentencing equalized. And in 1995, it seemed as if they might finally have succeeded. The United States Sentencing Commission, after studying the disparity, produced a recommendation that it be equalized. After investigating the issue, the Commission concluded that "the media and public fears of a direct relationship between crack and other crimes do not seem confirmed by empirical data."[147] But when the Commission moved to implement the recommendation, Congress passed a bill blocking the plan.

Black lawmakers called on Clinton to retain the Sentencing Commission's recommendation by exercising his veto power. Civil rights groups "led a telephone campaign to pressure the president to veto the bill."[148] Jesse Jackson said the president had the ability "with one stroke of your veto pen, to correct the most grievous racial injustice built into our legal system."[149] The Black Caucus said that the discrepancies "make a mockery of justice" and that it is "the first test of our seriousness . . . to aggressively root out and eliminate policies and practices that are patently unfair."[150] And the available political cover was clear: Clinton could simply claim that he deferred to the superior expertise of the Sentencing Commission, without needing to make a particularly spirited argument in favor of racial justice.

CLINTON SIGNED THE BILL INTO LAW, NULLIFYING THE Sentencing Commission's recommendation and retaining the 100-1 disparity. He defended his decision with a grand display of anti-drug tough talk. "I am not going to let anyone who peddles drugs get the idea that the cost of doing business is going down," Clinton said. "Tough penalties for crack trafficking are required because of the effect on individuals and families, related gang activity, turf battles and other violence."[151]

The civil rights community was livid. Clinton's decision to sign the legislation came just over one week after he had spoken publicly about racial inequities in the criminal courts. On the day of the Million Man March, Clinton had given a speech about race relations in which he declared that "Blacks are right to think something is terribly wrong... when almost one in three African American men in their 20s are either in jail, on parole or otherwise under the supervision of the criminal justice system."[152] Clinton said that it was unfair that a "disproportionate percentage" of black men were in prison for drug crimes "in comparison to the percentage of blacks who use drugs in our society."[153] Clinton's comments were made on October 16th. On October 27th, the press reported that he would be rejecting the recommendation to equalize crack and powder sentences.

The reversal was seen as an attempt to avoid upsetting white voters. As a Sentencing Commission official commented upon Clinton's signing of the bill, "[t]his is a total political call on their part... They are not going to do anything that will make the President look bad on the crime issue."[154] *The Washington Post's* editorial board criticized Clinton for making "the easy, politically safe choice," noting that the president "played down the real issue—terrible sentence disparity—and signed with a flourish and the usual anti-crime rhetoric."[155] By this point, though, the *Post* sighed, it was probably "unrealistic to expect the president to do the right thing" on such an issue.

But Clinton's stance was actually worse than it seemed. Not only did he not want to lower cocaine punishments, he wanted to *increase* them. Yet he made every effort to conceal his true position. Speaking to a group of black journalists, Clinton indicated that the crack/powder inequity pained him, saying that "the situation that exists is unfair, unjustifiable, and should be changed. And I'm going to do what I can to eliminate a huge percentage of the disparity."[156] One might think this flatly contradicted his actions. After all, a man who had wanted to "eliminate a huge percentage of the disparity" had signed legislation rejecting the Sentencing Commission's proposal to eliminate the disparity.

But there was no contradiction at all. What Clinton actually meant by "eliminate the disparity" was *raising* powder cocaine sentences in order to match crack sentences, rather than reducing crack sentences. He did not have in mind a proposal like that of the Sentencing Commission, which would have lowered the amount of time drug offenders spent in prison. As he said upon signing the legislation affirming the disparity, "when large-scale cocaine traffickers sell powder with the knowledge that it will be converted into crack, they should be punished as severely as those who distribute the crack itself."[157] Elsewhere, Clinton was even more explicit that his concern for "reducing the disparity" meant "injustice for all":

> QUESTION: *Well, would you raise the penalty for powder cocaine?*
> BILL CLINTON: *That's what I would do—yes... there's no question that the disparity is entirely too great in the sentencing. And I think when it comes to trafficking, they should raise the cocaine trafficking penalties.*[158]

Of course, this was like proposing to fix racial disparities in death penalty sentencing by simply finding more white people to kill. Perversely, Clinton's position made him appear to care about the inequity, while in reality not proposing to alleviate *any* of the punishment inflicted on people being convicted under the unjust crack laws. Fixing the disparity without lowering crack sentences presumed that those sentences were perfectly fair, but that powder cocaine users were simply getting off lightly. Its solution was to make members of all races suffer equally.

One of the key points made by opponents of the disparity had been that *all* cocaine starts as powder cocaine; crack is derived from powder. The result was that street-level crack dealers were punished more heavily than their suppliers. As the *Washington Post*'s Jefferson Morley explained:

> *Imagine two drug dealers, one a supplier and one a street dealer. The supplier sells the street dealer three grams of cocaine. The street dealer mixes the drug with baking soda, cooks it in his microwave oven, producing six grams of crystalline smokeable crack cocaine. If he gets arrested and sent to federal court, he faces a mandatory minimum of five years in jail. The supplier has to get caught with 500 grams of powder cocaine—about 1.7 pounds—to face that much time in federal prison.* [159]

Clinton's response to this was to concede that it was unfair, then to insist that the supplier be punished just as heavily. At every point, Clinton openly attempted to fudge and equivocate on the issue, so that black audiences would think he wanted to fix the disparity, while he simultaneously told white audiences that he would have no mercy when it came to the scourge of crack in American cities, and did not believe in being soft on drug dealers.

In 1997, the Sentencing Commission tried again, issuing a recommendation that the disparity be reduced to a mere 10-1. This time, Clinton signed on and promised to support the plan in his dealings with Congress. But the Congressional Black Caucus sensed Clinton's commitment was anemic, and insisted that having 10-1 racist sentencing was only somewhat better than having 100-1 racist sentencing. [160]

Ultimately the Black Caucus' view didn't matter; the proposal went nowhere and the law remained unchanged. As the CBC predicted, Clinton did not follow through on his promise to pressure Congress.

Still, Clinton now uses his tepid support for the 10-1 plan to portray himself as a crusader for reform. Asked by *Democracy Now!* in 2000 to defend his record on drug crime, Clinton boasted that "I did my best to persuade Congress to get rid of the discrepancy between crack and powdered cocaine in the sentencing guidelines."[161] To another journalist, Clinton blamed the right, saying that "by the time we got to this issue, the Republicans were in [the] majority and we just couldn't do it."[162] He did not mention that when he was afforded the unrestricted opportunity to eliminate that discrepancy entirely, he had chosen not to.

CLINTON SIGNED TWO FURTHER MAJOR PIECES OF ANTI-CRIME legislation. In 1996 came the Anti-Terrorism and Effective Death Penalty Act (AEDPA), which legal journalist Lincoln Caplan calls "surely one of the worst statutes ever passed by Congress and signed into law by a President."[163] As Caplan explains, "the heart of the law is a provision saying that, even when a state court misapplies the Constitution, a defendant cannot necessarily have his day in federal court."

AEDPA was a political response to the Oklahoma City bombing, and the perception that death row inmates were given unduly generous helpings of appellate procedure. It drastically accelerated executions, creating what judge Stephen Reinhardt called "a twisted labyrinth of deliberately crafted legal obstacles" that prevent death row inmates from raising issues successfully on appeal.[164]

AEDPA thereby inhibited the ability of judges to fix unsound convictions, and examine the substantive rather than procedural issues in a case. With the Supreme Court having interpreted AEDPA's requirements literally, according to Caplan, the law "has become an enormous source of frustration on the federal bench."[165] That's because it "trips up federal judges who try to undo unjust convictions, rendering them powerless to address procedural unfairness—and, at worst, preventing them from granting a potentially innocent person a new trial or release, or even stopping his or her execution."[166] One federal judge even admitted that "I suspect that there may well have been innocent people who were executed because of the absence of habeas corpus."[167]

Because habeus corpus is such a fundamental right, even some conservatives have looked askance at AEDPA. Republican-appointed judge Alex Kozinski of the 9th Circuit has called AEDPA "a cruel, unjust and unnecessary law that effectively removes federal judges as safeguards against miscarriages of justice."[168] And Daniel Patrick Moynihan argued that AEDPA would "introduce a virus that will surely spread throughout our system of laws."[169] Serious arguments have been made that the law should be declared unconstitutional, since it is a legislative attempt to eliminate a fundamental right.

AEDPA's harms are more than merely theoretical. According to a Columbia Law School study of death penalty cases from 1973 to 1995 "courts found serious, reversible error in nearly 7 of every 10 of the thousands of capital sentences that were fully reviewed during the period."[170] The errors were so numerous that "state courts threw out 47% of death sentences due to serious flaws, a later federal review found 'serious error'—error undermining the reliability of the outcome—in 40% of the remaining sentences."[171] As Lincoln Caplan explains, AEDPA eliminates the mechanism for correcting those mistakes. Without habeas corpus, "[i]nstead of later being found not to deserve the death penalty, as happened in seventy-three per cent of the cases, or instead of being found innocent, as happened in nine per cent of the cases, these defendants likely would have been put to death."[172]

But AEDPA was not the only way the Administration restricted criminal offenders' access to courts. Clinton also signed the Prison Litigation Reform Act, another legislative attempt to curb perceived excesses of justice. The PLRA was designed to restrain prisoners from filing lawsuits over their conditions; the perception was that too many inmates were complaining of having their rights violated. Instead of having these allegations dealt with by the courts, the PLRA tried to shift them back to the in-prison administrative grievance process.

Unfortunately, prison administrators are not terribly reliable at safeguarding prisoners' rights. The functional effect of the PLRA was therefore to allow for abuses of inmates to go unchecked. As Ian Head wrote in the *New Republic*, the Act "laid waste to the ability of incarcerated people to bring prison officials to court for violations of their constitutional rights, whether it be racial discrimination, lack of medical care, or brutality by prison guards."[173] *The New York Times* condemned the PLRA, writing that it "insulate[d] prisons from a large number of very worthy lawsuits, and allow[ed] abusive and cruel mistreatment of inmates to go unpunished."[174]

One particularly troubling aspect of the PLRA was its requirement that prisoners show "physical injury" in order to bring a successful suit over prison conditions. Because all kinds of conditions are abusive but do not cause lasting injury, this has severely circumscribed the brutalities that can be remedied. As the *Times* explained, the rule has been used to dismiss suits over all kinds of inhumane acts, including: "strip-searching of female prisoners by male guards; revealing to other inmates that a prisoner was HIV-positive; forcing an inmate to stand naked for 10 hours." Courts have also found that prolonged isolation and even prison rape do not necessarily meet the "physical injury" requirement.[175]

The PLRA also includes some almost gratuitous additional difficulties for inmates. Filing a case in federal court usually costs several hundred dollars, but courts can typically waive the fee for indigent litigants. The PLRA eliminates the fee waiver for prisoners. Instead, it "requires indigent prisoners to pay the filing fees for their lawsuits by paying part up front and then making monthly installment payments of twenty percent of their previous month's income until the fees are paid in full."[176] Of course, since inmates often earn something like $.40 an hour, this means months of work. The result is that thanks to the PLRA, any prisoner whose rights are abused and who needs a judicial remedy must effectively sign himself up for permanent indenture to the courts.

The PLRA contributed to the ever-expanding thicket of legal barriers between criminal offenders and the enforcement of their constitutional rights. It was one of several pieces of legislation that Clinton signed into law without objection, each punishing criminals further, without any evidence that doing so would have socially salutary effects.

But Clinton's pursuit of criminals went beyond signing Congress' bills; Clinton also incorporated the "tough on crime" attitude into the policies of administrative agencies under his control.

ANN GREENE WAS KNOWN AS "MAMA GREENE" AMONG residents of the Alemany housing project in San Francisco. She sat on the board of the tenants' association, and served as captain of her building. She always involved herself with the life of the community, "making sure the trash stays picked up and people don't play their music too loudly at night."[177] But when Greene's 38-year-old son, Ladell, who did not live with her, was arrested on drug charges, the San Francisco Housing

Authority immediately filed eviction papers against Ann Greene. The Housing Authority insisted that her son had stayed at her house, and that this was sufficient to evict her.

Greene's eviction notice came as a result of the "one-strike" policy adopted by the Department of Housing and Urban Development (HUD). The Clinton Administration introduced administrative guidelines that required public housing authorities to evict anyone who committed a drug crime. Previously, public housing authorities had been reluctant to evict tenants for criminal infractions, fearing constitutional concerns. The Clinton rule clarified that it was official administration policy to evict people after a single offense, no matter what.

The policy was personally directed by the President.[178] Speaking in defense of his decision, Clinton said:

> For some, one strike and you're out sounds like hardball. Well, it is. If you mess up your community, you have to turn in your key. There is no reason in the world to put the rights of a criminal before those of a child who wants to grow up safe.[179]

Clinton insisted that HUD would be taking vigorous measures to ensure local housing authorities were complying, promising that "there will actually be penalties for housing projects that do not fight crime and enforce 'one strike and you're out.'"[180] His speech announcing the rule included no acknowledgment of the possibility of error or overzealousness on the part of housing authorities, and Clinton bragged of the increasing numbers of drug arrests taking place in housing projects.

The one-strike policy had wide consequences for those seeking public housing. Tens of thousands of people were explicitly rejected for public housing on "one-strike" grounds annually. Human Rights Watch noted that given America's high felony conviction rate, 3.5 million people were made ineligible for public housing as a result of the rule.[181] But this understates matters, since the Clinton policy encouraged eviction for criminal *acts,* not criminal convictions. [182] That meant that even if a person was still under a presumption of innocence in the criminal courts, having not yet been convicted of anything, HUD could still move to take away their public housing. To say that one had not been convicted of a crime was no defense; even if a person was later found not guilty in a court, she could still be barred from public housing. In fact, one needn't even be *arrested* for a crime; the housing authority's word was sufficient. This gave housing authorities an extraordinary amount of discretion over eviction, and left tenants with few remedies when a "one-strike" eviction was initiated. Given that HUD adopted an explicit presumption of guilt, it was impossible to even know how to exonerate oneself and keep one's housing.

As a result, the horror stories were numerous. As Wendy Kaplan and David Rossman documented, evictions could happen over matters as trivial as "a petty fight between adolescent girls."[183] In one case, a family was evicted because the parents would not eject their 14-year-old son, who had been convicted of vandalizing school property (and received only community service from the juvenile court).[184] In another, a seriously ill 16-year-old was arrested for drug possession, and barred from public housing. When his mother let him stay one night in her apartment so that he could go to a doctor's appointment at the hospital next door, the housing authority began eviction proceedings against the mother. (The boy's charges would ultimately be dismissed in juvenile court, but this was irrelevant.)[185]

The one-strike rule meant that public housing tenants were at constant risk of eviction. They didn't just need to avoid arrest; they needed to avoid committing any act that would give the housing authority grounds to believe they had committed a criminal act. Tenants therefore had to be on edge at every moment, making sure not just to behave lawfully, but to behave in a manner that would please the authority. The effect was an extraordinarily intrusive regulation of poor people's behaviors, one that turned housing projects into unaccountable police states.

But even walking on eggshells was not enough. The Clinton Administration also insisted on construing the rules so that eviction could be initiated "without regard to the tenant's knowledge of the drug-related criminal activity."[186] That meant that even though a tenant may have had no idea a crime was being committed, they could be evicted anyway. Tenants were not only responsible for their own acts, but also those of their guests, including things the tenant did not know about and had no way to know. When an appeals court finally overturned this policy after Clinton left office, it noted the senselessness of punishing people for crimes they had no knowledge of. After all, "imposing the threat of eviction on an innocent tenant who has already taken all reasonable steps to prevent third-party drug activity could not have a deterrent effect because the tenant would have already done all that tenant could do to prevent the third-party drug activity."[187] Yet even though this policy was both unhelpful and unfair, the Clinton Administration went to court to defend it, insisting upon the right to evict people for offenses of which they were unaware.

The stepped-up enforcement meant that there were plenty of cases like that of Ann Greene. There, was, for example, sixty-three-year-old Oakland public housing resident Pearlie Rucker, who lived with a mentally disabled daughter, two grandchildren, and one great-granddaughter. The Oakland housing authority sought to evict her "because her daughter was found in possession of cocaine three blocks from the apartment" even though "Rucker [had regularly searched] her daughter's room for evidence of alcohol and drug use and... never found any evidence or observed any sign of drug use by her daughter."[188] Also in Oakland was seventy-one-year-old Willie Lee, who had resided in public housing for over twenty five years. When Lee's grandson, who lived with him, was caught smoking marijuana in the parking lot, the housing authority moved to evict Lee.[189]

The stories of elderly people being evicted are tragic; such individuals often have nowhere else to go, and face incredible difficulties after being turned out of houses they have inhabited for multiple decades. But the Clinton rule also had a particularly disruptive effect on the lives and well-being of children. The poorest children are the ones most likely to encounter juvenile courts at one point or another, and the HUD policy meant that, far from rehabilitating such children, encounters with the juvenile justice system would result in the child's entire family being evicted and left homeless.[190]

As a result, the "one-strike" policy provided no benefit. As Kaplan and Rossman document, "there is no evidence that it reduces crime in public housing but abundant evidence that it makes families homeless, puts children out on the street, leads police departments to breach laws concerning confidentiality of juvenile proceedings, and creates conflicts of interest between parents and their troubled offspring."[191] A one-strike policy therefore "causes more social ills than it cures." It also meant that the War on Drugs was explicitly escalated against poor people specifically; only poor residents of public housing stood to become homeless as a result of a drug charge, and only the poor had their constitutional protections erased.

In fact, the Clinton Administration exhibited a borderline obsession with increasing control over the lives of public housing tenants, to the point of being willing to subvert federal court decisions and the Fourth Amendment's restrictions on unreasonable searches and seizures. The Cato Institute's Timothy Lynch tells what happened:

> *In the spring of 1994 the Chicago Public Housing Authority responded to gang violence by conducting warrantless "sweeps" of entire apartment buildings.*

Closets, desks, dressers, kitchen cabinets, and personal effects were examined regardless of whether the police had probable cause to suspect particular residents of any wrongdoing. Some apartments were searched when the residents were not home. Although such searches were supported by the Clinton administration, Federal District Judge Wayne Anderson declared the Chicago sweeps unconstitutional. Judge Anderson found the government's claim of "exigent circumstances" to be exaggerated since all of the sweeps occurred days after the gang-related shootings. He also noted that even in emergency situations, housing officials needed probable cause in order to search specific apartments... The White House response was swift. President Clinton publicly ordered Attorney General Reno and HUD secretary Henry Cisneros to find a way to circumvent Judge Anderson's ruling. One month later the president announced a "constitutionally effective way" of searching public housing units. The Clinton administration would now ask tenants to sign lease provisions that would give government agents the power to search their homes without warrants.[192]

Thus in response to a judge's decision that its practices violated tenants' rights, the Clinton Administration simply forced tenants to sign away those rights as a condition of receiving housing to begin with.

There was some criticism of Clinton's decision. *The New York Times* editorial board said Clinton had "missed the point" of the federal court's ruling.[193] Harvard Law School's Charles Ogletree and Abbe Smith said Clinton was trying to "tear up" poor people's houses.[194] But the Administration did not back down; Clinton was consistent in insisting that the scourge of drug crime required intense surveillance of the lives of public housing tenants.

A NUMBER OF LOYAL DEMOCRATS HAVE ATTEMPTED TO DEFEND Bill Clinton's record on crime. They argue variously that while he may have presided over a drastic expansion of the prison system, (1) it did not begin with him, (2) it occurred mostly at the state level, (3) it wasn't the fault of the crime bill, (4) it was supported by black leaders themselves, and (5) it was more understandable in its historical context. When Bill Clinton was under fire for his comments in Philadelphia, writers in the liberal press gave lengthy and tortured justifications for Clinton's crime bill. *Slate* ran an article entitled "The Clintons Aren't to Blame for Mass Incarceration."[195] *RealClearPolitics,* under the heading "Don't Punish Clinton, Sanders for 1994 Crime Bill," pleaded that the bill was a sincere attempt to solve a complicated problem, while *Salon* suggested Clinton was following a "black silent majority" who supported the policies.[196] *The New York Times* immediately leapt to Clinton's defense with a highly opinionated news article entitled "Prison Rate Was Rising Years Before 1994 Bill."[197] These were predictable reactions to the criticism of the Clintons, given that Bill's remarks in defense of Hillary came at a politically vulnerable moment for the 2016 Democratic frontrunner. But as pieces of empirical reasoning, they are desperate; Bill Clinton's record on crime is unsalvageable.

To begin with, whether Clinton initiated versus expanded mass incarceration is of very little relevance. It's certainly more true to say that Clinton completed what Ronald Reagan started than that Clinton alone was chiefly responsible. But his culpability is not thereby diminished, it is merely shared jointly with other parties. The fact remains that the number of prisoners added under Clinton was larger than under any other president,[198] and to say that someone merely perpetrated the bulk of an atrocity rather than coming up with the idea for it is to say almost nothing at all.

Reagan and Bush might have had equally scant regard for the well-being of African Americans. But Reagan and Bush had never adopted the pretense of being interested in what the black community had to say to begin with. Only Clinton, with his egalitarian and empathetic rhetoric, and his warm spoken tributes to civil rights, can be accused of true *hypocrisy*. The Republicans may be equally to blame for the material consequences, but Clinton bears a special kind of blame; there is something especially disturbing about betraying black interests when it is done in the name of serving them.

I'T'S ALSO THE CASE THAT WHILE THE STATES CONTRIBUTED the largest fraction to the growth in inmate populations, the federal prison population grew at a comparable pace (see Fig. 1B). The number of federal prisoners "doubled during the Clinton years and grew more than during the previous 12 years of Republican control of the White House."[199] More than 60% of those federal inmates were there for drug crimes.[200] And when it comes to federal prisoners, the President is vested with extraordinary power, with the executive branch retaining wide discretion over which cases to prosecute, and the President personally having the ability to pardon federal inmates.

Clinton's control over prosecutions is important. Law professor John Pfaff has argued that contemporary mass incarceration was largely driven by discretionary decisions made by prosecutors rather than by changes in laws. "The primary engine of prison growth," Pfaff writes, "at least since crime began its decline in the early 1990s, has been an increased willingness on the part of district attorneys to file felony charges against arrestees... During a time of falling crime, prosecutors became more and more aggressive against offenders."[201] Prosecutors decide which crimes to go after, whom to charge, how many charges to bring, which plea agreements

FIGURE 1B

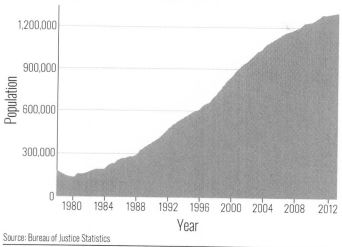

U.S. Federal Prison Population

Source: Bureau of Justice Statistics

to offer, and what sentences to ask for. Thus even though the legislative branch of government is the drafter of harsh laws, and the judicial branch is responsible for processing cases, the executive branch has an outsized role in determining what happens to criminal defendants. When prosecutors decide to either get tough or show mercy, the same set of laws can lead to radically different sets of outcomes. Because there are very few legal requirements for how many people prosecutors must charge, they have considerable freedom to bring as many or as few cases as they like.

The massive increases in the federal prison population during the Clinton years therefore could not have occurred without the Justice Department bringing scores of new charges against people. The Clinton Justice Department obtained more drug convictions than its predecessors (Clinton "averaged 17,767 convictions per year from 1993 to 1995 compared to 16,714 convictions per year under President Bush"[202]) and "during the

Clinton administration, the Department of Justice grew faster than any other agency of the federal government," according to the Justice Policy Institute.[203]

The President's pardon and commutation power is even greater. Article II of the Constitution grants the President the full authority to "grant Reprieves and Pardons for Offences against the United States,"[204] an ability that has been called one of the "least limited" powers in American government.[205] Presidential pardons and commutations cannot be revoked by acts of Congress, and the President is free to grant them to anyone he pleases.

Many presidents have taken full advantage of this extraordinary power. Upon his election in 1800, Thomas Jefferson pardoned those convicted under the Alien and Sedition Acts, which he opposed as unconstitutional.[206] Woodrow Wilson pardoned hundreds of people convicted under liquor laws in order to undermine Prohibition.[207] And Abraham Lincoln was so promiscuous with his pardons that his attorney general called him ""unfit to be trusted with the pardoning power" due to being "too susceptible to women's tears."[208] Harry Truman issued nearly 2,000 pardons; Franklin Roosevelt issued over 3,000.[209]

But in the Reagan/Bush/Clinton years, with the rise of the "get tough" consensus, use of the pardon declined. Despite pleas and petitions, Clinton was unwilling to use his constitutional authority. Even when the normally-reticent Justice Department supported prospective clemencies, Clinton refused to sign them; *Politico* reports that "[w]hile the Justice Department was often clearly reluctant to endorse pardons, [Clinton's internal] files also show that in 1998, there were almost three dozen cases where the department endorsed pardons but Clinton's own lawyers opposed them. The president sided with his aides and denied the pardons."[210]

In the final days of his presidency, Clinton indicated that he was considering offering "a broad clemency or amnesty for non-violent drug offenders who had served long prison terms."[211] As *USA Today* reported in December of 2000:

> *President Clinton is considering whether to offer clemency to scores of low-level drug offenders, raising the possibility that one of his last acts in office could be the broadest grant of clemency since presidents Ford and Carter pardoned thousands of Vietnam-era draft evaders more than two decades ago. The White House has been tight-lipped about what Clinton might do, but officials indicated Thursday that a decision could come as early as today. Several groups are trying to persuade the president to release some low-level drug offenders— perhaps as many as several hundred—before he leaves office, saying that their sentences were too harsh. Clinton gave them hope during a recent interview with Rolling Stone magazine, in which he hinted that he might act dramatically to shorten the five-, 10- and 20-year sentences of some non-violent drug offenders. Clinton said drug sentencing policies should be re-examined. 'The sentences in many cases are too long for non-violent offenders,' he said, adding that it was 'unconscionable' to punish crack cocaine offenders—more than 90% of whom are black—much more harshly than powder cocaine offenders—who are more likely to be white.[212]*

Clinton dangled the possibility of a large-scale amnesty, giving hope to those who had been unjustly imprisoned by his Justice Department. But when the list of 140 pardons and commutations was announced during the final few days of the presidency, only a couple of dozen were drug offenders. The handful of pardons was a pitiful disappointment, since, at the time, 58% of the country's

146,640 federal prisoners were there on drug charges.[213] Internal records show that Clinton considered, and rejected, a proposal to free nearly 500 prisoners.[214] *Politico* concluded that he must only have considered the amnesty idea "fleetingly," despite the hints his administration dropped in the press.[215]

Instead, the beneficiaries of Clinton's mercy consisted of a disproportionate number of Clinton's personal friends and political allies. These included such parties as (1) Marc Rich, a billionaire tax-evading fugitive who had made substantial donations to the Clinton library fund (2) Susan McDougal, a former law partner of Hillary's who had been convicted of contempt of court during the Whitewater investigation for refusing to tell a court whether Bill Clinton had lied under oath, (3) a Democratic congressman who had been convicted of soliciting child pornography, and (4) Clinton's brother Roger.[216] Clinton also issued a controversial pardon to two Florida carnival operators who had been convicted of bank fraud, had paid $325,000 in "consulting fees" to Hillary Clinton's brother, Tony Rodham,[217] and had been longtime donors to Bill's political campaigns.[218] Even though the Justice Department "strongly opposed" Clinton wiping the couple's federal bank fraud charges,[219] Bill Clinton urged a hasty approval of Rodham's pardon request for the couple, with the President writing in the memo that the fraudsters had been losing business over the convictions and needed to have the pardons granted quickly.

The failure of Bill Clinton to use his executive power to adjust drug sentences was an especially damning act. The pardon amnesty was morally correct, and moreover, easily doable. Nothing could more literally prove an unwillingness to "lift a finger" for black lives; the political expenditure necessary consists of picking up a pen. As the *Boston Globe* lamented, "both George W. Bush and Bill Clinton publicly called those laws unfair, and yet neither used their constitutional power to do something about it."[220]

The instance also disproves Clinton's self-portrayal as someone who tried hard for criminal justice reform, but was stymied by the need to maintain precious political capital. During the President's last days in office, he does not have to worry about the impact of his executive decisions on his ability to govern. There's no legislation left to push for, and the election has been held. At no point is a President freer to act as he pleases; he has unlimited Constitutional authority, and nothing to lose. The only damage that he can do is to his image. And Clinton *was* willing to risk having his image damaged; the pardons issued to disreputable cronies earned him considerable bad press. The Marc Rich pardon was condemned more than nearly any other act of Clinton's political career. *The New York Times* editorial board called it "indefensible" and "a shocking abuse of Presidential power."[221] *USA Today* said it showed a "hopelessly cracked ethical barometer," while George Stephanopoulos called it "outrageous" and Joe Biden said Clinton must have been "brain dead."[222] Representative Barney Frank, a strong ally of Clinton's, was deeply angered, saying "it was a real betrayal by Bill Clinton of all who had been strongly supportive of him to do something this unjustified. It was contemptuous."[223] Senator Patrick Leahy said the pardon was "outrageous," since Rich had been living a "life of luxury" overseas after evading taxes on 100 million dollars, and showed no remorse whatsoever.[224] The prosecutor in the Rich case, who had voted for Clinton three times, said:

> *Think of all the kids who hot-wire cars and go to jail. They don't get to choose between going behind bars or spending a rather comfortable exile... What was [Clinton] thinking?* [225]

Bill Clinton came to regret the Rich pardon. But not because it was a blatantly corrupt example of auctioning justice on the free market. Rather, he bemoaned the fact that "it wasn't worth the damage to my reputation."[226] The moral implications of the pardon never troubled Clinton at all; he defended it in a *New York Times* op-ed.[227] Clinton appeared unable to fathom why people might be upset that a tax-evading expatriate financier would earn his favor while thousands of crack addicts moldered in federal prison. If it was wrong, it was wrong because Clinton had miscalculated the costs and benefits to his personal interests and public image. (Fortunately, the Rich pardon led to dozens of speaking engagements and foundation donations; the long-term financial rewards largely balanced out the reputational harms.[228])

All of Clinton's rhetoric to black journalists and activists about his personal concern for the crack disparity was therefore false. In emotional tones, he promised African Americans that he would take whatever executive action he could to mitigate the problem. Yet when a clear opportunity arose, he expended his image for the sake of disgraced financial-sector associates instead. It's hard to avoid concluding that all of Clinton's professed sympathy over the injustices facing young black men was affected, that his tears were those of a very unscrupulous crocodile.

BUT THERE MAY BE A MORE FUNDAMENTAL MISTAKE IN judging Clinton's responsibility for mass incarceration by tallying quantities of inmates under his direct control. The presidency also carries a major "agenda-setting" role, one that not only creates specific federal policies with specific measurable consequences, but which also constrains or expands the set of perceived political possibilities and imperatives. In 1992, Clinton *deliberately moved the Democratic Party toward the Republican stance on crime,* with Clinton prominently displaying himself as a supporter and enforcer of the death penalty. By eliminating the liberal counterweight to punitive Republican policies, Clinton took "tough on crime" from being a contentious issue (on which the Democrats were in the minority) to a consensus one

(with Democrats, as Mark Warr noted, simply competing with Republicans to see who could be the least compassionate.)

Law professor John Pfaff believes blame for the Clinton incarceration increases should be attributed to the state rather than federal government, since "[t]here's very little the feds can do to the states," and "[t]hey can't change state law."[229] There is a mistake, however, in framing the question as "In what measurable way did the enacting of the 1994 crime bill directly initiate corresponding actions at the state level that clearly increased growths in prisoner populations?" That's important, but in order to understand their full role, we must also examine how Bill Clinton and the New Democrats shaped the nationwide political consensus on crime. Most tough on crime measures were implemented at the state level, but there must have been something occurring *nationally* in order for most of the 50 states to simultaneously head in the same direction. If it was a purely local development, one cannot explain how it seemed to occur everywhere at once. Thus while Pfaff is correct that there probably wasn't a particular federal policy that suddenly caused a change in state governments' behavior, it's a mistake to conclude from that that the acts of national politicians were not a major impetus toward state action. To solely ask whether the crime bill "created" mass incarceration, and then to argue that it didn't, is to deliberately frame the question so as to produce the answer most favorable to Clinton.

A minor right-wing think tank once came up with a public policy theory known as the "Overton window" in order to explain how ideas become accepted in national political discussions. The "window" comprises the set of beliefs along a spectrum that the public is willing to entertain as reasonable.[230] Some ideas, on the extreme right and the extreme left, are considered too radical to enter the mainstream public debate. Others are palatable enough to be discussed on the nightly news. The task of free-market evangelists, the think tank posited, was to move the Overton window closer and closer to their beliefs, making themselves more mainstream and consigning those who disagreed with them to the outer margins of the acceptable.

One of the harmful effects of Clinton's adoption of Republican crime rhetoric was that it created a shift in the Overton window: by abandoning left-wing criticisms of harsh and retributive crime control, Clinton's new platform moved the mainstream consensus on crime to the right. That meant there were fewer political bulwarks against abuses such as juvenile solitary confinement. Whereas previously, in the Dukakis era, the Democratic Party might have politely objected to such measures, Clintonian politics refused to make a fuss about it, on the grounds that doing so would be politically unpopular. With Clinton sounding less and less distinguishable from his Republican opponents on crime, the American Civil Liberties Union's perspective became steadily more marginal, and they were forced to fight on two fronts, against both Republicans and Democrats. This kind of shift in what constitutes the political mainstream is very difficult to quantify, and easy to ignore. Yet the development of a bipartisan consensus that mass incarceration was acceptable may well have filtered down to affect state policymaking, and the emergence of that consensus occurred largely because Bill Clinton and his allies in the centrist Democratic Leadership Council decided that traditional liberal values were too unpopular to be worth fighting for.

ONE OF THE MOST PERNICIOUS DEFENSES OF THE CRIME BILL IS the suggestion that African American leaders were in favor of it. A liberal blogger for *Mother Jones* magazine said that "the 1994 crime bill was supported by most black leaders at the time."[231] Bill Clinton himself, in defending the legislation, said that there had been "great demand, not just from America writ large, but from the black community, to get tougher on crime."[232] In the rush of liberal pundits to publish "it's more complicated than that" stories after Black Lives Matter confronted Clinton, there were numerous unseemly suggestions "that black citizens asked for it."[233]

To blame black people for the crime policies that made every interaction with police and courts an unmitigated terror is a distortion of history. In fact, black leaders were deeply divided on the crime bill. When the Democrats introduced the bipartisan crime bill in 1993, the NAACP called it a "crime against the American people."[234] Virginia Representative Bobby Scott recalls that "the Black Caucus was concerned because a lot of the provisions, in practice, adversely affect the black community disproportionately."[235]

In fact, when it was being crafted, the bill created an agonizing dilemma for the Congressional Black Caucus. Black communities were seriously afflicted by the violent crime wave, and CBC members were under pressure to support major legislative action. But they also knew that punitive crime control measures would end up disproportionately and unjustly hurting their constituents. Former Maryland Congressman Kweisi Mfume, who led the Black Caucus at the time of the crime bill, explained that:

> *The caucus was trying to bring a different perspective to the crime bill. On the one hand, we supported President Clinton's idea of adding 100,000 new policemen to the streets, and some of his other initiatives. On the other hand, we wanted to broaden the debate and temper the rush to solve the crime problem through solutions that had a disproportionate effect on blacks and Hispanics.*[236]

CBC members had to lobby hard to get preventive programs included in the crime bill, and even when they succeeded they were torn among themselves on the question of whether to vote for it. Ultimately, more of them voted for it than didn't, but newspaper accounts at the time noted that any support they gave was partly the product of party loyalty and intensive lobbying by Bill Clinton. The *Baltimore Sun* took note of "the extraordinary amount of presidential pleading required to secure the help of black lawmakers,"[237] and Black Caucus congressman Albert Wynn cited the caucus's "frustration" that black lawmakers were "being asked to bend more than most," being pressured to sacrifice their beliefs in order to preserve party unity.[238] Most black lawmakers ended up grudgingly supporting the final bill.

Some never came around, and were vocal in opposing the bill at every stage. CBC congressman Bobby Scott thought the idea of succumbing to draconianism in exchange for a few inner-city midnight basketball leagues was laughable: "You wouldn't ask an opponent of abortion to look at a bill with the greatest expansion of abortion in the history of the United States, and argue that he ought to vote for it because it's got some highway funding in it."[239] Surgeon General Joycelyn Elders was also extremely skeptical of the bill's benefits, saying "I look at our crime bill as one more expense... I don't see the great investment in prevention."[240]

In fact, the members of the Congressional Black Caucus had to work hard just to secure the modest quantity of prevention funding that did end up in the final bill. And in trying to tame the bill's excesses and secure social programs, the CBC received little support from the Executive Branch. As Anthony Lewis observed on the bill's passage, "the Justice Department did not work effectively against the worst features because President Clinton wanted something—anything—labeled 'crime bill.'"[241]

CBC members found themselves alone in trying to keep a bad bill from becoming worse. One of their key initiatives,

which received no support whatsoever from the Clinton administration, was a proposal to ban racial discrimination in the
administration of the death penalty. The Black Caucus' Racial
Justice Act would have allowed defendants to present evidence
of racism during their sentencing.

A seminal study by David Baldus and others in 1983 had
found that the death penalty was, indeed, deeply racist in its
administration. Black defendants in Georgia were nearly four
times more likely to be given the death penalty than white
defendants.[242] Cases with white victims were eleven times more
likely to lead to the death penalty than cases with black victims.[243] And while fewer than 40% of Georgia homicides were
against white victims, white-victim cases accounted for 87%
of death sentences.[244] It was disturbing data: the racial pattern
of punishment was unmistakable. A later study of Philadelphia death sentences confirmed the findings;[245] researchers
examined a series of variables that predicted whether a defendant would be sentenced to death and found that race was
undeniably affecting the results. They wrote that "it would be
extremely unlikely to observe disparities of this magnitude and
consistency if there were substantial equality in the treatment
of defendants in this system."[246]

But in 1987, the Supreme Court had rejected attempts to
introduce such statistics in death penalty cases. In *McCleskey
v. Kemp*, the Court ruled that the Baldus study was insufficient evidence to invalidate the defendant's conviction. This
was not because the Court deemed the study invalid, but
rather because it ruled that racial differences in application of
the death penalty were not unconstitutional. In a 6-3 opinion
written by Justice Lewis Powell, the Court held that "apparent
disparities in sentencing are an inevitable part of our criminal justice system," and worried that if it agreed that the
death penalty was applied in a racist manner, "we could soon

be faced with similar claims as to other types of penalty."[247]
The petitioner hadn't shown *why* black people were more
often sentenced to death, and the Court said it "decline[d] to
assume that what is unexplained is invidious."[248]

The *McCleskey* decision would become notorious in legal circles.
The Supreme Court's history might contain a long string of dishon-
orable blunders, but *McCleskey* stood out in its shamefulness even
for the Court. It all but acknowledged that the death penalty was
racist, then insisted that this wasn't the Court's problem. A survey
of legal scholars had branded *McCleskey* one of the worst Supreme
Court decisions since World War II.[249] NYU law professor Anthony
Amsterdam called the decision "the *Dred Scott* decision of our time."[250]
Justice Lewis Powell, asked after his retirement on whether he would
change any of his votes, replied: "Yes... *McCleskey v. Kemp*."[251]

The Black Caucus' Racial Justice Act was an attempt to undo
the embarrassment of the *McCleskey* decision. The *McCleskey* court had specifically stated that racial bias "arguments
are best presented to the legislative bodies," and so as duly
elected members of a legislative body, the Black Caucus took
the cue and intervened. (The Court had said it would defer to
the legislature to fix the problem because "it is not the responsibility—or indeed even the right—of this Court to determine
the appropriate punishment for particular crimes."[252] That was
not, in fact, the case. The Supreme Court is *constantly* determining appropriate punishments for crimes. It simply wasn't
moved by claims of racism.)

The Act was extremely modest in its provisions. It allowed
defendants to present evidence showing a pattern of racial bias
in the jurisdiction in which they were convicted, and placed a
burden on prosecutors to rebut that evidence. But it also allowed
a court to proceed with an execution if it found that the racial
injustice had been corrected; once prosecutors had satisfied the
court that there was no bias, the infliction of death could carry

on without further inconvenience or impediment. The only guarantee made to defendants would be that they were allowed to present certain evidence, and they were strictly limited in what kinds of evidence that could be. (They had to show a pattern of discriminatory application, not simply a greater rate of capital sentences by race.)

But Clinton wanted nothing to do with the Black Caucus' attempt to rid the death penalty of racism. He "refused to signal his support for the controversial measure despite the pleadings of members of Congress and the media."[253] In an editorial entitled "The Silent President," the *New York Times* chastised Clinton for his cowardice in refusing to comment on race and the death penalty. The *Times* wrote that "[i]t is time for President Clinton to take a stand for racial justice in administering the death penalty . . . [and] the president is silent about it."[254] This was especially galling, the *Times* said, because the White House had previously struck a deal with the Black Caucus, under which if the President lobbied for the racial justice provision, the Black Caucus would in turn support the crime bill:

> *The Congressional Black Caucus, which must accept all the bill's new death penalties in order to vote for it, thought it had a deal worked out with the Clinton Administration. The President, who has signed death warrants in Arkansas, would say publicly that the racial justice act was a desirable part of a balanced crime bill, and he would lobby for it. Caucus members and civil rights forces would join the lobbying. So far, however, not a sound has come from the White House or the Justice Department to advance or defend this provision.[255]*

Until the moment of the crime bill's passage, however, there was still some hope that Clinton would act. The *Times* reported a moment of political uncertainty, in which it was still possible for Clinton to step up and defend the principles of racial equity:

> *While Democrats compete with Republicans for ownership of the crime issue, President Clinton runs hard to keep up with the political pack. When the House and Senate negotiate over their bills and hundreds of pages of differences, will Mr. Clinton stake a legitimate claim to leadership? Will he help shape a strong public safety law that maintains such fair provisions as the Racial Justice Act? Those are the interesting questions now.*[256]

But these "interesting questions" turned out not to be very interesting at all. The answer to them was, predictably, no. The Act was dead before it was born. Republicans wouldn't hear of it, and Democrats were unwilling to support something that would undermine their commitment to a "new" crime politics. The words "racial justice" were verboten in New Democratic circles; they smacked of McGovernism and the Sixties and all the embarrassing progressive sympathies that the party was trying so very hard to erase. The Black Caucus found itself friendless. Its only remaining tactic was to negotiate for the inclusion of some funding for community-building initiatives, in the hope of mitigating some of the damage. After an exhausting tussle, they were given a limited number of concessions.

Torn between conflicting imperatives, knowing they couldn't get any more of their demands met, and needing to respond to their constituents' real concerns about crime, most of the Black Caucus ended up voting for the final bill. But they did so with no small reticence. Under the headline "Blacks Relent on Crime Bill, But Not Without Bitterness," *The New York Times* reported that:

> *The opposition of some black Democrats to the death penalty is so strong that 10 of the 38 black Democrats*

in Congress voted against the measure that would
have allowed the House to consider the crime bill,
even though it included millions of dollars in social
programs they say their communities sorely need.[257]

To lay responsibility for the crime bill on blacks is therefore a reprehensible form of victim-blaming. The truth is that some black politicians opposed the Clinton crime bill entirely, and "those who supported it weren't seeking punishment and nothing more; they desperately wanted massive investment in jobs and schools so the young people trapped in communities where work had suddenly disappeared would have some hope of survival."[258] As sentencing expert Marc Mauer writes:

While many African-American communities,
and others, were clearly concerned about crime
and violence, black political leadership did not
coalesce around the bill... The Black Caucus bill
emphasized support for crime prevention programs,
drug treatment, and creating job opportunities.[259]

One of the reasons that it looks, in retrospect, as if black leaders "supported" the crime bill is that the options they *did* support were simply not available to them, and they were given a false choice between watching their communities continue to be destroyed by crime and signing onto the incarceration-heavy program pushed by Clinton and Congressional Republicans. Milton Morris, a researcher on black economic issues with the Joint Center for Political and Economic Studies, spoke for a lot of black public policy professionals when he lamented in 1994 that "[a]ll the solutions before us are either Draconian, prison-oriented types of measures or the kind of costly long-term violence prevention efforts that I don't think the society right now has the patience or the will to take on."[260] Michigan Democrat John Conyers labeled the existing approach "simplistic," calling for a continued "uphill struggle" against senselessly punitive policies.[261]

All of this crucial qualification is missed by those who say black politicians "supported the crime bill." As Elizabeth Hinton, Julilly Kohler-Hausmann, and Vesla Weaver (two historians and a political scientist) have explained, white politicians (and those who now justify their behavior), have grossly distorted black demands:

> [E]ven at the time, many were asking for something different from the crime bill. Calls for tough sentencing and police protection were paired with calls for full employment, quality education and drug treatment, and criticism of police brutality. It's not just that those demands were ignored completely. It's that some elements were elevated and others were diminished—what we call selective hearing. Policy makers pointed to black support for greater punishment and surveillance, without recognizing accompanying demands to redirect power and economic resources to low-income minority communities. When blacks ask for 'better' policing, legislators tend to hear 'more' instead.[262]

Hinton, Hausmann, and Weaver write that "popular understanding of the rise of 'get tough' laws should not layer selective memory atop selective hearing of the past by justifying black incarceration with trite references to black voices."[263] In doing so, Clinton and his remaining supporters in the press exploit black perspectives for their own political ends; rather than listening to black demands, they simply use them, taking what they like and rejecting what they don't, and then abnegating responsibility when they are called to account.

A similar convenient selectivity occurs in the final common defense of Clinton's crime policies: they may seem racist and mercenary in 2016, but *things were different in 1994.* Explaining why Hillary Clinton had voiced strong support for criminal justice reform given her husband's '90s record, Hillary's spokesman Jesse Ferguson offered a variation on this defense: "[Hillary's] policy on internet might also be different than [Bill's] policy in 1994. Not because he was wrong but because times change."[264] A *RealClearPolitics* writer said that one might deplore the bill today "if you were a child, or not born yet, at the time of the bill's inception."[265]

But Clinton's crime policies were never reasonable, even at the time they were issued. As journalist Peter Beinart notes, "[t]he problem with this argument is that many of the crime policies the Clintons supported in the 1990s were probably wrong even back then."[266] "No one knew then that we'd seen the worst,"[267] said one of Clinton's defenders. But some people did.

Throughout the nineties, observers were commenting on the foolishness of reflexively punitive approaches. Even current NYPD police chief Bill Bratton, an early pioneer of "broken windows" methods, said in 1996 that national crime policies were failing to pay sufficient attention to preventing crime as well as punishing it, and that the existing political campaign rhetoric (not just on the Republican side) was unhelpful. Bratton said that:

> *The experts, whether from academia, law enforcement, sociologists, researchers, all believe that we need to do more on the preventive side, the treatment side, and it's not reflected in the funding decisions that are made and as you indicate, in the rhetoric that we hear, particularly in campaign years.*[268]

With Clinton trying to take teens' drivers licenses away and preventing courts from hearing death penalty appeals, it became impossible to have a serious conversation about how to actually deal effectively and humanely with criminal behavior. The crime bill itself was fully a political maneuver. *The Independent* noted that the bill "has great political significance" because it "lies at the heart of Mr. Clinton's effort to take the issue of crime from the Republicans."[269] The bill was urgently needed; not by the country, but by Clinton.

Predictably, then, the "get tough" measures implemented during the 1980s and 1990s were mostly useless. In defending the Violent Crime Control Act to the Philadelphia activists, Bill Clinton claimed that "because of that bill, we had a 25-year low in crime."[270] This is almost certainly false. The impact of the bill lay somewhere between the negligible and the trivial. Any increased incarceration was unlikely to have reduced crime.[271] As Liliana Segura of *The Intercept* explains, with crime rates already dropping, "the landmark features of the 1994 crime bill largely boiled down to posturing."[272] Even the COPS program, the 100,000 additional police on the streets that Clinton was so beamingly proud of, was in all probability a wash as far as crime-control was concerned.[273] The 100,000 number had been utterly arbitrary to begin with. Clinton's deputy issues director, John Kroger, recalled how it was arrived at: "Clinton had a big crime speech coming up. We had no idea how many extra cops would be a good thing. ... Bruce Reed and I called [Ron Klain] from Little Rock. He said, 'Would 100,000 be enough?'"[274]

The continuing growth of prisons was also a costly waste. The consensus among criminologists was that "increased incarceration at today's levels has a negligible crime control benefit," and that at a certain level, incarceration can actually have counterproductive effects.[275] The prison system was already so vast that most of the truly dangerous individuals had been put away, and there was nothing to be gained from feeding additional helpings of black bodies into the criminal justice system's ravenous maw.

CBC congressman Bobby Scott explains that the failure was perfectly predictable; after all,

> ...the Crime Bill did not look to research for its basis, but politics. Three-strikes-and-you're-out was found to be the number one vote-getting slogan of the 1994 election cycle. It beat anything you could say about Social Security, healthcare, or the environment. Three strikes and you're out got you more votes.[276]

Scott distinguishes between poll-based policymaking and evidence-based policymaking, and says that policies like three strikes "never made any sense" from a crime-prevention perspective, and that the crime bill as a whole was "a political document, not a crime-reduction document."[277] Former Deputy Attorney General Philip Heymann confirmed this, saying that the crime bill was "the most careful political calculation, with absolutely sublime indifference to the real nature of the problem."[278] Given that the bill was *never* a dispassionate attempt to create effective public safety policies, but was simply a bipartisan attempt to satisfy the public demand for some kind of major anti-crime initiative, it was not surprising that it did almost nothing, except to inflict further injustices upon vulnerable populations. "Everybody knew that was going to happen,"[279] says Bobby Scott.

The policies introduced by the 1994 crime bill were a cobbled-together mess, drawing on little research. As *The New York Times* observed upon the bill's passage, "[t]he law includes a sprawling array of programs, many of them untested, that taken together have little overall coherence... It reflects the ideological divisions that had stymied Congressional efforts to enact a crime bill for years as well as the pet projects of legislators whose votes were needed to pass it at last."[280] The included policies and programs were little more than a "a flimsy bauble to dangle before voters," a kaleidoscope of different impressive-sounding measures without any particular philosophy behind them. Or, as broken windows originator and erstwhile superpredator theorist James Q. Wilson said of the bill: "It's a Christmas tree designed by Salvador Dalí."[281] It's mistaken, then, to think of the crime bill as an honest and careful attempt to reduce crime rather than a very grand, very expensive, very inhumane political gesture.

WHEN HIS RECORD ON CRIME IS TAKEN AS A WHOLE, CLINTON cannot be treated as a sincere pragmatic progressive who only tried to balance citizens' legitimate fears of crime with a liberal concern for civil liberties. Political journalist Jamelle Bouie flatly summarizes what happened: "Democrats hungrily followed a conservative consensus on crime, government, and punishment, rejecting less punitive options in favor of federalizing draconian state and local policies that drove the growth in incarceration, all in an (ultimately failed) effort to bring suburban white voters back into the Democratic Party."[282] The idea that these policies were a legitimate response to the crime wave is revisionist. Each year there was more available data showing the declining crime rate, yet each year Clinton continued with more tough-guy grandstanding, unveiling useless severe initiative after useless severe initiative. Observers noted that Clinton's anti-crime rhetoric tended to escalate in accordance with the electoral needs of the Democratic Party. As political scientist Steven Puro noted in 1996: "In a political year, the get-tough rhetoric is the thing that seems to appeal to the American public. So the notion is on punitive procedures, punitive activities, such as Clinton's recent [drug testing for driver's licenses] proposal."[283]

Clinton stood out even among centrist Democrats for his advocacy of ruthless new crackdown measures against the criminal classes. Ever since his days as governor of Arkansas, President

Clinton had made punishing criminals central to his political appeal, and at Stone Mountain Clinton quite literally made a prop out of a group of convicts.

Some have been puzzled by Clinton's worsening of the criminal justice crisis. Vincent Schiraldi of Harvard's Kennedy School says "I remember thinking when Bill Clinton got elected that we would have a chance to turn things around [on criminal justice]. But I think we read the tea leaves wrong."[284] Thomas Frank exasperatedly asks about the crime bill:

> How could he sign such a thing right after giving a big speech deploring its effects? How can he and his wife now claim it was all an accident, when the consequences were being discussed everywhere at the time? When everyone was warning and even begging him not to do it? [285]

But the "how could he" question is only unanswerable if one makes certain assumptions about Clinton's values. If, on the other hand, one believes Clinton's actions came in response to the convenience of a political moment, where crime control was a sensible issue to "take" from the Republicans, there is no mystery. It wasn't about the human consequences, it was simply about the political usefulness of being Tough on Crime in positioning one's self as a "different" Democrat.

Of course, for millions of people, it was *very much* about the consequences. Get tough rhetoric has left the United States with the highest incarceration rate in the world, and a criminal justice system that seems to eat black communities alive. As Figure 1C (next page) shows, the United States now has a nationwide "prison archipelago," with thousands of jails and prisons housing multiple millions of people.[286] Its scale is almost incomprehensively large, its human costs incalculable. It is only because prisons are carefully kept out of sight (they are often in rural and remote areas) that the nationwide level of incarceration can be kept from truly being appreciated.

FIGURE 1C

The U.S. Prison Archipelago
State and Federal Correctional Facilities in the Contiguous United States

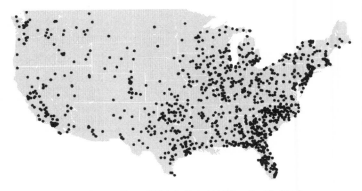

Source: Bureau of Justice Statistics, "Census Of State And Federal Adult Correctional Facilities."
Note: Map displays only prison facilities. In addition, there are approximately 750,000 inmates in more than
one thousand city and county jails. See Bureau of Justice Statistics, "Census of Jails: Population Changes,
1999–2013."

Much of the blame for that has to lie with Clinton, who not
only exploited fear of crime politically and abandoned all Democratic commitments to moderation, but squandered the chance
to walk back some of the crueler policies of the Reagan and Bush
years. During Clinton's presidency, the prisons grew more than
they ever had before, and he said and did nothing to stop it.
Quite the opposite: in addition to prosecuting countless federal drug cases and encouraging state adoption of three-strikes
laws, Clinton established policies that gutted the death penalty appeals system, removed remedies for abuses of prisoners'
human rights, and kicked families out of public housing over
minor drug offenses. Baltimore journalist and *The Wire* creator
David Simon notes that "[t]he administration that did the most
damage in terms of jailing Americans for nonviolent offenses is
the Clinton administration. By far." The Equal Justice Initiative's
Bryan Stevenson concludes flatly that when it came to the justice
system, "President Clinton's tenure was the worst."[287]

*Bill Clinton signs the 1995 Personal Responsibility
and Work Opportunity Act and smiles heartily.
(Lillie Harden on left, looking somewhat less enthused.)*

CHAPTER TWO

Welfare to Work

N 1992, WHEN BILL CLINTON ANNOUNCED THAT HE
planned to "end welfare as we know it," he was taking up
a unique position for a Democrat. The party of Lyndon
Johnson typically had to fight hard to preserve the country's
limited social safety net; it was unprecedented for a Democrat
to strongly disparage welfare and vow to destroy it. In fact,
when centrist political operative Bruce Reed heard Clinton give
his anti-welfare pitch, Reed was immediately struck by the fact
that "it wasn't the kind of thing most Democrats said."[288] (This
led Reed to enthusiastically join the Clinton campaign.)

The anti-welfare pitch was a key part of Clinton's 1992 platform. In Clinton's speech announcing his candidacy, he declared
that "[w]e should insist that people move off welfare rolls and
onto work rolls" and that "we should demand" that everybody
who can work and become "productive" does so.[289] With this
unprecedented rejection of New Deal language, emphasizing
"productivity" and "responsibility" over "guarantees" and "safety
nets," Clinton instantly changed the way Democrats talked
about welfare. Brendon O'Connor writes in *A Political History*

of Welfare that by intentionally bringing up welfare reform, and campaigning on it, Clinton "did crucially put time limits and workfare on the national agenda as a possible bipartisan position."[290] By promising to address welfare, Clinton also created public anticipation for a welfare reform measure. As O'Connor writes, "[t]his oft-repeated campaign rhetoric had consequences in that it heightened expectations for reform... [Clinton] helped create a perception that far-reaching reforms were necessary and that almost any other approach would be preferred to the then-current system."[291]

Clinton's idea to abolish welfare did not originate with his 1992 campaign. "I had long been committed to welfare reform," Clinton wrote in a 2006 *New York Times* op-ed presumptuously entitled "How We Ended Welfare, Together."[292] Clinton had introduced a "workfare" scheme in Arkansas and had promoted a 1988 welfare reform law requiring teen mothers to meet stricter conditions, like living at home, in order to receive benefits.[293] Clinton spoke of a "contract" with welfare recipients, whereby there would be no more free guarantees that were not coupled with personal obligations.[294] When asked by an interviewer about "demand[ing] a set of behavioral standards" for "15-year-old mother[s] on welfare," Hillary Clinton replied that she had "been talking about that since 1973" and was "one of the first people who wrote about how rights and responsibilities had to go hand in hand."[295] Hillary recommended the policy that Bill had introduced in Arkansas, by which "people who refused for whatever reason to participate had their benefits cut."[296]

For someone like Bill Clinton, concerned with recapturing white voters, welfare reform made sense as a pet issue to adopt. For many years, the Democrats had been the party of government social programs. The party was defined by the legacy of the New Deal and the Great Society, serving a motley coalition of the disadvantaged. But over the course of the 1980s and early

1990s, a backlash had developed against the social programs initiated by Franklin Roosevelt and expanded under Lyndon Johnson. An idea emerged that welfare programs were "broken," that they were breeding dependency and parasitism. Ronald Reagan notoriously told the story of a "welfare queen" whose government checks financed her brand-new Cadillac, and soon the idea of the welfare queen became a common cliché. (There *had* been a "welfare queen" in Chicago, a white woman who had bilked the government out of thousands of dollars, as well as being involved in kidnapping, extortion, and murder plots.[297] But nobody could ever seem to find another, and the welfare queen as a widespread social phenomenon was in all certainty a fiction. She became a kind of mythical creature, spoken of constantly while never seen.) As historian Daryl Carter documents, conservatives "stigmatized those on welfare, particularly women and minorities, as freeloaders, ne'er-do-wells, burdens on the taxpayer, and symbols of what was wrong with America."[298]

One cannot overstate the level to which this backlash was linked to race. Internal Democratic Party research had determined that white voters had turned away from the party in large part due to a perception that Democrats were the party of handouts to minorities. Conducting the largest study in its history, the Democratic National Committee found that white voters in focus groups were describing the Democrats as the "give away party, giving white tax money to blacks and poor people."[299] (The results of the survey were so ugly and embarrassing that the party quickly suppressed them, destroying nearly all copies of the report.[300]) Another study of white Reagan voters, by future Clinton pollster Stanley Greenberg, concluded that "[t]hese white Democratic defectors express a profound distaste for blacks, a sentiment that pervades almost everything they think about government and politics... Blacks constitute the explanation for their vulnerability and almost everything that has gone wrong in their lives, not being black is what constitutes being middle class, not being black is what makes a neighborhood a decent place to live."[301]

The data also confirmed that race was at the heart of the welfare issue specifically. An attempt by sociologists to determine which other beliefs were statistically correlated with support for welfare reform found that: "the one thing that did predict a negative view of welfare was negative beliefs about African-Americans, particularly a belief in black laziness" as well as "stereotypes of black women as being sexually irresponsible."[302] They also found that talking about welfare *in itself* changed people to have a more negative view of African Americans. "We found that as politicians talked more and more about welfare and what was wrong with the program, they moved people's racial attitudes. The people who were most likely to start seeing welfare as a big problem were actually those who shifted from not having negative views of African-Americans to steadily responding to this discourse by beginning to see race in a different way and seeing African-Americans in a much worse light."[303]

Race consequently became a key part of the political narrative around welfare. As sociologist Joe Soss summarizes, the story around welfare became a story of mooching, which:

> *...held that there were white people who played by the rules, and then there were people of color—and particularly black people — who were taking from those people in an illegitimate way. At the time, there was a lot of talk of the pathologies of the underclass. And many believed that it was really these liberal programs that were to blame for what was seen as a kind of crisis of crime and disorder and sexual irresponsibility and welfare dependence and all of these things.[304]*

There were political gains to be had in exploiting these prejudices. Sociologists Kenneth J. Neubeck and Noel A. Casaneve observed that by 2001, "[t]he racialization of welfare has reached the point where politicians can now exploit racial animus to promote their political ambitions and goals simply by speaking the word welfare."[305] In their book *Welfare Racism,* Neubeck and Casaneve examine the entire history of American social programs, showing that racism has been a core factor in determining how political discussions about welfare occurred.

Rutgers historian Donna Murch writes that the new centrist Democrats were willing to use this "illegitimate takings" story to reverse their political fortunes: "Bolstered with polling data and the crisis of the Reagan landslide, the New Democrats searched for ways to aggressively distance themselves from 'blacks' and to entice resentful white swing voters back into the fold. To do this, the New Democrats appropriated hot button issues from the Republican Party, later deemed 'dog whistle politics,' that invoked the specter of blackness without directly naming it."

It should perhaps be noted that all of the stories underlying the welfare panic were false. Not only was the welfare queen a mythical creature, the chupacabra of American social policy, but America was distinctly stingy with its social guarantees compared with the European countries. By the time Clinton took office, huge cuts to welfare spending under Ronald Reagan had already eliminated 400,000 people's eligibility for welfare, and one million people's eligibility for food stamps.[306] After adjusting for inflation, welfare benefits had fallen by 47% between 1970 and 1994.[307] Anger about benefits had thus increased at the same time as the benefits themselves were decreasing.

The arguments for links between illegitimacy and the receipt of welfare were also based on flimsy social scientific evidence. The infamous "Moynihan Report" (on the "tangle of pathology" afflicting the "negro family"[308]) had made for easy sound

bites about black family dysfunction and dependency. But the
concept was fundamentally unsound. First, the limited available
data had found that "welfare payments did not increase single motherhood."[309] But there were also fundamental correla-
tion/causation problems with the entire theory. Causal links
between phenomena are notoriously tricky things for social
scientists to make, and if one could argue that changes in black
family patterns caused lingering poverty, one could also argue
the reverse: the persistence of poverty was causing changes in
black family structures.

In fact, the very idea of welfare "dependency" was based on
a somewhat oblivious premise to begin with. Daniel Patrick
Moynihan himself took note of the fact that "it is the nature of
children to be dependent"[310]; there is no such thing as an independent infant. So, too, with single mothers. Since it's impossible to care for a child during the hours one is working a job,
and impossible to work a job during the hours one is caring
for a child, some level of dependence on outside assistance is
an inevitable aspect of poor motherhood. Yet "dependency" was
discussed as if it was by nature undesirable, something to be
eliminated by any means. Rarely did anyone venture to point
out that it may be a fact of social life that some who cannot
provide for themselves will always have to depend on others. The
rhetoric of mutual aid that had built the Great Society vanished,
as New Democrats joined the Republican attempt to eliminate
the dependency scourge.

WHILE REFORMING/ENDING WELFARE HAD BEEN ONE OF
his key proposals in 1992, once Clinton became president the issue lay somewhat dormant until 1995.
Up until that point, Bill Clinton remained preoccupied with
health care and crime, and the more liberal Democrats did
not care to bring up his welfare pledges. But with the Repub-

lican sweep of Congress in the 1994 elections, welfare once again entered the public discussion. The Republicans were eager to take Clinton up on his promise, and put pressure on him to follow through on ending welfare. As Joe Soss says, "Clinton found that he had painted himself into a corner, because of course the Republicans were willing to go much farther in this game than he was."[311]

The Republicans passed several welfare bills, each predictably unsparing in its elimination of benefits. Fearing the outright revolt of his liberal base, Clinton vetoed these bills twice, holding out for something that didn't seem *quite* like it had been lifted directly from the Contract with America. But Clinton knew the data on the popularity of cutting benefits, and knew that he would be held to account if he failed to make good on his unqualified pledge of 1992. It was Clinton who had helped to build the national consensus that welfare was "broken" and urgently needed "fixing," and thus he was expected to fix it. As Soss says, "for a public that had already learned to think of welfare as a black program—that had internalized these Republican calls to get tough on the welfare queens and whatnot—welfare now became center stage. The public was aroused, so something had to be done."[312]

That something was the dismantling of the Aid to Families With Dependent Children (AFDC) program. AFDC was a New Deal program founded in 1935, which offered cash payments to poor families. It was the core of the existing federal welfare system. Because AFDC offered aid without any work requirements, it was considered to be the root of the welfare "problem."

AFDC was also disproportionately received by black single mothers.[313] It was not the only program that offered government handouts with little expected in return (Social Security mailed millions of checks every month). But it was the program most linked in the public mind with "dependency."

The consensus among Republicans and right-leaning Democrats was that AFDC had to go in its entirety. Even the softened versions of the welfare bill did away with it. The central thrust of the plan to "end welfare as we know it" was that welfare should no longer be a federal guarantee of aid, but a quid-pro-quo in which limited assistance was granted in exchange for the fulfillment of various obligations. Welfare would not be a fallback for the destitute, but a program to incentivize employment.

With strong public support for this "welfare to work" philosophy, Clinton and the Republican congress seemed certain to succeed in removing AFDC. But since core Democratic blocs were disgusted by the welfare bill, it did not pass without controversy, and Hillary Clinton later recalled that she had to "work hard to round up votes for its passage."[314] As the bill moved closer to passing, the remaining liberals in the Democratic Party were scandalized. Lofty appeals to the better natures of the Congress and President were made throughout Washington. John Lewis took to the floor of the House and denounced the bill in especially uncompromising terms:

> *[This bill] is cruel. It is wrong. It is down right low down. The Republican welfare proposal destroys the safety net that protects our Nation's children, elderly, and disabled. It is an angry proposal, a proposal devoid of compassion, and feeling. Hubert Humphrey once said that "the moral test of government is how that government treats those who are in the dawn of life—the children; those who are in twilight of life—the elderly, and those who are in the shadow of life—the sick, the needy, and the handicapped." Mr. Chairman, this welfare proposal attacks each and every one of these groups. It takes money out of the pockets of the disabled. It*

takes heat from the homes of the poor. It takes food out of the mouths of the children... Vote against this mean-spirited proposal; raise your voice for the children, the poor, and the disabled... A famous rabbi, Rabbi Hillel, once asked, "If I am not for myself, who will be for me? But if I am only for myself, what am I?" What am I, Mr. Chairman? I am for those in the dawn of life, the children. I am for those in the twilight of life, the elderly. I am for those in the shadow of life, the sick, the needy and the handicapped.[315]

When the bill came up for a vote, Lewis pleaded: "How can any person of faith, of conscience, vote for a bill that puts a million more kids into poverty? What does it profit a great nation to conquer the world, only to lose its soul?"[316]

Other black Democrats made strong objections. Jim Clyburn of South Carolina told the House, "I find it ironic that at the same time our Nation's most vulnerable families are being required to do more for themselves, our states are being asked to do even less."[317] Black Democrats in Congress did not accept the argument that Democratic welfare reform was an improvement over that offered by the Republicans. Carol Moseley-Braun insisted the changes from the previously-vetoed Gingrich bills made little difference:

This bill is still an abomination, which is what I called the previous bill, and I intend to vote against it for precisely that reason—and I keep coming back to the question, and no one has answered the question: What about the children? What happens to them when all is said and done, with all the cuts and the changes that we are making with this legislation?[318]

Charles Rangel bitterly scoffed that "the Republicans will throw 2 million people, children, into poverty, and my President will only throw 1 million into poverty."[319]

THE APPEALS OF THE BLACK CAUCUS WERE INSUFFICIENT to sway Clinton. On August 22nd, 1996, he signed the Personal Responsibility and Work Opportunity Reconciliation Act (PRWORA) into law.

For those who had counted on Clinton to "end welfare as we know it," the PRWORA was not a disappointment. AFDC was gone in its entirety, along with the entire federal apparatus for directly administering welfare. In its place was a new system called Temporary Assistance for Needy Families (TANF), which completely transformed the country's public benefits system.

TANF ended the guarantee that poor mothers could receive assistance from the federal government. Instead, it imposed a five-year lifetime cap on benefits, and instituted a work requirement. Nobody could receive assistance for more than two years at a time. Immigrants (even lawful permanent residents) were barred from applying for aid. Most importantly, it decentralized the administration of benefits. Rather than being a federal program, TANF was delivered as a series of block grants to state governments, who were relied upon to make sure that the funds made their way into the hands of recipients. And the total amount spent by the federal government would be far less than its previous AFDC expenditures.[320]

This move was not just radical. It was an obliteration of the social guarantee to poor families that Democrats had spent decades building. When Clinton signed the bill, *The New York Times* did not underplay its significance, reporting that in a "sweeping reversal of Federal policy, President Clinton today ended six decades of guaranteed help to the nation's poorest children" and thereby "eliminated a pillar of Franklin D. Roosevelt's New Deal social welfare program, delighting the Republican-controlled Congress in this election year and incensing many of his fellow Democrats."[321] Clinton's Labor Secretary, Robert Reich, said Clinton had outright "ended the promise of help to the indigent and their children which Franklin D. Roosevelt had initiated more than sixty years before."[322]

Many Democrats found this impossible to endorse. Three senior officials in the Clinton Administration resigned almost immediately.[323] Even the conservative deregulation advocate Robert Rubin opposed Clinton's signing of the bill. Peter Edelman, one of the officials who had resigned, took to the pages of *The Atlantic* and called the bill "the worst thing Bill Clinton has done."[324] (Barack Obama said he found Clinton's signing of the bill "disturbing."[325])

Bill Clinton was open about the fact that his decision was at least in part motivated by political considerations (although George Stephanopoulos had told him that he was assured of reelection even if he did not sign the bill). "After I sign my name to this bill," Clinton declared, "welfare will no longer be a political issue."[326] But if Clinton thought he would appease Republicans with welfare reform, he was mistaken. The moment the bill was signed, Bob Dole declared that Clinton was transparently engaging in an "election year political calculation" and that "[b]y selling out his own party, Bill Clinton has proven he is ideologically adrift."[327] With AFDC dismantled, Republicans simply moved on to find other social programs, such as food stamps, to attack next.

AFTER THE ENACTMENT OF THE PRWORA, ITS SUPPORTERS almost instantaneously declared welfare reform a success. "We now know that welfare reform works," Clinton declared just a year after signing the bill.[328] But often one of their main criteria for "success" was whether people had been successfully removed from the welfare rolls. The Department of Housing and Urban Development claimed that switching from welfare to employment meant achieving "self-sufficiency," concluding that "welfare reform increased the rate at which families living in public housing or using vouchers at baseline became 'self-sufficient' in the sense that they were employed, no longer received welfare, and no longer had housing assistance."[329] A summary by the Republican House Ways and Means Committee claimed that "since it replaced the New Deal-era Aid to Families with Dependent Children (AFDC) program in 1996, Temporary Assistance for Needy Families (TANF) has been successful at cutting welfare dependence as caseloads have declined by 57 percent through December 2011."[330] Others, such as the Heritage Foundation, similarly phrased the decline in caseloads as a "decline in welfare dependence."[331] Conservative writer Heather Mac Donald wrote that:

> *Congress's wager paid off handsomely. Asked to look for work in exchange for their welfare checks, hundreds of thousands of women found jobs. From 1996 to 1999, employment among the nation's never-married mothers rose 40 percent. In 1992, only 38 percent of young single mothers worked; by March 2000, 60 percent of that group were employed. Another large portion of the caseload, faced with new participation requirements, simply decided that welfare was not worth the hassle. The result: a 52 percent drop in the caseload since August 1996, when TANF passed, to June 2001. Nearly 2.3 million families have left the rolls.*[332]

Hillary Clinton herself said she was proud that former AFDC recipients were "no longer deadbeats—they're actually out there being productive."[333]

All of these triumphant declarations by Republicans and the Clintons were curious. By conflating "no longer receiving welfare" with "no longer needing welfare," they avoided asking the question of how the actual life situations of the people who were removed from the rolls had changed. After all, "reducing the welfare rolls" is only a positive outcome if people are leaving the rolls because they no longer need assistance, rather than because they are facing new obstacles to obtaining it. Yet oddly, in the post-AFDC era, "declining caseloads" are often invoked, even by liberals, as a positive outcome. (In a critical assessment of welfare reform in the *Washington Post,* Dylan Matthews wrote that the declining number of recipients suggests that "some" of the support for welfare reform is justified.[334]) HUD's view was that less welfare meant more self-sufficiency. But a decline in caseloads said very little in itself; it was hardly unexpected that a law designed to reduce welfare access would end up reducing welfare access. The question was whether the particular people who would otherwise have been on welfare were better off.

THERE WERE EARLY SIGNS THAT THIS WAS NOT THE CASE, AND that while the PRWORA was, as *The New York Times* suggested, "effective in getting people off welfare, the system proved far less nimble at making them financially sound."[335] Senator Paul Wellstone of Minnesota was skeptical of the "boosterism" exhibited by the Democratic defenders of welfare reform:

> *There's been a flurry of credible reports suggesting that all is not well with welfare reform. But President Clinton and Vice President Gore continue to claim that welfare is `working'. What they overlook is why, at a time when the welfare rolls have been cut in half and the economy is booming, we now are finding that millions more children are going to bed hungry*

each night; demand for emergency food assistance is
growing; millions of poor families are dropping off
the Food Stamp rolls faster than economic indicators
would predict; and former welfare recipients are
losing their medical coverage, cannot make the rent
and utilities, and are unable to afford child care.
These are not the results of successful reform.[336]

Robert Reich was similarly unimpressed by Clinton's insistence that he had succeeded. Reich doubted the premise that declining welfare rolls necessarily meant a successful program:

The White House now claims that the 1996 welfare
bill has been a huge success, based on the large number
of people who have been removed from state welfare
rolls since then. But we have no way of knowing how
many of these people are in permanent jobs paying a
living wage, or are in temporary jobs paying so little
that they have to double up with other family members
and leave their children at home alone during the
day, or are living on the street. And we may never
know, even after the economy slides into recession,
and the ranks of the unemployed begin to grow once
again. The sad truth is that America has embarked on
the largest social experiment it has undertaken in this
half of the twentieth century without even adequate
base-line data from which researchers can infer what
has happened, or deduce what will happen, to large
numbers of poor people who no longer receive help.[337]

One problem in testing these assertions was that by getting rid of federal involvement in welfare, Clinton had also gotten rid of a core accountability mechanism. The states were being entrusted to administer welfare, but they were not required to demonstrate that they had used the money well. And measuring outcomes across fifty different state systems, and trying to determine the extent to which each program was succeeding or failing, would have been an impossible research task.

Thus, just as Jim Clyburn had noted, while welfare recipients were being saddled with new obligations, states had to meet very few requirements in exchange for their own handouts. TANF dollars flowed in regardless of how well a state's program was doing. Compounding the problem was the fact that states could actually reallocate TANF money toward other programs if they felt it necessary. Consequently, as the Center on Budget and Policy Priorities reports, the block grants ended up being used to "plug state budget holes" rather than providing cash assistance to the poor.[338]

Other provisions similarly incentivized states to restrict assistance. A "caseload reduction credit" lowered the obligations states had to meet for their work programs if they could demonstrate they had removed people from the rolls.[339] And while states were evaluated on whether they had put people to work, they were not evaluated on whether they had provided adequate assistance to families, encouraging states to move the poor into low-wage jobs to rid them from the rolls as quickly as possible.

WHAT CAME NEXT WAS ALMOST AMUSING IN ITS PREDICTABILITY. Because TANF's effectiveness depended on the competence and benevolence of state governments, levels of TANF assistance varied considerably across states. In some parts of the country, TANF benefits were sufficient to elevate a family to nearly 50% of the poverty line, though nowhere did benefits do any better than reaching half the federal poverty level. But across much of the South (including many of the country's poorest states), TANF recipients were lucky if their benefits got them to 15% of the poverty line, a sum impossible

Maximum TANF Benefits Still Leave Families Well Below Federal Poverty Level

Maximum TANF grant for family of three as a share of the federal poverty level
10-20%   20-30%   30-40%   40-50%

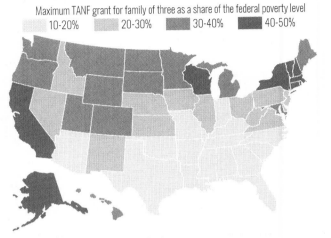

Note: TANF = Temporary Assistance for Needy Families.
Hawaii and Alaska poverty measurements are higher than other 48 states.
Source: Center on Budget and Policy Priorities (CPBB), calculated from 2013 Department of Health and Human Services Poverty Guidelines and CBPP-compiled data on July 2013 poverty levels

to subsist on. The states with the highest African American populations extended the stingiest TANF benefits. Alejandra Marchevsky and Jeanne Theoharis of *The Nation* go so far as to say that in the post-welfare era, "a revival of Jim Crow–like practices and exclusions have flourished, as Southern states have largely dismantled their welfare systems and pay some of the lowest benefits in the nation."[340] And because African Americans face intense job discrimination (they are less likely to receive callbacks than their equally-qualified white counterparts[341]), the work requirements are already likely to be disproportionately difficult for African Americans to fulfill.

Nor is the program improving. The value of TANF checks keeps dropping, making its benefits ever more meager. Federal funding has been stagnant for twenty years, and doesn't change in response to recessions. Thus recipients generally get by during prosperous times like the final years of the Clinton Administration, but when the economy contracts, TANF does little to help families survive hard times.

Welfare reform did succeed in moving many single mothers into jobs, if only because the disappearance of benefits left little other option than to accept whatever employment was available. But the evidence on whether the increased employment actually increased these mothers' overall well-being is mixed. Conservatives and the Clintons tended to speak of full-time employment as if it was in itself the desirable state of being for single mothers; to be "productive" meant no longer being a "deadbeat." But this was not necessarily so. A mother who had to travel on an hour-long commute to a dead-end job, thus never seeing her child, may have increased her "productivity" while becoming worse off. If a mother's increased earnings are spent on childcare for the time she spends at work, and her parenting suffers as a result of her mandatory employment and her exhaustion after a day's work, moving mothers from welfare to work could damage the lives of poor children *even as it increases both employment and earnings among single mothers.* The fetishization of work, and the corresponding obliviousness to other important life outcomes, can make welfare reform appear more successful than it truly was.

Former welfare mother Diana Spatz explains that welfare reform wrongly assumed that work automatically improves mothers' lives, when certain types of work are themselves barriers to education and self-improvement:

> *"Any job is a good job" was the slogan emblazoned on*
> *the walls of county welfare agencies across the country,*
> *as tens of thousands of low-income mothers were made*
> *to quit college to do up to thirty-five hours per week of*
> *unpaid "workfare": sweeping streets, picking up trash*

*in parks and cleaning public restrooms in exchange
for benefits as low as $240 a month. Contrary to
"welfare queen" stereotypes, like most welfare mothers,
I worked first. Work wasn't the problem; it was the
nature of the work—low-wage, dead-end jobs with
no benefits and little chance for advancement—that
kept families like mine on the welfare rolls.*[342]

In assessing welfare reform's results, if we examine it fairly,
what we see generally is a bifurcation. Those who were successfully "moved to employment" saw their earnings increase. But for
others, conditions not only stagnated, but worsened. In particular, those at the "bottom of the bottom" suffered. In the years
since welfare reform, the percentage of families in extreme poverty
increased by 50%.[343] And there is evidence to suggest that large
numbers of people live on incomes as low as $2 a day, with many
selling plasma in order to survive.[344] As Ron Haskins, a Republican
who helped write the welfare bill, notes, because of the structure
of TANF "any mom who does not have the ability to maintain her
household and work at the same time is going to have trouble."[345]

TANF can leave such people stuck in deep poverty. Previously,
under AFDC, a mother could receive benefits while attending
school full-time, thus enabling her to get a degree and gradually
move off welfare. But TANF did not count higher education
as fulfilling the work requirement, thus women were unable to
support themselves while being educated. Consequently, while
in 1995, "649,000 student parents were receiving cash assistance
while enrolled full-time in education programs, only 35,000
full-time students received TANF aid in 2004."[346]

Because of TANF's restrictive conditions, mothers who cannot
work or struggle to meet their obligations are unlikely to receive
benefits. There has consequently been a decline in the percentage of poor families that receive benefits. While under AFDC,

FIGURE 2B

Welfare Reform and the
Decline of the Social Safety Net

Number of families receiving benefits for every 100 with children in poverty

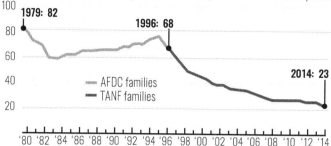

Note: TANF = Temporary Assistance for Needy Families, AFDC = Aid to Families with Dependent Children, Deep poverty = income less than 50% of the federal poverty line

Source: Center on Budget and Policy Priorities (CPBB), analysis of poverty data from the Census' Current Population Survey and AFDC/TANF caseload data from Department of Health and Human Services and (since September 2006) caseload data collected by CPBB from state agencies

FIGURE 2C

TANF Lifts Many Fewer Children out of
Deep Poverty Than AFDC Did

TANF (2010)

Lifted 24% of children who would otherwise have been in deep poverty

**629,000
children**

AFDC (1995)

Lifted 62% of children who would otherwise have been in deep poverty

**2,210,000
children**

Note: TANF = Temporary Assistance for Needy Families, AFDC = Aid to Families with Dependent Children, Deep poverty = income less than 50% of the federal poverty line

Source: Center on Budget and Policy Priorities, analysis of Census' Current Population Survey, additional data from Heath and Human Services' TRIM model

68% of families with children in poverty were receiving some form of benefits, by 2014, that number had declined to 23% (See Figure 2B). And while AFDC had succeeded in lifting 62% of children out of deep poverty, for TANF that number was only 24% (See Figure 2C).

Welfare reform was therefore precisely what its liberal critics said it was: little more than the elimination of the safety net. The Center on Budget and Policy Priorities concludes that "[TANF], the cornerstone of the 1996 reforms, is not the success that some proclaim and should not be used as a model for other safety net programs."[347] Marchevsky and Theoharis, in *The Nation*, summarize the best available empirical findings on welfare reform's success:

> *[M]ost studies of the effects of this legislation, including our own, have concluded that it has only succeeded in pushing people out of the welfare system—not helped the vast majority out of poverty. Even during the boom years of the late 1990s, when former recipients were job hunting in a robust labor market, research showed that poor mothers were channeled into low-wage, dead-end jobs, and that many who "timed out" or were "sanctioned out" of TANF could not find work because they needed more education and training...* *[TANF] traps poor mothers into exploitative, poverty-wage jobs and dangerous personal situations, deters them from college, and contributes to the growing trend of poor mothers who can neither find a job nor access public assistance.*[348]

BILL CLINTON STRONGLY DISAGREES THAT SIGNING WELFARE reform was inherently damaging to the interests of the poor. During his testy 2016 exchange with the Black Lives Matter protesters in Philadelphia, Clinton attributed all of welfare reform's failures to the actions of state governments, who stripped benefits. "We left them with enough money to take care of all the poor people who couldn't go to work, on welfare," Clinton insisted. "We left them with the money they had before the welfare rolls went down 60 percent. The Republicans took it away and they're blaming me."[349] The fault therefore lies not with the federal government, says Clinton, but with the states to which it handed over authority.

But this is a bit like saying "Don't blame me, I just handed the baby to the dingo, I didn't know it was going to eat it." One would have to be spectacularly unfamiliar with the centuries-long history of Southern legislatures to believe they would cheerfully, efficiently, and effectively administer the distribution of welfare benefits to poor black mothers. Clinton may pronounce himself shocked that once given the ability, the Southern states kicked people off the welfare rolls en masse, but as Eric Levitz of *New York* magazine wrote, "[o]ne problem with Clinton blaming Republicans for 'taking away' people's welfare is that, without *his* law, they wouldn't have been able to."[350]

By simply blaming the states, Clinton is also forgetting the extent to which he was the architect of the unforgiving time-limited benefit restrictions, and his own promotion of the idea of a "dependency crisis." Clinton himself publicly deployed the "declining caseloads" metric of welfare reform's success, without considering whether those declining caseloads could be concealing the existence of deprivation. As Peter Edelman, himself an old friend of the Clintons, says of them, "[t]hey don't acknowledge the number of people who were hurt. It's just not in their lens."[351]

The welfare bill was never in any sense a compromise for Clinton. The elimination of welfare was something Clinton *introduced* into the 1992 race, something he fundamentally *made an issue* in the first place. In 1996, Bob Dole was so flustered by Clinton's "tough welfare talk" that he accused Clinton of engaging in "petty theft" of Dole's platform.[352] And it's not as if Clinton came to regret what he had wrought; 10 years after it passed, free to speak his mind without fear of political consequence, Clinton proudly wrote that "the 1996 Welfare Act shows us how much we can achieve when both parties bring their best ideas to the negotiating table and focus on doing what is best for the country." Clinton said that "we never betrayed our principles and we passed a bill that worked and stood the test of time."[353]

Clinton therefore stood proudly behind his repudiation of Roosevelt and Johnson. Most disturbingly, he refused to acknowledge the part that race played in turning welfare reform into a winning political issue. As Neubeck and Casavere write, "[t]he ease with which political elites abolished the Aid to Families with Dependent Children program—the primary safety net protecting poverty-stricken mothers and children—would have been impossible had not many politicians, along with policy analysts and the mass media, spent decades framing and morphing welfare into a supposed 'black problem.'"[354] Clinton rode this "black problem" to the presidency in 1992, then worked with Newt Gingrich to intensively address it by stripping away the public benefits that most assisted African American women. As a result, he made life harder for millions, and eroded the core of the Democratic Party's commitment to supporting the poor.

Lillie Harden was a black Arkansas mother who had spent time in the AFDC program. When Bill Clinton met her at an event, he was instantly impressed by her story. Harden had gone from being on welfare to having a job at a supermarket. For Clinton, she was the perfect poster woman for his welfare reform plans. Clinton cited her repeatedly in his pitches for the personal responsibility bill. He dwelled particularly on something she had told him about why she was proud to have a job instead of living on welfare: "When my boy goes to school and they say what does your mama do for a living, he can give an answer."[355] Clinton invited Harden to the signing ceremony for the welfare bill, where she was seated next to him as he eliminated AFDC.

But while Lillie Harden made for a useful welfare-to-work anecdote in Clinton's speeches, her life did not turn into the kind of success story Clinton spoke of. As Marchevsky and Theoharis note, "had the Clintons maintained an interest in Harden, they would have discovered that her 'success' was short-lived."[356] She continued to struggle with poverty, and her son ended up in prison. In 2002, she suffered a stroke. Harden's application for Medicaid was denied, though she had been given access to Medicaid when she was on AFDC.[357] As a result, she could not afford her $450 prescription medication, and Harden died at the age of 59 in 2014. Heartbreakingly, when Harden was interviewed by a journalist, she requested that he relay a message to Clinton asking the former president to help her get Medicaid. Of her job, she said only: "it didn't pay off in the end."[358]

During a debate with Bob Dole in 1996, Clinton declared that "I want to make more people like that woman, Lillie Harden. So I've got a plan to do it. And it's just the beginning."[359]

Clinton was not wrong. He did indeed make more people like "that woman," Ms. Harden.

And it was indeed just the beginning.

Dr. Joycelyn Elders, the first African American to serve as
Surgeon General of the United States,
as well as the first African American to be fired from the position of
Surgeon General of the United States

CHAPTER THREE
Black Appointees

OUT OF THE 100 STUDENTS IN JOYCELYN ELDERS' entering class at the University of Arkansas medical school, three were black, and three were women. Elders was the only one who was both.[360] From a childhood of hardship, through indefatigable hard work, Elders built an extraordinary career as a pediatric endocrinologist and dedicated ambassador for public health. When she became the United States Surgeon General in 1992, she would be the first African American, and only the second woman, to be hired for the position. Fifteen months later, however, she would find herself the first African American, as well as the first woman, to be summarily fired from the position.

Dr. Joycelyn Elders began her life as Minnie Lee Jones in the tiny hamlet of Schaal, Arkansas, population 98 (or "99 when I'm home," as Elders would say),[361] where her family lived in an unpainted, three-room shack without electricity. She was the eldest of eight children, born to sharecropper parents in a "rural, segregated, poverty-stricken pocket" of the state. Much of Elders' childhood was spent doing farm chores, milking cows and slopping hogs. The local schools were in session only part of the year; the rest of the time, children would be doing farm labor.

Elders' father, she recalls, was a quiet, hardworking man who spent spring through fall "plowing, planting, chopping, picking, cutting, or baling," and the winters hunting and trapping raccoons, possums, squirrels, and minks. Elders' mother had an eighth grade education (which was considered extremely advanced for a black woman at the time), but was determined to make sure all of her children were well-schooled.

The family's situation was precarious; Elders recalls when swarms of locusts came ("like a black horror coming through the sky, making a kind of ungodly zinging noise"), devouring the cotton plants, wiping out the cash crops upon which her parents' living depended. There were no doctors; the family had no car and no money, so medical care was impossible to obtain. As a young girl, Elders watched relatives die of treatable illnesses; she herself had never met a doctor before arriving at college.

The expectation for girls like Elders was that they would become domestic help. Elders remembers hearing the district school supervisor say to her home economics teacher "Now you be sure and train your girls to become good maids."[362] But Elders had no intention of becoming a maid. Inspired after meeting Edith Irby Jones, the first African American to attend the University of Arkansas School of Medicine (like Elders, the daughter of a sharecropper), Elders resolved to become a doctor. A succession of achievements followed: a scholarship to Philander Smith College at the age of 15, a B.S. in Biology by the age of 18, and a three-year stint as an Army physical therapist (where she treated President Eisenhower). Elders then applied to, and was accepted at, the University Arkansas School of Medicine. She was only the second African American woman ever to attend, the first being Edith Irby Jones herself.[363]

Elders experienced predictable bigotries. The medical school lunchroom was whites-only. At one point her white roommate, a fellow medical student, was approached by a group of white neighbors, who told her they "didn't consider it right or proper" for her to live with a black person.[364] Professors would find themselves accidentally using the n-word around her, then apologizing.[365] One of Elders' professors told her "You know, you have as much education as a lot of white people."[366] (Elders, by then a fourth-year medical student, responded "Doctor, I have more education than *most* white people."[367]) In her second year of medical school, Elders remembers taking her brothers and sisters to a drive-in showing of *Old Yeller,* and being humiliatingly confronted by an attendant after she had parked in the "white" section close to the screen.[368]

Nevertheless, Elders thrived. Consumed by her work, she paid little attention to the inevitable countless petty injustices. Her intense ambition and diligence took her from achievement to achievement: an internship at the University of Minnesota Medical Center, multiple master's degrees, dozens of published articles on pediatric medicine, and a fellowship from the National Institutes of Health. At the age of 30, she was the chief pediatric resident at the University of Arkansas Medical Center. Within a few years, she would be an assistant professor at the university, then an associate professor, then a full professor. For anyone, this would have been an incredible record of accomplishment. For the girl from Schaal, it was a stunning feat of talent, intelligence, and diligence.

It is not surprising, then, that Governor Bill Clinton should have chosen Joycelyn Elders to head the Arkansas Department of Health in 1987. A more capable individual could not have been found.

Still, Clinton may not have known quite what he was getting. If he expected a demure and pedestrian bureaucrat, he would be sorely let down. Upon taking office, Elders immediately launched a series of new initiatives to improve public health. She promoted awareness of AIDS and teen pregnancy, and presided over a "tenfold increase in the number of early childhood screenings annually and a near-doubling of the immunization rate for two-year-olds in Arkansas."[369] At her urging, the Arkansas legislature introduced its first comprehensive K-12 sex education and health program.

Elders did not shy away from politically controversial decisions, if she felt they were necessary to serve the public health. Infamously, she publicly stated that abstinence-only sex education was ineffective. And at her very first news conference, she infuriated conservatives with her answer to the question of whether condoms should be distributed in school clinics: "Well, we're not going to put them on their lunch trays," Elders said. "But, yes."[370]

Elders rarely let pragmatic politics intrude on her decision-making. Here, she recounts an instance of her general approach:

> *The department heads were briefing me on our list of programs, which all seemed more or less straightforward until we got to an AIDS education grant that was supposed to go to a gay and lesbian organization. 'Oh,' I heard, 'there could be a real bad flare-up over this one, Dr. Elders. We could get some serious criticism here. They've put out a good proposal, and I think they'd do excellent work, but if we fund them, there's going to be political fallout. Of course, it's your decision, Dr. Elders.' The whole rest of the discussion that phrase kept popping up: it was my decision. Try as I might, I wasn't getting any clear advice, except on whose decision it was, which I already knew. The gay and lesbian group had a good track record. On the other hand, the new legislative session where they were going to be*

debating our budget was coming up soon. Right now might not be the best time to look like we were encouraging homosexuals by giving them money. Then again, it was my decision. 'We're going to fund this group,' I said. 'Whatever the political fallout is, we'll just take it.' [371]

For her fearless avowal of distinctly progressive positions, Elders received hate mail from all over Arkansas, and the state "Right to Life Committee" described her as "a very dangerous woman."[372] But she amassed a formidable track record, having made demonstrable public health gains in a state plagued by poverty and illness. Thus when Bill Clinton became president, Elders followed him to Washington as Clinton's nominee for Surgeon General. *The Washington Post* reported that Elders' right-wing opponents in Arkansas were "personally thrilled they may never have to be in the same room with her again."[373]

Her nomination immediately irritated congressional Republicans. Her "loud, clear, and flamboyant" advice to teens was alternately praised and despised.[374] The pro-life movement went apoplectic upon hearing that Elders had described the Christian Right by saying "they love little babies, as long as they're in somebody else's uterus."[375] Her support for medical marijuana, and her description of teen motherhood as being comparable to slavery, drove additional interest groups bananas. Trent Lott was horrified to hear that Elders displayed an item in her office called an "Ozark Rubber Plant," a novelty flower made of curly condoms.[376]

Ultimately, after a months-long fight, and close congressional scrutiny of every part of her past, Elders was confirmed in the Senate 65-34, with some Democrats dissenting to oppose her, and a handful of Republicans defecting and supporting her. From living in a tiny shack in the segregated South of the 1930's, Elders had risen to become the nation's most prominent medical official.

Immediately, as she had been in Arkansas, Elders was unapologetically assertive in Washington. And just as immediately, she got into trouble for it. In December of 1993, only three months after taking office, in response to a question at the National Press Club, Elders said that drug legalization ought to be studied and could foreseeably have positive social effects. Elders did not advocate anything stronger than conducting further inquiry into the matter, but her remarks were portrayed as calling for the full legalization of all manner of mind-bending opiates. Strongly committed to its signature War on Drugs, the Clinton Administration instantly rebuked her and publicly disavowed her comments.

As the months went on, Elders continued to attract new controversies. She became known for her persistent frank endorsement of covering contraceptive use in sex education. She did not back down on her comments about studying drug legalization. She said abortion providers helped women. In an interview, she suggested that conservatives' fear of sexuality was causing their homophobia.[377] The political right "got angrier and angrier."[378] (They were also handed further ammunition against Elders when her 28-year-old son Kevin was arrested on drug charges.[379])

The Administration began to distance itself from its Surgeon General. She was "warned repeatedly by the White House to mind her tongue," *The New York Times* reported, but "proved unwilling to listen."[380] When the Clintons put together the healthcare reform initiative, Elders was shut out, "only allowed minimal input."[381] Instead, the Clintons chose to include Ronald Reagan's Surgeon General, C. Everett Koop. Koop, a sincere (white) Christian with a grandfatherly deportment and chin-strap beard, was considered a national treasure. (Just like Elders, Koop had also advocated for condom use and sex education in schools.[382] But Koop could get away with more; he was the spitting image of Uncle Sam.)

Still, as Surgeon General, Elders was an extremely effective advocate for public health. She was in high demand for public speaking engagements, and traveled to conferences, schools, churches, and colleges to deliver lectures. She was a captivating speaker, "arguably the best orator among all the surgeons general."[383] She had a flawless command of the scientific evidence, and "spoke from the gut about the poor and disenfranchised and children at risk." Historian Mike Stobbe writes that:

> *Many public health veterans were deeply impressed. 'Listen to her, and you'd be sitting on the edge of your chair, practically. She was that good,' Lee said. Some remember one of her first trips to visit the CDC in Atlanta, speaking to a science-oriented crowd not known for being a passionate audience. 'She got three standing ovations. Three,' one former CDC official recalled. The reaction was even stronger in a speech she gave to a large crowd of Georgia state health department employees, many of them African American. 'It was so thrilling to see so many of my staff, who never would respond to me that way, get that excited about being in public health and see a leader they could relate to,' recalled Kathleen Toomey, a Public Health Service veteran who at the time was Georgia's state epidemiologist. 'People were crying. When she finished, they had their hands up, trying to touch her. I had to whisk her off so she wouldn't get trampled. It was like dealing with Mick Jagger.'*[384]

But while Elders may have been a sensation on the lecture circuit, she continued to be denounced in Congress and the D.C. press, and Clinton was becoming frostier and more impatient with her. Beloved by health workers or not, Elders was simply too colorful, too loud, too opinionated. She was a political liability. It would only take one more comment from Elders to convince Clinton to fire her.

Ironically, the remark that got Elders flung out of government was one of her least outrageous. At a United Nations event on AIDS, Elders was asked whether masturbation should be taught as a way to prevent AIDS. Thinking a moment, Elders said that "perhaps" it should: "I think that it is something that's part of human sexuality and it's part of something that perhaps should be taught."[385] It was about as mild a statement on sex education as could be expressed. In fact, for several days, it barely received any notice at all. But when the Clinton Administration found out that the *U.S. News and World Report* was planning a piece on the comments, Clinton refused to stand by Elders. He instantly demanded she resign. Her remarks were deemed a "last straw," and Leon Panetta confirmed to the press that "[i]f she had not resigned, she would have been terminated."[386]

After just 15 months, the first black Surgeon General was no more. Joycelyn Elders returned to the practice of medicine, and took up a pediatric medicine professorship back at the University of Arkansas. "I came to Washington, D.C., like prime steak and after being here a while, I feel like poor-grade hamburger," she said.[387] Characteristically, though, Elders displayed not a shred of regret:

> *I said that we were going to talk about the things that were the greatest cause of poverty, ignorance, and enslavement in the United States. And we did. I didn't survive it, but our adolescents did. I'm proud of those fifteen months. Maybe nobody else is... I did the very best job that I knew how. And if I had to do it all over again, I'd do it the same way.*[388]

Indeed, Elders had been fired despite offering opinions that fell well within the medical consensus. The National Guidelines for Sexuality Education has advocated that masturbation be taught to children ages 5 to 8.[389] And as Elders herself quipped, "[w]e know that more than 70 to 80% of women masturbate, and 90% of men masturbate, and the rest lie."[390] Elders may have been brazen, but she always adhered closely to the facts. As Mike Stobbe notes, hate her as they may have, "[n]one of her many critics ever really succeeded in making a case that she had her facts wrong."[391]

It was never the facts that got Joycelyn Elders into trouble. It was that she defended her values, loudly and proudly. "I never learned to tone it down,"[392] she concedes. As Patricia Ireland, president of the National Organization for Women, observed at the time, Elders' firing amounted to a demand that women keep quiet on matters of gender and sexuality:

> *This says to all of the women's-rights advocates in the administration: Don't talk out loud. It won't be tolerated... Joycelyn Elders was a lightning rod because she spoke the truth: that the religious right wants sex education without educating about sex.*[393]

She would not keep quiet. Thus Joycelyn Elders, a trailblazing physician and brilliant public health advocate, was fired. Fired for being too lippy. Too forthright, too rambunctious. Too "uppity," perhaps. We might even say... too black.

After firing Dr. Elders, Bill Clinton never spoke to her again.[394]

Lani Guinier's background was in many ways the opposite of Elders'; where Elders grew up in in a poor rural community, where few had attended high school, Guinier's family was cosmopolitan and urban, part of the American academic elite.

Guinier's father, Ewart Guinier, had been the first chairman of Harvard's Department of Afro-American Studies. In his undergraduate class at Harvard, Guinier had been the only black student, until he was forced to leave after being unable to pay the tuition.

Guinier's mother, Eugenia "Genii" Guinier, was a speech therapist and English teacher. Though she was white and Jewish, Genii
"took up the cause of racial justice as her own," boycotting Wool-
worth's and joining the 1963 March on Washington for Jobs and
Freedom. "Any group functioning for the betterment of black
people, Genii was there," said her friend Vera Shorter.[395] Genii
Guinier "was extremely conscious of the ills of the time against
black people, and she did what she could to change this."[396] When
she died in 2009 at 91, she was described as "a teacher, dancer,
water colorist, lover of music and social activist."[397]

Lani Guinier herself quickly became accomplished, attaining
nearly every one of the American meritocracy's most respected
distinctions and accolades. She attended Radcliffe, then Yale
Law School (alongside a certain future presidential power couple), and went on to a federal judicial clerkship. She spent four
years as a special assistant for civil rights in the Carter Administration's Justice Department, then became an NAACP litigator
before settling into a comfy academic position at the University
of Pennsylvania School of Law. By 1992, she had passed a few
years there, spending her time producing thoughtful (though
somewhat arcane and circumlocutory) law review articles. Her
resume qualified Guinier for nearly any position in the highest
ranks of the legal profession. She was, as the judge she clerked
for described her, "a shining example of a brilliant woman."

Guinier would have therefore been a logical choice for Assistant Attorney General for Civil Rights, even had she not been
a longstanding friend of the Clinton family. When Bill Clinton
nominated her for the post in April of 1993, he was not only
selecting the first black woman to hold the post, but the first
experienced civil rights lawyer.[398]

But trouble came quickly. Conservatives immediately went
on the attack against Guinier. The day after her nomination,
the *Wall Street Journal* ran an op-ed piece suggesting she was a

dangerous radical, a "civil rights ideologue" bent on imposing anti-democratic racial quotas and undoing the fabric of American governance. [399] The rest of the political media piled on, and Guinier's confirmation process swiftly became a battle.

At the center of the controversy were Guinier's law review articles, which concerned race and representation in elections. Guinier had made a number of complex, scholarly arguments about race and the Voting Rights Act, in which she suggested that "majority rule" often afforded insufficient protection to minorities, and that voting systems could be adjusted in order to ensure that minority voices were not always outvoted. Guinier suggested that forms of proportional representation could better serve to protect minority interests than "one-man, one vote" systems.

Conservatives insisted this was outrageous. Guinier, they said, was trying to bring back the "in your face civil rights agenda" of the 1960s. [400] Guinier wanted to create a "racial spoils system" that prioritized minority interests over majority ones; she was a "radical" unfit to serve.

The irony of this was that Guinier's positions were almost entirely the opposite of conservatives' interpretations of them. Conservatives believed Guinier wanted to create race-based voting systems give handouts to minorities. In fact, Guinier's entire point was to *criticize* race-based voting systems, and call for race-neutral ones. In order to ensure the representation of racial minorities in Congress and state legislatures, voting districts were often drawn along explicitly racial lines. A squiggle of a district would attempt to capture all of the black voters living within a particular geographic area, so that black voters could be assured that they would have a representative. (If districts weren't drawn on racial lines, white voters would simply predominate in every district, ensuring that black voters could never elect anyone. With a single majority-minority district, black voters could always win one—but only one—seat.)

Guinier was heavily critical of the idea of drawing districts based on race. She argued that creating black districts was of limited effectiveness in causing black political interests to be represented in the lawmaking process. After all, if there were 25 state senate seats, with 24 always held by white senators and one always held by a black senator, the black senator would simply always be outvoted. The situation wouldn't really have changed from when black voters lost *all* of the elections. In fact, things might be even worse for black voters, because the problem would appear to have been addressed without actually being addressed at all. As Guinier explained:

> *Creating majority black, predominantly poor districts is one way to ensure at least physical representation of black interests. This makes sense to the extent that electoral control insures accountability and influence. But racial districting also means that the electoral success of white legislators in white districts is not dependent on black votes. The direct consequence of majority black districts is that fewer white legislators are directly accountable to black interests. In this way, districting may reproduce within the legislature the polarization experienced at the polls; token electoral presence is replaced by token legislative presence.*[401]

Guinier suggested that a fair system needed to ensure that the majority would pay attention to the minority in making decisions. Otherwise, the majority could simply exercise whatever tyrannies it pleased, and the minority would be powerless to stop it, despite have elected representatives. Strict majoritarianism makes little sense; in a system where 51% of people have one set of interests, and 49% of people have a very different set of interests, if the majority always ruled, nearly half the population would always go totally unrepresented. In this respect, Guinier mirrored the concerns of James Madison and the framers of the Constitution, who worried about what would happen when simple majorities could impose whatever they pleased on minority groups. The entire Bill of Rights was an attempt to address the problems that come with majority rule.

Guinier suggested that rather than electing officials by simple-majority votes in racially-drawn districts, the United States should adopt systems of proportional voting, devised to make sure majorities had an interest in appealing to minority voters. Such systems, she said, had been adopted around the world with success. In an article for the *Boston Review,* Guinier had explained how it worked:

> *Instead of dividing a city with seven elected officials into seven wards or districts, all city voters get seven votes. Voters can use their seven votes in any combination to support candidates of their choice. They could vote all seven for one candidate, or divide their votes, putting three on one candidate and four on another. In corporations that use cumulative voting, each shareholder—even so-called minority shareholders—gets the same number of votes as there are directors. If five positions exist for the corporate board of directors, each holder of stock gets five votes per share. In a corporation with one hundred shares of stock, a shareholder with twenty shares can put all her votes on one director-candidate, thus assuring the candidate's election to one of the five seats.* [402]

Guinier pointed out experiments in cumulative voting by corporations and local city councils and county school boards. She noted that it was used in South Africa to ensure that white Afrikaners would be represented despite being a demographic minority. And she explained that it was race-neutral, because it wasn't set up to favor a particular racial group in any way.

But to the conservative media, by criticizing "majoritarianism" and "tokenism," Guinier had signaled that she rejected democracy. It did not matter that Guinier's beliefs actually comported with many of conservatives' ostensible principles (e.g. race neutrality, countering the tides of populism). And it did not matter that, as William Coleman wrote in *The New York Times,* "[d]uring the Bush Administration, the Justice Department approved [similar] alternative voting systems in at least 35 different jurisdictions."[403] Guinier was a quota queen who hated the Voting Rights Act, and she needed to be stopped. The rest of the press didn't help matters. *The New York Times* ran an editorial that implied Guinier had a radical agenda that would worsen American racial tensions.[404] *The Washington Post* quoted the head of the American Jewish Congress suggesting Guinier had a "a very troubling race-based politics."[405] The papers quoted Guinier as having said that fair outcomes mattered just as much as fair procedures, and then quoted commentators characterizing this as a desire for the race-based redistribution of justice.

With so much negative press being directed at Guinier, even liberal members of the Senate began to experience doubts. But President Clinton made matters worse. He made no effort to defend Guinier. As the pressure increased for an "explanation" of Guinier's "troubling views," there was silence from the White House. Guinier was also asked to remain quiet, even as Democratic senators were lining up to oppose her, on the grounds that, in the words of Vermont's Patrick Leahy, she would turn the Civil Rights Division into a "complete aberration" that would "in no way be acceptable."[406] When Guinier went on television and publicly demanded that the Senate give her a hearing before mischaracterizing her views, the White House was furious. Guinier says she was then "forbidden to do more interviews,"[407] and told flatly that "you are not a team player and you weren't the right person for this job."[408] White House officials, sensing that her nomination was doomed and unwilling to expend political capital to save it, began to pressure Guinier to voluntarily withdraw. Guinier, however, was adamant that she be given a chance to explain herself to the Senate, an insistence that further infuriated Clinton officials. She condemned "the distortions which have been picked up by the media and have been echoed in a game of telephone in which I haven't even had access to the initial speaker" and asked for "an opportunity to respond to those distortions and correct the record."[409] According to Daryl Carter, this assertiveness "rankled" in the Administration. [410]

Eventually, Guinier was called in for a meeting with Clinton himself. Clinton explained that he found her writings troubling, that he thought her proposals were "balkanizing."[411] Guinier spent an hour attempting to explain her views to Clinton, but he explained that he was facing a politically difficult situation.[412]

Half an hour later, Clinton telephoned Guinier to tell her that the nomination was being withdrawn. At a press conference, Clinton suggested Guinier had not been properly vetted:

> At the time of the nomination I had not read her writings. In retrospect, I wish I had. Today, as a matter of fairness to her, I read some of them again in good detail. They clearly lend themselves to interpretations that do not represent the views that I expressed on civil rights during my campaign...[413]

Clinton went on to call those writings "anti-democratic" and "difficult to defend."[414] After withdrawing the nomination, Clinton never spoke to Guinier again. [415] He did, however, attempt to make amends by making the odd public declaration that "I think she's wonderful. If she came to me and asked for $5,000 I'd go down to the bank and give it to her, no questions asked."[416]

The Guinier episode "sent shock waves through traditional civil rights groups," who had already been dubious about Clinton.[417] The NAACP chairman said Clinton had "kicked us in the teeth" by withdrawing Guinier[418] Guinier was just "the latest in a string of jilted appointees dumped once controversy arose,"[419] as Randall Kennedy writes. Clinton had already withdrawn the nominations of two other women, Zoë Baird and Kimba Wood, over their hiring of unauthorized immigrants as nannies. (In fact, some women had not even made it to the appointment process. Dr. Johnetta Cole, the president of Spelman College, had been considered a major contender for the position of Secretary of Education. But Clinton struck Cole's name from the list when the press mentioned her "reported affiliation with a pro-Palestinian group" and characterized her as "far left."[420]) Clinton's refusal to stick up for women he had nominated began to seem like a pattern. As Randall Kennedy observed, "Clinton has shown that, unlike Presidents Reagan and Bush, he has no strong sense of attachment to people whom he exposes to attack."[421] The *New York Times* said Clinton "handled [Guinier's] nomination miserably" and was "unwilling to fight."[422]

THE ELDERS AND GUINIER APPOINTMENTS AND SUBSEQUENT abandonments may seem to be mere footnotes in the Clinton presidency. Many other Clinton policies had more systemic consequences for African Americans; it might seem that the only people truly affected by Clinton's scrapping of Elders and Guinier were Elders and Guinier themselves. But these incidents are important in understanding both Bill Clinton's political values and the way those values affected African Americans.

The important thing to note about Elders and Guinier is that they were fundamentally concerned with crafting *ideas and programs* that would make a more decent society, and eliminate racial inequities. This focus on fighting for outcomes put them at odds with the New Democratic program. As historian Daryl Carter explains, "at the heart of the [Democratic Leadership Council's] vision on racial issues was that equal opportunity was the primary goal, but if that goal created strenuous political difficulties, then it would be dispensed with."[423] Since, in practice, seeking equal opportunity will *always, by necessity* create strenuous political difficulties (because changing the allocation of power is never easily consented to by the powerful), the DLC's commitment to equal opportunity was no commitment at all. It was simply a commitment to remain rhetorically committed to the *words* "equal opportunity," with the full knowledge that no political capital was to be spent in the attempt to pursue any actual realization of those words.

Guinier's belief in substantive racial equality therefore conflicted with Clinton's politics of infinite compromise and appeasement. As Daryl Carter explains: "[Guinier] also seemed to conflict with New Democratic attempts to downplay the importance of race in American life… Placing conciliatory approaches above confrontational ones, New Democrats saw Guinier's full-throated support for innovative approaches to problems of racial equality at the end of the twentieth century as destructive to the policy and electoral interests of the Democratic Party."[424]

Guinier, *The New York Times* reported, was "interfering with the President's efforts to reclaim the political center."[425] But the end result of those efforts was that anyone who believed in fighting for anything had no place in the party. To the extent that black women were appointed, they needed to not have actual, substantive commitments to political principle. The result was a form of tokenism; Clinton would make many black cabinet appointments, but whenever a black appointee displayed any distinctively black *politics,* they would be gotten rid of. Ironically, or perhaps not, this was one of the very issues that Lani Guinier had been criticized for writing about; she suggested that mere minority representation was of very little meaning in itself, if it did not lead to substantive differences in outcome. Because of that very commitment to outcomes over the mere appointment of representatives, Guinier could not be appointed as a representative, since Clinton's politics were predicated on deemphasizing outcomes.

THE LIVES AND BACKGROUNDS OF JOYCELYN ELDERS AND LANI Guinier are worth reviewing, because they offer a poignant study in contrast. When we see how hard these women were willing to work in order to reach the highest points of their profession, and we set it next to how hard Bill Clinton was willing to work in support of them, every one of Clinton's excuses for himself seems pitiful. Joycelyn Elders went from slopping hogs in Schaal to being chief pediatric resident at the University of Arkansas. How much fight did this take? How much grit, how much fortitude? And yet how much exertion would Clinton expend in order to let this woman do her job? Not just "barely any." Zero. Lani Guinier was a distinguished scholar and Yale Law School graduate, with an exemplary record of scholarship and teaching, who had worked diligently on behalf of the disenfranchised in the South with the NAACP. When she saw injustice, she fought it, with intelligence, creativity, and assiduity. How much effort would Clinton spend on Guinier's behalf? None. He was content to have these women serve him, but when called upon to do an act of service for *them*, he ditched them both and never spoke to either one again. Contrast how hard someone like Elders worked to get where she was with how little Clinton worked to save her. Consider what vermicular cowardice Clinton showed in the face of a level of adversity that paled next to the adversity Elders herself had faced.

But the word "cowardice" mischaracterizes the problems with Clinton's treatment of his black female nominees. The ugly truth is not that Clinton was too afraid to fight for them, it was that he *did not believe they were worth fighting for.* Clinton did not just withdraw Guinier's nomination; he used the press conference afterward to denounce her views as antidemocratic. Clinton insisted that while he may have fired these women for being mouthy, it was not because *he* had a principle of not wanting strong black women in his administration, but because the Republicans "made" him. He emphasized in his meeting with Guinier that he was under intense political pressure. But he went beyond giving in to political pressure. He reinforced the Republican characterization of Guinier, and refused to give her a chance to defend herself. He insisted that she was antidemocratic, when he knew she was anything but.

The end result of Clinton's appointment politics was that black women were faced with the same Faustian bargain that Clinton presented to the country: abandon your most fundamental beliefs, or be cast aside. Keep your mouth shut or be fired. Joycelyn Elders, Lani Guinier, and prospective education secretary Johnetta Cole spent their lives working toward justice, finally reaching the pinnacle of their achievement, only to find themselves used and discarded by Bill Clinton, precisely because of their serious moral commitments.

Bill Clinton enjoys a visit with Rwandan children, 2006

A roomful of skulls from the 1994 Rwandan genocide

CHAPTER FOUR

CLINTON IN AFRICA
I. Rwanda, Part One

*Rwanda will never ever leave me. It's in the pores of my body. My
soul is in those hills, my spirit is with the spirits of all those people
who were slaughtered and killed that I know of, and many that
I didn't know. ... Fifty to sixty thousand people walking in the
rain and the mud to escape being killed, and seeing a person there
beside the road dying. We saw lots of them dying. And lots of those
eyes still haunt me, angry eyes or innocent eyes, no laughing eyes.
But the worst eyes that haunt me are the eyes of those people who
were totally bewildered. They're looking at me with my blue beret
and they're saying, 'What in the hell happened? We were moving
towards peace. You were there as the guarantor'—their interpretation—'of the mandate. How come I'm dying here?' Those eyes
dominated and they're absolutely right. How come I failed? How
come my mission failed? How come as the commander who
has the total responsibility—We learn that, it's ingrained in us,
because when we take responsibility it means the responsibility
of life and death, of humans that we love.*[426]*
—Romeo Dallaire

WHEN PAUL RUSESABAGINA DISCOVERED A WORKING FAX
machine in his hotel, he was immensely relieved. By mid-
April of 1994, most of the phone lines in Kigali had been
shut down or destroyed; to be able to send a fax was "miraculous." As the killing continued day after day outside the hotel gates,
Rusesabagina's only hope was to reach someone outside Rwanda.[427]

Crammed into the Hotel Milles-Collines were over 1,200 refugees, whom Rusesabagina was trying to shelter from the ongoing genocide. As the hotel's manager, Rusesabagina attempted to preserve the Milles-Collines as a sanctuary, while across the country hundreds of thousands of Rwandans were being hacked to death with machetes. Each day, soldiers would arrive at the Milles-Collines, deciding whether to massacre the guests. Each day, Rusesabagina would invite them in and ply them with cognac, negotiating with them to spare the lives of the hotel's residents. The people in the hotel were, as Romeo Dallaire describes it, "like live bait being toyed with by a wild animal, at constant risk of being killed and eaten."[428]

Rusesabagina knew he couldn't negotiate forever. So he placed his hope in the miraculous fax machine. Staying up until 4 a.m. many nights, Paul sent faxes all over the world, to the U.N., the Peace Corps, the Belgian Foreign Ministry, the Quai D'Orsay, everyone he thought might stand a chance of intervening to stop the genocide.

Many of Rusesabagina's faxes were to the White House, addressed to Bill Clinton personally. He followed them up with phone calls. He pleaded with White House staff for answers, begged them to put him through to someone who could do something. He was rebuffed each time; told he needed to call a different agency, who told him he needed to call a different agency, who told him...

At last, after 76 days, the genocide concluded when troops from the rebel Rwandan Patriotic Front recaptured Kigali. But by that point, 800,000 Rwandans were dead, in one of the worst mass killings of modern history. The blood of the Rwandan genocide permanently stained the international community's reputation; what were "global policemen" like the United States and the UN even good for if they wouldn't stop a genocide? It was almost as if all the windy post-Nuremberg "never again" speechifying was little more than hollow rhetoric...

It didn't matter that the White House wouldn't put Rusesabagina through to the right official. Even if they had, nothing would have changed. The failure to intervene did not occur because political decision-makers were unaware of the genocide, but because they consciously decided not to act to stop it. It was, as Timothy Longman writes, "[t]he lack of political will, rather than the lack of information, [that] prevented the world from acting to stop the killing."[429] There was nothing Paul Rusesabagina could tell the White House that they were not already fully aware of.

"IF THE HORRORS OF THE HOLOCAUST TAUGHT US ANYTHING," Bill Clinton said before becoming president, "it is the high cost of remaining silent and paralyzed in the face of genocide. Even as our fragmentary awareness of crimes grew into indisputable facts, far too little was done. We must not permit that to happen again."[430]

Clinton's words were stirring, but they reflected a broad consensus among the Western powers after World War II: another Holocaust could not be allowed to occur. It was a vow that American presidents consistently made. As Samantha Power documents:

> In 1979 President Jimmy Carter declared that out of the memory of the Holocaust, 'we must forge an unshakable oath with all civilized people that never again will the world stand silent, never again will the world fail to act in time to prevent this terrible crime of genocide.' Five years later, President Ronald Reagan, too, declared: 'Like you, I say in a forthright voice, 'Never again!' President George Bush Sr. joined the chorus in 1991. Speaking 'as a World War II veteran, as an American, and now as President of the United States,' Bush said his visit to Auschwitz had left him with 'the determination, not just to remember, but also to act.'[431]

By the time of the Clinton Administration, this had become an article of American political faith, one of the country's few solid moral commitments: whatever other misfortunes we might inflict through our actions and inactions across the globe, the United States would never permit the tragedies of 1939-1945 to replay themselves.

The events in Rwanda during 1994 would be the true test of the country's commitment to the principle. It was the precise scenario that each president had solemnly sworn an oath to prevent. Moreover, the country had the resources, opportunity, and knowledge necessary to help. It was, fundamentally, an event that could have been stopped, or at least significantly mitigated, through the taking of steps that were known and feasible. But over the course of 100 days, as literally hundreds of thousands of bodies piled up in Rwanda, President Clinton did exactly what he had promised he would never do; he remained "silent and paralyzed in the face of genocide," and even as his "fragmentary awareness grew into indisputable facts," he lackadaisically "permitted it to happen again."

The most important thing to understand, in analyzing international responsibility for the genocide, is how much information was available to the decision-makers. A person cannot be held accountable for not stopping something he did not know was occurring. Indeed, Bill Clinton "is said to have convinced himself that if he had known more, he would have done more."[432] He claimed in 1998 that he did not "fully appreciate the depth and the speed with which [Rwandans] were being engulfed by this unimaginable terror."[433] Now, Clinton can offer his present-day charitable works in Rwanda as proof that once he is made aware of suffering there, he will dedicate himself diligently to alleviating it, that he would never leave Rwanda to perish if he knew he was capable of acting.

But Clinton's claim not to have fully understood the situation is a lie, or at least only not a lie if the word "fully" is used as a syntactical escape valve, as doubtless Clinton intended it to be. None of us "fully" understands anything, thus even if Clinton "*appreciated* the depth and the speed with which Rwandans were being engulfed by unimaginable terror," he can truthfully claim that he did not *fully* appreciate them. No amount of proof that Clinton knew what was going on can prove that he *fully* knew what was going on; he did not, for example, know each of the victims by name. With such "incomplete information," Clinton reasons to himself, he could not have been expected to intervene.

In any reasonable sense of the term, however, Clinton knew. Knew there was a genocide, knew its scale. People at all levels of government knew. It was all over the press. In fact, the idea that any informed official at the time could plead ignorance to the Rwandan genocide is laughable. As time passes, it may be easier and easier to blur the history, to suggest that everything was opaque and uncertain and that it would have taken impossible omniscience in order to understand. But the violence in Rwanda was *in the newspapers.* It wasn't just the stuff of minor internal State Department memoranda and overlooked faxes at the bottom of receptionists' inboxes. It was in *The New York Times* and *The Washington Post.* The administration's spokespeople were being regularly asked about it.

It's easy enough, if we know nothing about it, to accept the proposition that the scale of the Rwanda genocide became clear only after the fact. Fog of war and all that. It certainly comports with the received image of Africa as a dark and unfathomable continent, out of which reliable information never flows. But any glance through contemporary sources instantly invalidates this view of history. To say one didn't know is not just implausible or unlikely. It is a lie.

In order to assess the question of "knowledge," and the subsequent issue of culpability, it is vital to understand the timeline of the genocide, and to figure out what information was available at what points. Again, keep in mind that President Clinton, in tearfully apologizing to Rwandans, said he did not "fully appreciate the depth and the speed" with which Rwandans were being engulfed by this unimaginable terror."

On April 6th, 1994, the day before the Rwanda genocide began, the country's president had been assassinated, his plane shot down over Kigali by parties unknown. It was the small spark necessary to trigger a genocide; the president was a Hutu, and the killing provided the necessary pretext for the country's military forces to carry out a plan they had been working on for some time: the extermination of their ethnic rivals, the Tutsi minority.[434]

On April 7th, a motley assemblage of paramilitary forces, under the direction of high-ranking members of the political elite, began a concerted program of mass slaughter. Inspired by an apocalyptic "Hutu Power" ideology, and fueled by "hate radio" stations commanding ordinary citizens to kill, groups of machete-wielding death squads roamed through the country, killing every Tutsi they could find, as well as moderate Hutus. In this nationwide paroxysm of stabbing, raping, and shooting, hundreds of thousands would be killed over the next 100 days.

Before the genocide even began, the signs of approaching violence in Rwanda had been present for months, if not years. As Clinton himself acknowledged in 1998, "these killings were not spontaneous or accidental… The ground for violence was carefully prepared."[435] In fact, "U.S. officials in Rwanda had been warned more than a year before the 1994 slaughter began that Hutu extremists were contemplating the extermination of ethnic Tutsis."[436] In August of 1992, the U.S. Embassy's deputy chief of mission in Kigali, sent a diplomatic cable to Washington, citing "warnings that Hutu extremists with links to Rwanda's ruling party were believed to be advocating the extermination of ethnic Tutsis."[437]

But even if one could plausibly forgive a failure to appreciate the warnings, once the killings began, the situation became very clear to all. An examination of the timeline, and the relevant press reports, shows just how much was known at what points.

The Rwandan president was assassinated on the 6th, a Wednesday. The killings began on Thursday the 7th and lasted three months. On the Thursday, members of the Presidential Guard killed eleven Belgian UN peacekeepers, as well as the Rwandan prime minister. On Friday the 8th, Bill Clinton publicly stated that the prime minister had been "sought out and murdered."[438] *Reuters* described a "wave of bloodletting"[439] in which "embers of the security forces and gangs of youths wielding machetes, knives and clubs rampaged through the capital, Kigali, settling tribal scores by hacking and clubbing people to death or shooting them."[440]

On Saturday, April 9th, Clinton included references to Rwanda in his weekly radio address (which was "otherwise devoted to crime and other domestic issues"[441] and focused largely on Clinton's pitch for his crime bill.) Of the situation there, he said:

> *Finally, let me say just a brief word about a very tragic situation in the African nation of Rwanda. I'm deeply concerned about the continuing violence... There are about 250 Americans there. I'm very concerned about their safety, and I want you to know that we're doing all we can to ensure their safety. I ask you to join together this morning in praying for their safety and for a return to peace in Rwanda.*[442]

That same day, United Nations observers in Kigali witnessed a massacre that took place in a Polish church, in which over one hundred people including children were brutally hacked to death.[443] *The New York Times* described Rwanda and Burundi as "two nations joined by a common history of genocide," raising the specter of the g-word.[444]

On the 11th, *The New York Times* published the accounts of Americans who had recently evacuated:

> 'It was the most basic terror,' said Chris Grundmann, 37, an American evacuee, describing the fears of the Rwandan civilians and officials who were targets of the violence. He and his family, hunkered down in their house with mattresses against the windows, heard the ordeals of Rwandan victims over a two-way radio. 'The U.N. radio was filled with national staff screaming for help,' he said. 'They were begging: 'Come save me! My house is being blown up,' or 'They're killing me.' There was nothing we could do. At one point we just had to turn it off.' Since Wednesday, it is estimated that more than 20,000 people have been killed in fighting between the Hutu majority and the Tutsi minority that have struggled for dominance since Rwanda won independence from Belgium in 1962. On Friday alone, the main hospital had many hundreds of bodies before noon. Mr. Grundmann, an official with the Centers for Disease Control [said that] the family's cook, a Tutsi, came to their home begging for help on Friday after having spent three days pretending to be dead. 'He told us that on Wednesday night someone had thrown a grenade into his home… He escaped through an open window, but he thinks his wife and children died. For 36 hours he played dead in a marsh. There were bodies all through the marsh. He said there were heads being thrown in.'

On April 12th, *The New York Times* published a profile of several Adventist missionaries who had fled:

> "Now that we are out," Mr. Van Lanen said today, "I fear, in a way, that we have betrayed the people we came to help. Now, they fear that most of those

people—deprived of their protection—will become victims of the bloodletting that has set the majority Hutu tribe of Rwanda against the minority Tutsis. Red Cross officials estimate that the violence has taken more than 10,000 lives in Kigali alone, and as many or more in the countryside.[445]

That same day, Toronto's *Globe and Mail* ran a report containing interviews with traumatized Canadians who had evacuated:

There were bodies everywhere. Wounded people were not getting any attention. Women with children on their backs were hacked to pieces. I saw one man still alive who was disembowelled, another had almost been cut in half with a panga (a long, sharp knife).

Kigali, they reported, was like a "slaughterhouse" and "blood was literally flowing in the gutters."[446]

On the 15th, *The New York Times* published a report about the refugees gathered in Paul Rusesabagina's Hotel Milles Collines:

In Kigali, scores of Rwandans have taken refuge at the Hotel Mille Collines. There is an uneasy, nervous coexistence there between the families of the Rwandan military and some middle-class Tutsis who were unable to leave the city. Both are convinced they will be massacred. They congregate in the dark hallways, whispering for hours, virtual prisoners. As United Nations soldiers came to take the foreign journalists to the airport, dozens of the Rwandans crowded around and begged to be evacuated, fearing that the departure of Westerners would mean sure death for them. Their pleas were rejected by the troops. As the convoy left, many gathered silently in the driveway and stared.[447]

On the 16th, the Montreal *Gazette* published a desperate plea from a Rwandan exile, under the headline "Don't abandon us":

> *[Fidele Makombe] says he was stunned by the orgy of murder, rape and torture unleashed in the small central African nation... Human-rights observers are convinced that the coterie of ethnic Hutus around the president used the incident as a pretext to unleash a reign of terror... Makombe, who runs the Rwandese Human Rights League from his base here, is appealing to the world not to kiss off Rwanda as another African human-rights basket case, but to understand the true nature of the conflict...*[448]

The killings in Rwanda were no secret, then. Every day, the papers were full of them; one could offer many, many more clippings from the *Washington Post, The New York Times,* and the various wire services, and these were just from the first weeks of a genocide that went on unimpeded for three months. By April 24th, the Sunday *Washington Post* was filled with pleas from Human Rights Watch, who explained unequivocally what was going on:

> *We put the word genocide on the table. We don't do it lightly. There is clearly here an intention to eliminate the Tutsi as a people... This is not "inter-tribal fighting" or "ethnic conflict." First, it's not fighting, it's slaughter...*[449]

A front page *Post* story from the same day described "the heads and limbs of victims... sorted and piled neatly, a bone-chilling order in the midst of chaos that harked back to the Holocaust."[450]

To not "fully appreciate" what was going on would have required not glancing at a newspaper for the three months from the beginning of April to the beginning of July.

It's important to provide excerpts from some of these contemporary media accounts, so as not to accidentally lapse into believing that the genocide was something hidden or unknown. After such a calamity, for which so many are culpable, a great number of people have vested interests in downplaying the extent to which the genocide was (1) knowable and (2) preventable. If only to spare themselves a lifetime of guilt, they must publicly repeat that the situation was unclear, and that nothing could be done. But the historical record says otherwise; very little was unclear, and even those things that were unknown on April 8th were certainly clear by the 20th, when fleeing survivors' reports of genocide were being recounted in the press daily. As April turned to May, the nation's papers were openly puzzled by Clinton's refusal to do anything. On May 2nd, the editorial board of *USA Today* angrily denounced Clinton for his uselessness:

> *Imagine the horror of watching 25 mutilated bodies float down a local river—every hour. Try to picture 250,000 North Carolinians abandoning their homes and belongings in a terrified run for their lives from machete-wielding madmen. That's what life is like these days in Rwanda, a small but densely populated Central African nation where as many as 200,000 men, women and children have been slaughtered in the past three weeks… Where is the world's horror? And, more immediately, where is the world's outrage? Surely, if hundreds of thousands of innocent civilians were hacked to death in France or Germany, the international call for action would be swift and strong. But Rwanda is in Africa. And, unfortunately, the Western world reacts slowly to black-on-black violence. President Clinton, who criticized George Bush for not doing more to stop ethnic cleansing*

*in Bosnia, certainly took his time getting around
to this genocide. Only last weekend did he finally
deliver a radio address, broadcast in Rwanda,
pleading for an end to the violence. That's about three
weeks—200,000 victims—too slow.*[451]

But if the editors at *USA Today* thought Clinton would
spring into action after 200,000 victims, they were mistaken.
Besides the evacuation of Americans, Clinton's radio address to
Rwandans, which Human Rights Watch called "so mild as to
be worthless,"[452] would constitute the full extent of the U.S.'s
action in the country until July.

In fact, there was a conscious commitment to inaction among
Clinton officials. As Princeton Lyman, then serving as U.S.
Ambassador to South Africa recalls, "[p]eople knew what was
going on…There certainly was information flowing in. The
African Bureau at the State Department was pleading for the
Pentagon to bomb the hate radio stations. People had informa-
tion. There was just a reluctance to do very much."[453] Former
State Department military advisor Tony Marley describes a
meeting at the State Department:

*One official even asked a question as to what
possible outcome there might be on the congressional
elections later that year were the administration to
acknowledge that this was genocide taking place
in Rwanda and be seen to do nothing about it.
The concern obviously was whether it would result
in a loss of votes for the party in the November
elections… I was stunned because I didn't see what
bearing that had on whether or not genocide was,
in fact, taking place in Rwanda. Partisan political
vote-gathering in the U.S. had no bearing on the
objective reality in Rwanda.*[454]

Marley said that even modest proposals for action were instantly rejected. When Marley suggested that they at least attempt to jam the frequencies of the hate radio stations that were fueling the genocide, a State Department lawyer told him it would go against the spirit of the U.S. Constitution's commitment to free speech.[455] (For the record, United States constitutional law does not protect the right to order a genocide on the radio.)

Michael Barnett, of the U.S. Mission to the U.N., describes the attitude he witnessed:

> INTERVIEWER: *What were your instructions, or what was the attitude of your superiors at the U.S. U.N. Mission?*
>
> MICHAEL BARNETT: *The general attitude was that "We now have to close down the operation."*
>
> INTERVIEWER: *Close it down?*
>
> MICHAEL BARNETT: *Close it down.*[456]

B UT THE CLINTON ADMINISTRATION ACTUALLY DID SOMETHING much, much worse than failing to intervene. It deliberately attempted to downplay the atrocities, refusing to refer to them publicly as genocide, for fear that doing so would obligate them under the U.N.'s Genocide Convention to take action. As *The Guardian* reported in 2004, "President Bill Clinton's administration knew Rwanda was being engulfed by genocide in April 1994 but buried the information to justify its inaction, according to classified documents... Senior officials privately used the word genocide within 16 days of the start of the killings, but chose not to do so publicly because the president had already decided not to intervene."[457] "Detailed reports" were reaching the top levels of government; Secretary of State Warren Christopher "and almost certainly the president" had been told mid-April that there was "genocide and partition" and a "final solution to eliminate all Tutsis."[458] The CIA's national intelligence briefing, circulated to Clinton, Al Gore, and other top officials, "included almost daily reports on Rwanda," with an April 23 briefing saying that rebels were attempting to "stop the genocide, which… is spreading south."[459] As William Ferroggiaro of the National Security Archive explained, declassified documents show that "[d]iplomats, intelligence agencies, defense and military officials - even aid workers - provided timely information up the chain… That the Clinton administration decided against intervention at any level was not for lack of knowledge of what was happening in Rwanda." Joyce Leader, U.S. Embassy's deputy chief of mission in Kigali, admitted in 2014 that "We had a very good sense of what was taking place."[460]

But nobody in the United States government was willing to use the word "genocide" publicly. The United Nations Convention on the Prevention and Punishment of the Crime of Genocide contains a binding requirement that countries prevent genocide, so acknowledgment of the genocide would have created a legally binding mandate to stop it. Even though internally, members of the Clinton Administration were referring to a genocide, publicly their spokespeople were under strict orders to refuse to confirm that a genocide was occurring. "Be careful," warned a document from the Deputy Assistant Secretary of Defense's office, "Legal at State was worried about this yesterday – Genocide finding could commit U.S.G. to actually 'do something.'"[461]

The resulting press conferences took Clintonian hairsplitting to its most absurd outer limits. Here, reporters try to pin down State Department spokesperson Christine Shelley and Secretary of State Madeleine Albright:

> REPORTER 1: —*comment on that, or a view as to whether or not what is happening could be genocide?*

CHRISTINE SHELLEY (STATE DEPARTMENT): *Well, as I think you know, the use of the term "genocide" has a very precise legal meaning, although it's not strictly a legal determination. There are—there are other factors in there, as well. When—in looking at a situation to make a determination about that, before we begin to use that term, we have to know as much as possible about the facts of the situation.*

REPORTER 2: *Just out of curiosity, given that so many people say that there is genocide underway, or something that strongly resembles it, why wouldn't this convention be invoked?*

MADELEINE ALBRIGHT: *Well, I think, as you know, this becomes a legal definitional thing, unfortunately, in terms of—as horrendous as all these things are, there becomes a definitional question.*[462]

Finally, at the end of May, as hundreds of thousands lay dead across Rwanda, the Clinton Administration changed its policy and began using the term. But *even then* they took great pains to use a carefully-constructed legalism; while they would admit that there may have been "acts of genocide" occurring, they drew a distinction between these and "genocide," believing this would keep them from triggering the Genocide Convention. Again, reporters tried to get a straight answer:

CHRISTINE SHELLEY: *We have every reason to believe that acts of genocide have occurred.*

ALAN ELSNER (REUTERS): *How many acts of genocide does it take to make genocide?*

CHRISTINE SHELLEY: *Alan, that's just not a question that I'm in a position to answer.*

ALAN ELSNER: *Is it true that the—that you have specific guidance not use the word "genocide" in isolation, but always to preface it with this—this word, "acts of"?*

CHRISTINE SHELLEY: *I have guidance, which— to which I—which I try to use as best as I can. I'm not—I have—there are formulations that we are using that we are trying to be consistent in our use of.* [463]

Alan Elsner later described his incredulity at the Administration's non-responsiveness:

The answers they were giving were really non- answers. They would talk in incredibly bureaucratic language. In a sense, it was almost like a caricature. If you look at it now, it looks utterly ridiculous. These were all kind of artful ways of doing nothing, which is what they were determined to do. [464]

Not only did the Clinton Administration adopt a policy of refusing to recognize the genocide, but it pressured other countries to do the same. Former Czech Ambassador to the U.N. Karel Kovanda recalled that his government was pressured by the U.S. not to use the term:

KAREL KOVANDA: *I know that I personally had an important conversation with one of my superiors in Prague who at American behest suggested that they lay off.*

INTERVIEWER: *Lay off calling it genocide?*

KAREL KOVANDA: *Yeah. Lay off pushing Rwanda, in general, and calling it genocide specifically.*

INTERVIEWER: *So the Americans had actually talked to your government back in Prague and said, 'Don't let's call it genocide.'*

KAREL KOVANDA: *In Prague or in Washington, but they were talking to my superiors, yes.* [465]

There is much to be revolted by here. Despite Clinton's promise that he would never sit idly by while genocide was occurring, not only was he doing exactly that, but his administration actually perpetrated a *planned act of genocide denial* specifically in order to avoid having to prevent a genocide from occurring. As *The Guardian* reported, the Clinton Administration, "felt the US had no interests in Rwanda, a small central African country with no minerals or strategic value."[466] Thanks to Rwanda's lack of minerals, the world's most powerful nation was content to let 800,000 people have their faces chopped off with machetes.

But this underplays the Clinton Administration's responsibility. It's true that the U.S. government both deliberately refused to send forces to Rwanda and deceived the world about whether a genocide was occurring. It's also true that both then and now, Bill Clinton pretended that there was too little information to come to any conclusions all while receiving detailed briefings on the genocide (as it was simultaneously splashed across the daily papers). But perhaps even worse, the Clinton Administration actually took affirmative steps to keep the United Nations from sending a force to Rwanda. As Samantha Power explains:

> In reality the United States did much more than fail to send troops. It led a successful effort to remove most of the UN peacekeepers who were already in Rwanda. It aggressively worked to block the subsequent authorization of UN reinforcements. It refused to use its technology to jam radio broadcasts that were a crucial instrument in the coordination and perpetuation of the genocide.[467]

"Recall," said former special envoy to Somalia Robert Oakley, "it wasn't just not sending U.S. forces: we blocked a security council resolution to send in a U.N. force."[468] Indeed, the Clinton Administration deliberately stalled United Nations efforts to coordinate an intervention. According to *Foreign Policy*, "[w]hen the genocide began, the United States launched a diplomatic campaign aimed at bringing the U.N. peacekeepers home. Initially, Washington sought to shutter the mission entirely."[469] On May 17th, *The New York Times* reported that "[t]he United States forced the United Nations Monday to scale down its plans and put off sending 5,500 African troops to Rwanda in an effort to end the violence there... Washington argued that sending in a large peacekeeping force raised the risk of the troops› being caught up in the fighting."[470] There was "a decisive U.S. role in the tragic pullout of United Nations peacekeepers"[471] and each time the United Nations attempted to formulate a modest plan for reprieve, the United States stalled it, even to the extent of using its Security Council veto power over other nations. As renowned Rwanda scholar and Human Rights Watch official Alison des Forges, concluded, "the U.S. was the primary stumbling block" to international efforts to stop the massacres.[472] The president of Refugees International, Lionel Rosenblatt, said "[t]he ball was not only dropped by the U.S., it was blocked by the U.S."[473]

To the extent that the Clinton Administration did exert itself over Rwanda, it was entirely to assist the handful of Americans who were there. As *PBS* documented "In the first days of the genocide, the Clinton administration was focused not on the Tutsis, but on what was happening to the 255 Americans in Rwanda" (this was clear from Clinton's radio address of the 10th).[474] The President held meetings on Rwanda on both April 7th and 8th with the Secretary of State and Secretary of Defense, but they were concerned entirely with American lives. The meetings concluded that "the top priority should be to evacuate Americans from Rwanda."[475] In fact, this was the *only* priority.

One may wonder why the Clinton Administration acted so callously in the face of such a preventable catastrophe. But one need not wonder long. The relevant considerations were explained by Bill Clinton during his commencement speech at the Naval Academy in May of 1994, during the middle of the genocide:

> *Now the entire global terrain is bloody with such conflicts, from Rwanda to Georgia... Whether we get involved in any of the world's ethnic conflicts, in the end, must depend on the cumulative weight of the American interests at stake.*[476]

There, in plain language, was Clinton's philosophy. "The cumulative weight of the American interests at stake" were the deciding factor when it came to "ethnic conflicts" like the Rwandan genocide. With few American interests in Kigali (no minerals), there was little that needed to be done.

Clinton's close political advisor, Dick Morris, was even more explicit in describing the president's reasoning:

> *The real reason was that Rwanda was black. Bosnia was white. European atrocities mattered more than African atrocities—not to Clinton himself, but to the media, which covered the grisly deaths in Yugoslavia but devoted considerably less attention to the genocide in Africa. And without the media dogging him to take action, Bill Clinton...wasn't about to pay attention.*[477]

The words of a jaded and disreputable operative like Dick Morris may of course be taken with some skepticism. But it's hard to believe that if the same circumstances had occurred in a European country, Clinton would have shown the same level of indifference. The president's treatment of Rwanda had everything to do with a political calculus; Administration officials were openly concerned with the situation's effects on the November election. (They lost anyway.) And since there was simply not much political value to intervening in Rwanda, Clinton had no desire to. Dick Morris' point is especially useful because it illustrates one of the fundamental truths about Clinton and race: Clinton is not a racist, he simply makes his decisions on the basis of their perceived value to his political capital and self-image. But because black lives are less valued, and making black lives better offers fewer political rewards, Clinton nevertheless ends up making a pattern of racist decisions.

Bill Clinton has struggled to explain why he did not intervene in Rwanda. In 1998, he visited Kigali and offered what some have described as an "apology," though as Samantha Power notes, it was actually little more than a "carefully hedged acknowledgment."[478] In that statement, Clinton admitted that "[i]t may seem strange to you here, especially the many of you who lost members of your family, but all over the world there were people like me sitting in offices, day after day after day, who did not fully appreciate" the depth of the terror.

Indeed it did seem strange, because it was, in fact, impossible. As Rwanda scholar Timothy Longman wrote, "Clinton's claims were false. It is not that the U.S. government didn't know what was happening in Rwanda. The truth is that we didn't care."[479] And as Power concluded, "[a]s the terror in Rwanda had unfolded, Clinton had shown virtually no interest in stopping the genocide, and his Administration had stood by as the death toll rose into the hundreds of thousands."[480]

Even as he constructed the appearance of regret, then, Bill Clinton was engaging in political spin. Dana Hughes of *ABC News* reports on an internal memo from late in 1994, offering talking points with which the president could cover himself. The memo:

> ...*suggests the president argue that the United States took appropriate and swift action in Rwanda after it was clear there was genocide, and that the U.S. was*

one of many countries who authorized the United Nations to pull out of the country right before the atrocities began. In short, says the memo, the U.S. 'did the right thing' and shares no responsibility for allowing the genocide to occur. Clinton himself echoed these sentiments in comments to the press a few months earlier where he said he had 'done all he could do' to help the people of Rwanda.[481]

If all of Clinton's statements of regret come loaded with implicit self-exonerations, to what extent can they count for anything at all? Rwandan genocide survivors Alice and Claude Gatabuke summarize their revulsion at Clinton's display of quasi-contrition:

Former President Clinton's words rang hollow both in material and delivery. Instead, they conjured up images, of white foreigners being evacuated from Rwanda to safety at the outset of the genocide. The rest of us, the innocent civilians, were provided with neither the option of evacuation, nor the decency of protection, but were left, amidst a bloody war and genocide, come what may. It is almost impossible to articulate the depth of betrayal felt at this profound sense of political expediency.[482]

One of the most disturbing aspects of Clinton's conduct around Rwanda is that he has been willing to lie about it and spin it in order to paint himself as sincerely oblivious and well-intentioned. The existing evidence incontrovertibly proves that Clinton failed to intervene because he didn't see anything to be gained domestically. This is not a conspiracy theory, or a speculative hypothesis. Clinton's own words from the time of the genocide, about the "cumulative weight of American interests," affirm what witnesses from his Administration have said.

The evidence also proves that the Clinton Administration went far beyond inaction. It also attempted to stop others from acting. But worst of all, it adopted a conscious policy of genocide denial. It knew there was a genocide, but publicly fudged the truth so as not to have to stop it. This is actually far, far worse than even Holocaust denial; after all, the most harmful time to deny a genocide is while it is occurring, especially if your denial is made deliberately so that nobody will stop the genocide. At the peak of one of the 20th century's worst mass slaughters, Bill Clinton presided over an act of institutionalized genocide denial so as to allow the killing to continue.

We were pretending to be dead. They took stones and smashed the heads of the bodies. They took little children and smashed their heads together. When they found someone breathing, they pulled them out and finished them off. They killed my family. I saw them kill my papa and my brother, but I didn't see what happened to my mother.[483]
—RECOLLECTION OF A TUTSI WOMAN

All of the refugees were running in front of the trucks in order to stop them leaving. And I remember hanging on to a UNAMIR truck and asking the soldier, "Are you really abandoning us? We'll all be killed. Why are you leaving?"[484]
—FLORIDA NGULINZIRA, RWANDAN REFUGEE

We all knew we would die, no question. The only question was how. Would they chop us in pieces? With their machetes they would cut your left hand off. Then they would disappear and reappear a few hours later to cut off your right hand. A little later they would return for your left leg etc. They went on till you died. They wanted to make you suffer as long as possible. There was one alternative: you could pay soldiers so they would just shoot you. That's what [Tatiana's] father did.[485]
—PAUL RUSESABAGINA

Note:

None of those taking refuge in Paul Rusesabagina's Hotel Milles-Collines was killed; all 1,200 survived the genocide. Rusesabagina's story was preserved in the 2004 film *Hotel Rwanda,* in which he is played by Don Cheadle. He was eventually awarded the Presidential Medal of Freedom...by George W. Bush.

II. AIDS and South Africa

ODAY, THE CLINTON FOUNDATION IS WIDELY KNOWN FOR ITS work on AIDS in Africa. But as on so many things, Clinton's attitude toward the African AIDS crisis was starkly different during his time in office.

In the late 1990s, tens of millions of Africans were HIV-positive. Nearly 80% of those dying globally of AIDS were in Sub-Saharan Africa.[486] AIDS was (and remains to this day) a debilitating scourge. South Africa was suffering acutely from AIDS, and the country had the highest absolute number of people infected.[487] With an average income of $2,600 per year,[488] few South Africans could afford antiretroviral drug treatment, which cost up to $10,000 annually. Faced with an extraordinary number of AIDS cases, and an impossible cost of treatment, the South African government introduced a measure that would allow for the importation or local production of generic drugs. The law, which paid a fixed fee to patent-holders, would reduce the cost of drugs by up to 90%. The legislation was signed into law by Nelson Mandela (whose son would ultimately die of AIDS in 2005).[489]

But Pharmaceutical and Research Manufacturers of America (Pharma), an alliance of 100 of the largest American drug companies, were furious. Claiming that their intellectual property rights had been violated, and labeling South Africa's action "piracy," they challenged the law in South African courts and began vigorously campaigning against it in Washington.[490] Pharma hired a U.S. lobbying firm, what is today called the Podesta Group, to bring pressure on South Africa.

The Podesta Group was founded by brothers Tony and John Podesta in 1988. It was a fruitful partnership; Tony became one of D.C.'s most influential fundraisers, working on behalf of BP, Bank of America, and the Egyptian government, and bundling contributions for Bill Clinton, Ted Kennedy, and other major Democrats.[491] John became Clinton's chief of staff, and would go on to found the Center for American Progress think tank, before being invited to lead Barack Obama's transition team. The Podesta Group itself became an extremely powerful political force, with prominent corporate clients including Wal-Mart and Lockheed Martin.[492] The Podestas were therefore a fine choice to help Pharma get the ear of Washington.

With John Podesta still serving as Chief of Staff, the Clinton Administration "went to war" over the generic-drug legislation, putting "immense" pressure on South Africa to honor the patent rights of American companies.[493] They insisted, wrongly, that South Africa had violated World Trade Organization rules on patents.[494] The U.S. trade representative rescinded South Africa's trade benefits, refusing to grant tariff breaks on exports.[495] The Clinton Administration even put South Africa on the "Super 301" trade watch list, a special designation meant to "prise open recalcitrant foreign markets under threat of retaliation."[496] (The Administration had adopted the same strong-arm tactics against Thailand. *The New York Times* said U.S. pressure "caused the country to put restrictions on its manufacture of cheap patented drugs and ban their import, which AIDS doctors say reduced the country's ability to fight the disease."[497])

Vice President Al Gore was designated to lead negotiations with South African President Thabo Mbeki. Gore, however, firmly stood by the drug companies' position, refusing to grant South Africa concessions. As *The Guardian* reports, "[f]or 18 months, Mbeki urged and pleaded with Gore to intervene on behalf of his government and its struggle against HIV"[498] yet Gore "not only refused [but] "put intense pressure on Mbeki to drop the legislation and comply with the drug companies'.[499]

The Clinton Administration came under criticism for its efforts to punish South Africa for its desperate attempt to stanch the tide of AIDS deaths. The editorial board of the *New York Times* said the Administration's policy had been dominated by "the desire to protect American pharmaceutical patents," and insisted that "Washington should stop pressuring South Africa to change the law."[500] When Al Gore began running for president, AIDS activists disrupted his campaign events to protest his role.[501]

Under scrutiny, Clinton relented. The Administration "was so embarrassed by the public outrage that it backed off,"[502] and announced that it would "no longer seek increasingly tough standards on protection of intellectual property and will instead enforce minimum standards."[503] By then well into the final year of his presidency, Clinton performed a rapid *volte-face* and began promising sweeping new anti-AIDS initiatives, despite the fact that AIDS had "scarcely surfaced" as an issue on previous Clinton trips to Africa.[504]

Clinton also gave Africans a lecture on self-reliance and responsibility, telling the National Summit on Africa"[505] that "cultural and religious factors" were getting in the way of disease prevention. "We shouldn't pretend that we can give injections and work our way out of this," he said. "We have to change behavior, attitudes."[506]

It was understandable that Clinton would emphasize personal behavior and de-emphasize the provision of drugs. This was in keeping with the Administration's approach to Africa more broadly, which had proposed a "shift from aid to trade"[507] that de-emphasized the provision of material support. As one Democratic representative put it, Africa would move from having a "donor-recipient relationship" with the U.S. to being an "economic partner."[508] This would, in the words of the U.S. Ambassador to Uganda, "bring confidence to American corporations,"[509] with the White House promoting Africa as "an untapped market of 700 million people."[510]

When the shift was announced, according to *The Independent*, it "was seen in Washington as a move by the US to pre-empt criticism from other G7 countries, notably France, that it was not doing as much as it could to assist developing countries in general, and African countries in particular" after U.S. overseas aid in 1996 fell below that of France for the first time.[511] The African National Congress in South Africa was highly critical of the Clinton move, which they saw as "neo-colonialist" and supported "only with the greatest reluctance."[512]

Throughout his presidency, Clinton's attitude toward Africa was viewed with skepticism by Africans and African Americans. In 1994, Congressional Black Caucus actually boycotted a conference on Africa held by Clinton, believing it was a public relations stunt to disguise Clinton's lack of actual material support for Africa. "I don't think there has been a focus on Africa ever in any administration, including this one," said one CBC congressman.[513] When Clinton visited South Africa in 1994, it was reported that South Africans received his visit frostily, and "suspect[ed] Clinton has come only to revel in the public relations boost of Mandela's company and has little to offer beyond symbolic gestures of support."[514]

Indeed, aid to Africa dropped throughout the Clinton years, and would only rise again during the presidency of George W. Bush. Even Clinton's friend and fellow philanthropy-mogul Bill Gates has acknowledged that "the low point in terms of U.S. aid generosity was at the end of the Clinton administration."[515]

And while Clinton gave emotional speeches about the end of apartheid, he kept Nelson Mandela's name on the U.S.'s terrorist watch list, meaning Mandela was subject to travel restrictions.[516] Mandela's name would finally be taken off by Bush, during the last year of his presidency.[517]

In fact, George W. Bush's Africa policy would offer a striking contrast from that of his predecessor. Ironically, given his well-deserved reputation for overseas bungling and malfeasance, Bush's initiatives on Africa were far more ambitious and generous than Clinton's. Bush founded a $1.2 billion anti-malaria initiative, and soon after taking office initiated a vast new program for AIDS treatment in Africa. The President's Emergency Plan for AIDS Relief (PEPFAR) committed $15 billion to fighting AIDS, delivering cheap medication across the continent.

The results are widely seen as being incredibly successful. As Eugene Robinson of *The Washington Post* summarizes:

> *When the Bush administration inaugurated the program in 2003, fewer than 50,000 HIV-infected people on the African continent were receiving the antiretroviral drugs that keep the virus in check and halt the progression toward full-blown AIDS. By the time Bush left office, the number had increased to nearly 2 million. Today, the United States is directly supporting antiretroviral treatment for more than 4 million men, women and children worldwide, primarily in Africa.*[518]

Importantly, this success partially occurred because Bush rejected the "conventional wisdom" that anti-AIDS treatments that worked elsewhere would not work in Africa due to cultural and behavioral problems. Such arguments, of the type furthered by Clinton at the Conference on Africa, "turned out to be categorically wrong."[519]

Bush's AIDS initiative was a triumph, delivering an unprecedented amount of funding and giving millions access to medication. (President Obama would later come under significant criticism from anti-AIDS activists for failing to maintain the intensity of commitment to the issue that Bush displayed.[520]) Clinton spent years in office trying to keep South Africa from giving away cheap drugs and damaging American pharmaceutical profits. Yet it is Clinton who is more widely known for his AIDS work. "George Bush has actually delivered more resources, but Clinton is ten times more popular in Africa," said Princeton Lyman, the former Ambassador to South African under Clinton. "That's because, just like he does everywhere, he portrays that sense that he cares."[521]

III. AL-SHIFA

The first thing Amin Mohamed knew about America's last war on international terrorism was when the roof caved in. "Allah Akbar! It's the end of the world!" he screamed as 14 cruise missiles landed next door to the sweet factory he was guarding. The 40-year-old ran with a broken leg for three miles to the Nile, before realising that al-Shifa, Sudan's main pharmaceutical factory, was the only building that had been hit. "The walls just disappeared," he says. "One moment I was lying down, listening to the sound of planes. The next, everything was smoke and fire. I didn't know there were such weapons." Three years on, the sweet factory has a new roof and Amin's leg has mended. Fadil Reheima, also on duty that night, squats nodding and smiling beside him. Fadil, 32, cannot tell me what he remembers, however, because he has been deaf and dumb since the attack.
—from James Astill, "Strike One," *The Guardian* (Oct. 2, 2001).

BEFORE FOURTEEN CRUISE MISSILES TURNED IT INTO A HEAP of twisted steel and medical detritus, the Al-Shifa factory in Khartoum was the largest manufacturer of medicines in all of Sudan, producing over half of the country's pharmaceutical products and specializing in anti-malaria drugs.[522] But on August 20th, 1998, the plant was "pulverized," reduced to nothing but "broken concrete and iron bars," leaving "thousands of brown bottles of veterinary and other medicines" littered across the sand.[523] Fourteen years later, its wreckage remained, a shrine to an incident that locals still refer to as a terrorist attack.

The Al-Shifa plant had been taken out on the direct orders of Bill Clinton.[524] The strike was in retaliation for Osama bin Laden's recent bombings of the U.S. embassies in Kenya and Tanzania. In addition to destroying the Al Shifa, the administration targeted a group of Al-Qaeda training camps in Afghanistan.

When it was pointed out to the Clinton Administration that they had just eliminated one of Sudan's major medical suppliers, spokespeople "claimed the plant was actually a disguised chemical weapons factory." They insisted that "soil samples taken outside the plant had shown the presence of a substance known as Empta, whose only function was to make the nerve gas VX."[525] The plant, they said, "was heavily guarded… and it showed a suspicious lack of ordinary commercial activities."[526]

All of this turned out to be false. As Richard Bernstein explained:

> [A] British engineer, Thomas Carnaffin, who worked as a technical manager during the plant's construction between 1992 and 1996, emerged to tell reporters there was nothing secret or heavily guarded about the plant at all, and that he never saw any evidence of the production of an ingredient needed for nerve gas. The group that monitors compliance with the treaty banning chemical weapons announced that Empta did have legitimate commercial purposes in the manufacture of fungicides and antibiotics. The owner of the Shifa factory gave interviews in which he emphatically denied that the plant was used for

anything other than pharmaceuticals, and there was never persuasive evidence to contradict his assertion. At the same time, members of the administration retreated from claims they made earlier that Osama bin Laden had what [Defense Secretary William] Cohen called "a financial interest in contributing to this particular facility." It turned out that no direct financial relationship between bin Laden and the plant could be established.[527]

Striking the Al Shifa facility had been contentious within the Clinton Administration. *The New York Times* reported that "the voices of dissent were numerous"[528] and that "[o]fficials throughout the Government raised doubts up to the eve of the attack about whether the United States had sufficient information linking the factory to either chemical weapons or to bin Laden, according to participants in the discussions."[529] As the U.S. ambassador to Sudan conceded afterward, "[t]he evidence was not conclusive and was not enough to justify an act of war."[530] *Slate* journalist Timothy Noah goes further, writing that any suggestion the plant was making nerve gas components was "desperate conjecture"[531] on the Administration's part.

After the attack, public calls were made for the Clinton Administration to justify the bombing. Human Rights Watch wrote a letter to Clinton in which it said:

The U.S. government has not explained why its investigation of the site was sufficiently diligent in light of the fact that U.S. officials now admit that they did not know the plant manufactured legitimate pharmaceuticals. The evidence these officials cite for their belief that the plant had no legitimate civilian purpose - unlike the web sites of other known pharmaceutical manufacturers in

Sudan, this company's web site did not mention any products - is hardly conclusive... The U.S. government should attempt to ease these concerns by providing further elaboration of the diligence of its pre-bombing investigation of the plant.[532]

HRW criticized the Clinton Administration for "resisting a proposal to send U.N. chemical weapons investigators to Sudan to examine the al Shifa factory"[533] in order to examine whether the Administration's justifications were true. But the Clinton Administration was extremely reluctant to allow such a move; after all, it knew what the likely outcome would be. The Administration instead worked hard to make sure the sloppy decision-making behind the bombing was not revealed. As *The New York Times* reported, "[i]n the aftermath, some senior officials moved to suppress internal dissent... Secretary of State Madeleine K. Albright and a senior deputy, they said, encouraged State Department intelligence analysts to kill a report being drafted that said the bombing was not justified."[534]

Regardless of the cover-up, though, the damage could not be undone. The factory was completely destroyed, never to be rebuilt, an enormous supply of medicine wiped out in an instant. The factory's owners sued in U.S. federal court in an attempt to receive compensation for the destruction, but the court dismissed their suit, reasoning that "the enemy target of military force" has no right to compensation for "the destruction of property designated by the President as enemy war-making property."[535]

The human costs, however, far exceeded the property damage. As James Astill reported in *The Guardian*, Al Shifa was:

...one of only three medium-sized pharmaceutical factories in Sudan, and the only one producing TB drugs - for more than 100,000 patients, at about £1 a month. Costlier imported versions are not an

option for most of them - or for their husbands, wives
and children, who will have been infected since. Al-
Shifa was also the only factory making veterinary
drugs in this vast, mostly pastoralist, country. Its
speciality was drugs to kill the parasites which pass
from herds to herders, one of Sudan's principal causes
of infant mortality. Since the bombing, "people have
gone back to doing without," says Eltayeb, with a
shrug.[536]

Some, like Germany's then-Ambassador to Sudan, Werner Daum, estimated that the destruction of the Al Shifa plant may have led to thousands of deaths,[537] though there does not actually appear to be reliable data on the public health consequences of the bombing. Jonathan Belke, in the *Boston Globe*, reported that the factory's destruction likely exacerbated a medical catastrophe:

Without the lifesaving medicine it produced,
Sudan's death toll from the bombing has continued,
quietly, to rise... this factory provided affordable
medicine for humans and all the locally available
veterinary medicine in Sudan. It produced 90
percent of Sudan's major pharmaceutical products.
Sanctions against Sudan make it impossible to
import adequate amounts of medicines required to
cover the serious gap left by the plant's destruction.
Thus, tens of thousands of people—many of them
children—have suffered and died from malaria,
tuberculosis, and other treatable diseases...[538]

But whatever the specific cost in human lives, the destruction of an enormous storehouse of life-saving medicines, in a country with which the United States was not at war, was nevertheless an extraordinary act to be taken without diligence.

Why did Clinton bomb the Al-Shifa factory? He was not, presumably, consciously attempting to destroy Sudan's supply of malaria drugs. But since Clinton had been given ample reason to doubt that the factory was making chemical weapons, and senior officials were offering grave doubts as to the wisdom of destroying the factory, why did he go through with it?

Some have posited a "wag the dog" story to explain Clinton's conduct; the bombing coincided with Monica Lewinsky's testimony in front of a grand jury, and the hypothesis is that Clinton urgently wanted a strike against al-Qaeda as a distraction, leading him to ignore evidence of the factory's innocence out of a wish to hastily blow something up. That's a deeply cynical interpretation, and unfounded. But we can believe the second half without necessarily buying the conspiratorial first half; whether or not it had anything to do with Lewinsky, Clinton wanted to strike back at Al-Qaeda after the embassy bombings, and his desire for a bombing overtook his desire to make sure that bombing was against the correct target. As *The New York Times* reported, "[s]ome officials said they were told that the President and his aides approved the operation… to show that the United States could hit back against an adversary who had bombed American embassies simultaneously in two countries."[539] It's not that Clinton *knew* the building was a medicine factory, then, it was that he *didn't care enough to find out*.

This interpretation, which fits well with the facts, suggests once again that Clinton's strategic calculus rarely gives any real weight to black people's lives. For Clinton, if there was a chance that the factory was producing nerve gas, that was sufficient reason to destroy it, period. But for a moral human being, the chances that the factory is producing nerve gas must be set against the chance that it is an aspirin factory, and the potential human toll of a mistake should be factored into the decision-making. Given how serious the doubts about the factory were, and how decisive Clinton was against the advice of his senior officials, we must conclude that Clinton was simply not very concerned with the black lives that were at stake in the question of whether the intelligence was reliable.

Al-Shifa may not have been the kind of extraordinary bloodbath that Rwanda was. (Though poor Fadil Reheima was blinded for life, and an impoverished country's supply of valuable medicines was obliterated by guided missiles.) But Clinton's behavior was consistent. In each instance, the interests of America (and more importantly, of Bill Clinton) were the only factor given any consideration. The interests of the anonymous Africans who stood to bear the consequences were given no consideration at all.

IV. CLINTON AND KAGAME

It's hard to describe...I wish I could. It's hard to describe.
At first, I just thought it was in a movie. I never knew that I
would see him like that. It took time to adjust [to the fact that it]
was actually him. His shirt was his, his fingers were his,
his forehead was his, his jeans, the shoes on the floor...
it was him, but I didn't want to believe it was him.[540]
—DAVID BATENGA, asked how he felt upon finding the
dead body of his uncle, Patrick Karegeya

BEFORE PATRICK KARYEGA WAS STRANGLED TO DEATH IN A Johannesburg hotel room, he had been afraid for his life. "I am already a dead man," he had told those who spoke with him.[541] Karyega had once served as the chief intelligence officer under Rwandan President Paul Kagame. But after being ousted by Kagame in 2006, Karyenga was forced into exile in South Africa. There, he became publicly critical of Kagame's regime. Karyega confirmed what many reports had long suggested: that Kagame stifled human rights, restricted free speech, and regularly ordered the assassination of dissidents. Asked why he opposed Kagame's regime, Karyega said that "the problem I have" with the Rwandan president is that "[h]e believes in killing his opponents... there is a long list of people that have died politically."[542] Soon, Karyega himself would become an entry on that list. Believing himself safe in South Africa, Karyega agreed to meet with an acquaintance at the ritzy Michaelangelo Towers hotel. By the time Karyega's nephew found him, he had been smothered to death with a pillow in an upper-floor suite.

President Paul Kagame initially denied having ordered Karyenga's assassination. But later public statements somewhat sabotaged his credibility on the matter. Kagame insisted that those who attempted to undermine Rwanda's government "will pay the price wherever they are."[543] In an interview with the BBC, Rwanda's ambassador to the U.K. made only the most half-hearted attempt to avoid admitting that the country's government ordered Karyenga's assassination. The Ambassador attempted to claim that Kagame's "pay the price" remark had nothing to do with Karyenga's killing (nor did the Rwandan defense minister's suggestion that traitors would "die like dogs"):

> AMBASSADOR: *What president Kagame is saying does not necessarily have to do with Karyenga, it has to do with everyone who betrays the country.*
> INTERVIEWER: *Did Mr. Karyenga betray the country?*
> AMBASSADOR: *Of course. Karyenga has been on record as a declared enemy of the state...*
> *[...]*
> INTERVIEWER: *...[W]hen your defense minister is quoted saying 'Ignore those making noise that someone was strangled with a rope on the seventh floor in a certain country,' we know who he is talking about, and goes on to say 'If you choose to be a dog, you die like a dog.'...*

AMBASSADOR: *I think the metaphor refers essentially to people who have become useless. As far as Rwanda was concerned, Karyenga had become a declared enemy of the state. He had been on record saying that he advances the overthrow or government change through violent means. To the extent that he takes that position, he loses value, he is no longer useful to us as a country because he is an opponent of the state.*[544]

Beyond the ambassador's frank justification for ridding the world of "useless" people, Kagame himself then said that he "wished" he had ordered Karyenga's death, and refused to rule out the use of political assassinations.[545]

During the BBC's interview with the Rwandan ambassador, the interviewer pressed the ambassador on the question of why other Rwandans in exile had been warned that their lives were in danger from their own government. The Ambassador's response did not offer reassurance:

AMBASSADOR: *That was a result of allegations that have never been proved. Anyone who threatens the life of the country and the lives of the 11 million or so people who live in the country needs to be held to account.*
INTERVIEWER: *And how will they be held to account?*
AMBASSADOR: *Different ways. Like the President says, if you threaten the state, the state has a right to defend itself.*[546]

I N 1998, ON PRESIDENT CLINTON'S TRIP TO AFRICA, HIS SPEECHES emphasized the strides African leaders were making toward embracing free markets and enlightened governance. Clinton spoke especially of a "new generation of African leaders."[547]

Unlike the old communist-leaning strongmen, these new leaders understood the importance of economic liberalization and Western democracy. They signaled the continent's break from the unfashionable socialists like Nkrumah, Lumumba, and Mugabe that had previously characterized African leadership.

Foremost among these new leaders was Paul Kagame. During the 1994, Paul Kagame had been the head of the Tutsi-dominated rebel forces, the Rwandan Patriotic Army (RPA). When Kagame and the RPA successfully recaptured the country and brought the genocide to a close, they created a new government, in which Kagame himself would serve as Vice President and Minister of Defense, before ultimately becoming President in 2000.

But Paul Kagame's leadership quickly became notorious. In 1995, as the RPA took over the country, Kagame "killed civilians in numerous summary executions and in massacres" and "may have slaughtered tens of thousands" in revenge killings over the genocide.[548] In 1996 and 1998, Kagame committed what the United Nations described as war crimes and acts that "if proven before a competent court, could be characterized as crimes of genocide."[549]

Once in office, he became one of the most vicious despots in Africa. Kagame suppressed opposition newspapers, kicked out human rights observers, and all but eliminated freedom of speech, with dissidents being sentenced to long prison terms for genocide denial.[550] He became especially known for murdering members of the opposition. As *The Independent* reports:

> *Enemies of Kagame – the despot so beloved by Western democratic leaders and charity dupes – seem to have a strange habit of dying in disturbing circumstances. Over the years a succession of prominent critics and campaigners, judges and journalists, have been killed. They have been beaten, beheaded, shot and stabbed, both at home in Rwanda and abroad in nervous exile.[551]*

As one of Kagame's former officers explained, "[i]f you differ strongly with Kagame and make your views known from the inside, you will be made to pay the price, and very often that price is your life."[552] In 2011, the British government warned two Rwandan exiles living in London that "the Rwandan government poses an imminent threat to your life," a threat that could not be controlled even on British soil.[553]

THROUGHOUT ALL OF THIS, BILL CLINTON'S PRAISE FOR KAGAME has been unqualified. The two forged what the *New York Times* described as a "deeply respectful friendship." Clinton called Kagame "one of the greatest leaders of our time."[554] "From crisis," Clinton said, "President Kagame has forged a strong, unified, and growing nation with the potential to become a model for the rest of Africa and the world." Clinton has referred to Kagame by saying "I know this guy. He's a G.S.D. guy... Gets stuff done."[555]

Few would dispute that Kagame gets stuff done. Unfortunately, a large amount of the "stuff" in question appears to be the assassination of dissidents and the perpetration of war crimes. Rwanda scholar Filip Reyntjens calls Kagame "probably the worst war criminal in office today."[556]

Bill Clinton knows about Kagame's record. But, in a tactic that recalls his treatment of the 1994 genocide, he has responded by insisting that the facts are unclear, that nobody knows the real truth. "It's complicated," Clinton has said, and "the matter has not been fully litigated."[557] Speaking of the killings Kagame perpetrated in the Congo, Clinton said this was simply the U.N.'s opinion: "[t]he U.N. said what it did about what happened after the [Rwandan] genocide, in Congo... Kagame strongly disputes it... Right now I'm not going to pre-judge him because there's this huge debate about what happened in the Congo and why, and I don't know."[558]

But as a Human Rights Watch researcher exasperatedly explained in response: "It is not a matter of pre-judging. The facts are well-established... There is no doubt that Rwandan troops, together with their Congolese allies, committed large-scale massacres and other grave human-rights violations against Rwandan and Congolese civilians. The evidence is there for all to see. What more does Clinton need?"[559] "Either he's completely uninformed about what we know about Kagame or he's in total denial," said Filip Reyntjens.[560]

Clinton has rejected this criticism, citing Kagame's record of improving the public infrastructure of Rwanda. Clinton replied that "there's some people in the human rights community who believe that every good thing that has happened in Rwanda should be negated by what they allege that they have done in the eastern Congo."[561] The Clinton Foundation's foreign policy director has said that Rwanda is simply a messy place, and moral judgments are misplaced: "There are lots of countries in the world that are complicated and it's not our role to pass judgment... The ethos we have here, and it comes from [Clinton himself], is that there are plenty of other people who are focused on those issues."[562]

But many human rights groups and Rwandan dissidents have said that by publicly supporting Kagame, and refusing to make any attempt to modify Kagame's behavior, Clinton enables the abuses to continue. They "argue that Mr. Clinton's continuing embrace helps validate Mr. Kagame and buffers him from international pressure."[563] "How much longer will the international community continue to endorse this repressive regime?" asked Reporters Without Borders.[564] "You just feel anything can happen, especially when nothing is done at the international level against Kagame," said a Rwandan opposition activist living in Britain. "It is like he has a license to kill."[565] Frank Habineza of the Democratic Green Party, who was forced to flee the country after his deputy was mysteriously decapitated, said that "[i]f the international community took a stand on political space and democracy, that would be the most helpful to us."[566] Unfortunately, Clinton, as well as Tony Blair, has not only embraced Kagame as a friend, but have actively downplayed the extent of his atrocities.

One person who pleaded with Clinton to stop supporting Kagame was Paul Rusesabagina of the "Hotel Rwanda," who wrote Clinton a letter begging him to at least make an effort to rein in Kagame or recognize the extent of his abuses. "Dear President Clinton," Rusesabagina wrote, "your mission to 'build a world where people everywhere have the chance to support their families, uplift their communities and live out their dreams' is not a sentiment shared by Kagame's administration, as evidenced by governmental actions in DRC and the disparities and corruption present in Rwanda." Rusesabagina cited Kagame's imprisoning of opposition electoral candidates, and pointed to numerous reports from human rights groups detailing Kagame's abuses of power. "For the good of all Rwandans, this must not be allowed to continue," Rusesabagina concluded.[567]

But Clinton paid no more attention to the letter than he did to Rusesabagina's desperate faxes to the White House at the height of the genocide. Just as he did in 1994, Rusesabagina misunderstood the problem. He believed that if he could only draw the facts to Clinton's attention, Clinton would be compelled by his conscience to reverse course. But just as he did during the genocide, Clinton has indicated that he knows full well the nature of Kagame's murderous regime.

Clinton's support for Kagame is easy enough to understand. Facing heat for his actions during the genocide, Clinton sought to redeem his image by funneling a large quantity of Foundation cash into Rwanda. Embracing the new Tutsi government was a way to show the world that Clinton had been on their side, and to reinforce the idea of his being a caring person who made a mistake. Thus once Clinton had embraced Kagame, he became extremely reluctant to admit Kagame's war crimes, even as the evidence became overwhelming. Doing so would mean that Clinton's efforts at redemption had done nothing.

But note how sinister this is: Clinton refuses to admit that Paul Kagame is one of the world's worst war criminals, because Clinton doesn't want to make himself look bad. It is not simply a matter of making a pragmatic compromise for the sake of doing good. Clinton is not being asked to sacrifice his charitable ventures, but to merely stop actively working to downplay the veracity of the claims of human rights groups. It's also the case that Clinton's friendship with Kagame gives him a tremendous ability to pressure Kagame, who depends on Clinton for his access to the global elite. Yet Clinton chooses not to exercise this power; his Foundation sees human rights as the concern of "other groups."

Finally, there's no reason that pulling out of Rwanda entirely would have to inhibit Clinton's ability to do good; after all, there are plenty of other needy countries that are *not* ruled by the world's worst war criminal. It is solely because Clinton wants to publicly redeem himself on Rwanda that it is *this country specifically* that he feels the need to work with. Thus Clinton finds himself supporting a murderous dictator, and helping to muffle the human rights groups who are trying to democratize the country, solely to preserve Clinton's own self-image.

v. Clinton and Africa, Appraised

How should Clinton's Africa legacy be assessed? On the one hand, he runs a charitable foundation that has made considerable investment in Africa. On the other hand, he denied a genocide, fought against AIDS treatment measures on behalf of U.S. businesses, bombed a medicine factory, and covered up human rights abuses by a terrifying and ruthless dictator. His record is therefore what we might call "mixed." One should not be unduly cynical about Clinton's present-day charitable efforts in African countries. But there's a chance, just a chance, that Clinton partially engages in these because of their benefit to his image.

The head of George W. Bush's Africa initiative has voiced his frustration that Bush is "reluctant to let us tell the world he's doing it,"[568] and indeed, Bush's multi-billion dollar, life-saving programs are publicized very little. By contrast, Clinton's Africa initiatives land with a considerable media splash. Journalist Carol Felsenthal, who has extensively examined Clinton's post-presidency, suggests Clinton's actions are part of a "striving for respectability" aimed at restoring his image after the public disgrace that marked his last years in office.[569] Clinton, she says, has made no secret of the fact that with his Foundation work, he is "angling for the Nobel Peace Prize"; he is a person who "feeds off public acclaim," and therefore needs a successful charity to helm.[570] Yet the Clinton Foundation's achievements on AIDS in Africa, Felsenthal reports, are mostly the work of Ira Magaziner, the tireless subordinate who runs the Clinton Global Health Initiative. Clinton himself has a "tendency to take too much credit" and makes African health workers "wince" when he "seems to want to don a Superman cape and put himself at the center of every rescue."[571]

The Clinton Foundation itself is not strictly a charity, either. *The New York Times* has described the Foundation as "more a nonprofit global consulting firm than a traditional philanthropy."[572] Its primary mission, says the *Times*, is "not to provide direct humanitarian aid"; instead it "is known for sending bright but inexperienced recent graduates to work as technical advisers to government ministries."[573] Ira Magaziner has said of their work that "the whole thing is bankable... It's a commercial proposition. This is not charity."[574] Instead of aid, the Clinton Foundation spends much of its effort "creating new markets," finding lucrative investment opportunities in the developing world for Western private capital.[575] These have included everything from "using business methods to streamline fertilizer markets in Africa" to "working with credit card companies to expand the volume of low-cost loans offered to poor inner city residents."[576] (Note that typically, enticing poor people into taking on large amounts of credit card debt is not among the activities of a charitable foundation.) Clinton is open about the fact that in this work, he is trying to help corporations profit from the developing world. He attempts to "reinvent philanthropy" as a lucrative enterprise for his partners because, in his words, "I think it's wrong to ask anyone to lose money."[577]

The Foundation's spending is also somewhat opaque. Bill Allison of the pro-transparency Sunlight Foundation has said that the organization operates as a "slush fund for the Clintons."[578] Charity Navigator, a watchdog group, has added the Clinton Foundation to its watch list of problematic charities, because its "atypical business model... doesn't meet our criteria."[579] Only a small percentage of the Foundation's money is spent on direct charitable grants,[580] and of the rest, only 1/3 is spent outside of the United States.[581] While the Foundation apparently uses most of its money for its programs, it has been reluctant to have the programs themselves evaluated. The Clinton Health Access Initiative has refused to allow the charity evaluation organization GiveWell to analyze its outcomes,[582] and the Better Business Bureau has listed the Clinton Foundation as failing to meet the basic standards for reporting the effectiveness of its programs.[583]

Certain expenditures have also appeared unduly lavish. The Foundation spends $8 million in annual travel expenses (the Clintons fly on private jets), and universities that invite Clinton to speak can find themselves hit with unexpected invoices for $1,400 hotel phone bills and $700 dinners-for-two.[584] The Foundation itself bought a first-class plane ticket to bring Natalie Portman (and her prized Yorkie) to an event, and funds a "glitzy annual gathering of chief executives, heads of state, and celebrities."[585]

Despite this, the organization has extracted money from smaller, less wealthy philanthropic groups, offering to have Bill Clinton speak at their fundraising events in exchange for their donating huge sums to the Clinton Foundation. The head of one small school-building charity, which tried to get Clinton to accept an award at its annual fundraiser, was told by Clinton Foundation that "they don't look at these things unless money is offered, and it has to be $500,000."[586]

Bill Clinton's own motivations for the charitable work can be called into question. Clinton Foundation gatherings are packed with celebrities and CEOs, and whatever good the organization may do across the globe, it certainly brings Clinton himself both luxury and adulation. Lawrence O'Donnell has offered a particularly acidic take on Clinton's philanthropy:

> *It's all self-glorifying. If we wanted to sit down and say 'Let's construct a path for glorification of Bill Clinton in a postpresidential environment,' we could say 'It would be great if he did a lot of good works in Africa.' Look. My resistance to being impressed by Bill Clinton's charitable work comes from his obvious, desperate desire for me to be impressed by it. And his extremely calculated desire for me to be impressed by it. This is a person as calculating about public image as exists in the world. He's as extreme a narcissist as politics produces—but he is, fundamentally, what politics produces. They're virtually all like him, to some*

lesser degree. But they are all somewhere on that narcissistic trip he's on. It's inevitably part of what these people do.[587]

Note that O'Donnell does not dispute the positive material consequences of Clinton's endeavors in Africa. Doing things for narcissistic reasons does not mean that one will not do good things. It simply means that one will only do good things when there happen to be self-interested reasons for doing them. Clinton intentionally defied the Genocide Convention in order to let hundreds of thousands die in Rwanda, since there was nothing to be gained from intervening. But since fundraising for charitable initiatives in Rwanda makes Clinton seem very good indeed, and helps reinforce the image that his actions during the genocide were well-intentioned ignorance rather than deliberate indifference, he is perfectly happy to dedicate himself to fundraising in Rwanda.

Perhaps this perspective is unfair, and attributes to Clinton an extraordinary amount of bad faith. But once someone deliberately orchestrates the denial of a genocide so as not to have to stop it, we might want to raise an eyebrow at all future gushing professions of their sincere humanitarianism. We might suspect that, if their humanitarian good works can equally well be explained by a love of self, vanity may be the more plausible motive.

But we know full well how to test these two theories against one another. We know a person is not acting selfishly if they *would do the same thing even if it did not serve their self-interest.* The question, in understanding whether Clinton is using black people or merely failing them, is what he does when the cameras turn off.

For this, Haiti serves as a useful case study.

Bill Clinton vigorously explains something to a Haitian man.

CHAPTER FIVE
Clinton in Haiti

P RESIDENT JEAN-BERTRAND ARISTIDE'S ELECTION IN 1990 had been seen as an encouraging harbinger of a new, relatively more peaceful and democratic era in Haitian politics. Aristide was a liberation theologian and orphanage proprietor who had spent years preaching about the well-being of the poor, sick, and hungry.

After the country had survived multiple decades ruled by the Duvaliers *père* and *fils* (a pair of murderous grifters who financed their upscale dictator-chic lifestyles by trafficking in the body parts of dead Haitians[588]), the frugal curate Aristide was a welcome relief.

The peace did not last. Aristide was overthrown in a military *coup d'etat* the next year, and the country collapsed into disarray. The new junta government swiftly introduced the usual program of arrests, tortures, and mysterious disappearances, with all opposition subject to terror and suppression.[589] Faced with violence and economic collapse, hundreds of refugees began to flee the country in tiny boats, bound for U.S. shores.[590]

United States law allows political refugees to apply for asylum if they have a "well-founded fear" of political persecution, which plainly the Haitians did.[591] But the George H.W. Bush administration refused to let the Haitians go through the asylum process. Instead, it followed a formal policy of simply dispatching the Coast Guard to scoop the fleeing Haitians from the water, then immediately sending them back to Haiti.[592]

The Bush policy was condemned by human rights groups; after all, the entire purpose of political asylum is to ensure that people are not being returned to countries where their lives are in danger, yet the U.S. government was openly sending thousands of Haitians back to a country where their lives were in danger. It was also seen as discriminatory, even racist: refugees from Cuba were routinely granted asylum, but Haitians were not. (Of nearly 25,000 Haitians interdicted by the U.S. from 1981-1991, only eleven were allowed into the country to be given asylum hearings.[593]) The brazen inhumanity of the administration's actions shocked many, and throughout his 1992 campaign, Bill Clinton had pledged unequivocally that he would end the policy immediately upon taking office, criticizing the practice as "cruel" and "immoral."[594] Clinton said that by contrast to Bush:

> *If I were President, I would—in the absence of clear and compelling evidence that they weren't political refugees—give them temporary asylum until we restored the elected Government of Haiti.*[595]

The promise was an unusually forceful one for Clinton; it was markedly free of his usual qualifications and hedges. There was no real argument that the refugees were political. They were fleeing a military dictatorship. The granting of political asylum would also be within the President's powers; there was no obvious legal impediment to his carrying out the promise.

But shortly after being elected, before he had even taken office, Clinton reversed himself. In what the *New York Times* called a "bluntly worded" radio address, Clinton announced that:

> *The practice of returning those who flee Haiti by boat will continue, for the time being, after I become President... Those who leave Haiti by boat for the United States will be intercepted and returned to Haiti by the U.S. Coast Guard.*[596]

Asked about the switch, Clinton said his "campaign rhetoric had been sorely misunderstood." Clinton maintained that "people who didn't qualify as refugees still shouldn't be here," and the Haitians were fleeing for "economic" rather than "political" reasons, and thus didn't qualify as refugees.

This was news to the Haitians, who had thought they were fleeing political violence. It also angered human rights advocates, who had believed Clinton's word that he would end the Bush policy. The Lawyer's Committee for Human Rights was stingingly critical of the Clinton double-cross. The head of the National Coalition for Haitian Refugees said he was "shocked and dismayed that President-elect Clinton would go back on his word."[597] After all, he said "[t]he policy violates the most basic tenet of refugee protection. People at least deserve to be heard to demonstrate a fear of persecution before they are returned."[598]

The reversal also alienated black Democrats, who had relied on Clinton to show more respect for the rights of poor black refugees than Bush had. Kweisi Mfume, then head of the Congressional Black Caucus, later recounted his anger at Clinton over the blatant abandonment of his promise:

> *Barely one week after Clinton's inauguration... the President decided to reverse his campaign promises about Haiti. Throughout his campaign, Clinton had assured voters that he was going to end the Bush policy of sending Haitian refugees back to the country they had risked their lives to escape. The Haitians, he told us, were fleeing their native land seeking a safe*

*haven and political asylum. Black people all across
this country gravitated to Clinton's message because
he was moving beyond Bush's inhumane policy,
which turned a blind eye to conditions in Haiti—
men being tortured and maimed, women being
raped, and the bodies of children found washed up
on the shore. Yet, in Clinton's first week in office, he
announced he would continue to maintain the Bush
policy of repatriation, mumbling some kind of poor
excuse for his decision.*[599]

Mfume said that in his opinion, "Clinton could not have
done such a thing without taking the black vote and the Caucus for granted."[600]

The reasons for Clinton's change of mind were never made
public, but the *New York Times* suggested one explanation,
reporting that "[m]embers of Mr. Clinton's foreign-policy
team have expressed concern that celebrations surrounding Mr.
Clinton's inauguration, which will be widely televised, will be
marred by news footage of Haitian boat people drowning…"[601]
Naturally, who would wish to see such celebrations marred?

The forced repatriation policy was not the only way in which
the U.S. violated the Haitians' rights, however. As disagree-
ments over the refugees' status had gone through the courts,
the Bush administration had begun a policy of storing refugees awaiting transfer at the Guantánamo naval base in Cuba.
Because Guantánamo was not U.S. soil, detaining people was
thought to avoid the triggering of legal procedural protections
that may have been granted to those who were actually being
held in the country.

Bill Clinton continued the Bush policy of keeping refugees
at Guantánamo indefinitely. But Clinton introduced a new
policy as well: testing the Haitians for HIV, and segregating

those who tested positive. In doing so, he created "the world's first HIV detention camp."[602]

Conditions in the HIV camp were horrific. The facility was a "leaky barracks with poor sanitation, surrounded by razor wire and guard towers,"[603] and numerous detainees were housed in tents. Many of the refugees were gravely ill with AIDS, and the crowded facility was characterized by fear, squalor, and uncertainty. After being held for more than a year, some of the refugees began a hunger strike. (The military retaliated by putting the leader of the hunger strike in solitary confinement.[604]) Communications home had to be smuggled out.[605] As one refugee wrote in a letter to her family, "I have lost in the struggle for life... There is nothing left for me. Take care of my children, so they have strength to continue my struggle... I have lost hope. I am alone in my distress."[606] Another recalled:

> We had been asking them to remove the barbed wire; the children were playing near it, they were falling and injuring themselves. The food they were serving us, including canned chicken, had maggots in it. And yet they insisted that we eat it. Because you've got no choice. And it was for these reasons that we started holding demonstrations. In response, they began to beat us. On July 18th, they surrounded us, arrested some of us, and put us in prison, in Camp Number 7... Camp 7 was a little space on a hill. They put up a tent, but when it rained, you got wet. The sun came up, we were baking in it. We slept on the rocks; there were no beds. And each little space was separated by barbed wire. We couldn't even turn around without being injured by the barbed wire.[607]

In the tiny, cramped cells, "[t]here was no privacy. Snakes would come in; we were lying on the ground and lizards were climbing over us. One of us was bitten by a scorpion... there were spiders. Bees were stinging the children, and there were flies everywhere: whenever you tried to eat something, flies would fly in your mouth."[608]

The military doctors began giving women birth control without the women's knowledge or consent.[609] Yet at the same time Clinton Administration refused to provide the AIDS-infected refugees with life-saving medical care, which almost certainly hastened their deaths. The U.S. military had recommended that the sickest refugees be airlifted to hospitals within the United States for treatment. But the administration, not wishing to let any of the Haitians onto U.S. soil, refused. As a result, there were "a huge number of unnecessary early deaths."[610] When asked why they were refusing to provide medical treatment, a spokesman for Clinton's Immigration and Naturalization Service said bluntly: "They're going to die anyway, aren't they?"[611]

Eventually, after human rights lawyers filed suit, the federal courts stepped in to put a stop to Clinton's actions. A federal judge called the treatment "outrageous, callous and reprehensible" and criticized Clinton for imposing on refugees "the kind of indefinite detention usually reserved for spies and murderers... The Haitians' plight is a tragedy of immense proportion, and their continued detainment is totally unacceptable to this court."[612]

Thanks to judicial intervention, then, the HIV camp was finally closed. But for some, the court order did not come soon enough. A detainee named Joel:

> ...died just days after he was freed from the camp, at the age of 26. For months, human rights attorneys had begged the Immigration and Naturalization Service (INS) to send Saintil and other gravely ill Haitians for treatment in the United States, but the agency had refused until a federal district court judge

ordered the sickest released. Saintil was flown to his
father's house in Florida, but it was already too late.
He became one of the camp's first casualties.[613]

Even for the survivors, the nearly two years spent in Clinton's detention camp had lasting psychological effects:

> *Annette Baptiste still cries when she thinks about what*
> *the United States did to her ten years ago on its Naval*
> *Base in Guantánamo, Cuba. Sitting in her Brooklyn*
> *apartment, she recalls how the United States detained*
> *her and 276 fellow Haitians in the Alcatraz of refugee*
> *camps, imprisoning them for some eighteen months*
> *simply because they, or their loved ones, had HIV. "I*
> *relive Guantánamo every day," she says in Creole. "It's all*
> *in my head." Guantánamo is also in Pierre Avril's head,*
> *say the friends who looked after him in the United States.*
> *Avril was just 14 when he arrived at Guantánamo, and*
> *the trauma of the experience—the fear, the uncertainty,*
> *the stigma—left permanent damage. Today he is once*
> *again in detention, this time in a psychiatric correctional*
> *facility in upstate New York.*[614]

Even after action by the courts stopped the Clinton policy, the administration was still reluctant to process refugee claims from Haitians. When President Aristide was finally returned to power, and Clinton's government announced that the refugees would finally be freed from detention, the administration was sure to declare that "under no circumstances will any Haitian currently at Guantanamo be admitted to the United States."[615]

Freeing the detainees had not come easily, because Clinton fiercely defended his government's right to indefinitely imprison Haitians. In doing so, he "helped pave the way for" the future justifications for indefinite detention at Guantánamo made by

his successor, George W. Bush. As law professor Brandt Goldstein explained, Clinton's lawyers followed the exact same logic
that Bush would use just a few years later to defend the same
kind of imprisonment:

> *The Clinton White House justified this atrocious
> conduct in terms that sound strikingly familiar
> today. Justice Department attorneys maintained
> that foreigners held by the United States at
> Guantánamo Bay have absolutely no legal rights,
> whether under the Constitution, federal statutes,
> or international law. According to this logic, the
> Clinton White House was free to treat the detainees
> however it pleased.*[616]

But the court decisions surrounding the Haitian refugee crisis would not come up during the debate over Bush's detention
practices. Clinton Administration lawyers had fought to have
the decisions questioning the legality of detention removed from
the books, and the case would disappear.

CLINTON'S RECORD ON HAITI DID NOT GET BETTER. WHILE
the Administration publicly opposed the removal of President Aristide, it covertly supported the right-wing death
squads that had assisted the coup. The leader of the brutal
Front for the Advancement and Progress of Haiti (FRAPH),
Emmanuel Constant, had been on the CIA's payroll for
years.[617] American officials admitted to both working with him
and encouraging him to form FRAPH in the first place. U.S.
intelligence called him "a young pro-Western intellectual...
no farther right than a Young Republican" even though his
organization was, as sociologist William Robinson explains, a
"well-organized instrument of repression, operating in a death-
squad manner to continue the process of decimating popular

sector organization" and "bent on preserving an authoritarian political system."[618] The organization, "carried out much of the reign of terror that led to the killing of more than 3,000 Haitian civilians in three years" and "shot into pro-democracy crowds celebrating Aristide's planned return, killing eight people and wounding many others."[619]

Despite this string of atrocities, the United States continued to provide support to Constant and the FRAPH, some of which was more overt than covert. *The Los Angeles Times* reported on one of Constant's speaking events:

> Constant appeared on a public podium with a sound system, allegedly supplied by the U.S. Embassy, flanked by a row of U.S. soldiers to protect him from a seething crowd. He then read a speech, reportedly drafted by U.S. Embassy officials, that cast him as a democrat ready to help heal the wounds of the nation.[620]

When the United States restored President Aristide to power, Constant was sheltered on U.S. soil, despite Haiti's pleas that Constant be deported and tried for war crimes in his home country. At first, Constant was held in detention, and was ordered deported by a judge. But after Constant threatened to publicly expose the CIA's links to his organization, "the Clinton administration released him into the United States rather than return him to Haiti, provided him with a work permit, and required that he abide by a gag order."[621]

The Clinton Administration attempted to cover up its involvement with FRAPH after Aristide's restoration. When FRAPH massacred pro-Aristide protesters, the U.S. raided and destroyed FRAPH headquarters. In the process, it seized FRAPH's internal documents and brought them back to the United States. The Administration refused to accede to Aristide's request for the return of the documents, which Human Rights Watch said contained "intact evidence of death-squad crimes."[622]

The seizure and retention of the documents was a blatant violation of Haiti's sovereignty. In a report, the Congressional Research Service concluded that because "[u]nder international law, official government documents are property that belongs to Haiti as a state. . . their retention by the U.S. government violates Haiti's ownership rights."[623] HRW's Advocacy Director noted that the withholding of the documents was inhibiting Haiti's ability to prosecute criminals, saying "[t]hese thugs terrorized Haiti for three years, murdering, torturing and raping... The United States has taken away a potential goldmine of evidence which could help bring some of these people to justice and now won't give it back."[624]

The withholding of the documents was reportedly an effort to keep the CIA's links with the FRAPH a secret; *The New York Times* cited the Clinton Administration's "implicit fear that some documents might mention American intelligence links to members of the discredited former Government that ousted Mr. Aristide in a military coup in 1991."[625] The U.S.'s refusal was condemned by the United Nations' independent human rights envoy to Haiti, who said he believed that "the U.S. administration is trying to cover up some of its wrongdoing in that period."[626] Even when the U.S. finally agreed to return the documents, a State Department spokesman said processing them would involve first censoring them and "blocking out American names in the papers."[627] This despite the fact that the documents had been seized, without apparent legal justification, from the sovereign territory of another country.

The U.S.'s support of FRAPH made for an apparent irony. Allan Nairn, a journalist for *The Nation* who won a Polk Award for his reporting on Haiti and the CIA, said that "many of the officials whom Clinton was claiming to be fighting were actually his employees."[628] Nairn observed that if "Clinton had simply cut them off, completely ended their support, the Haitian public itself most likely could have brought down the coup regime without a US occupation."[629] Even as the U.S. professed itself flummoxed as to how to restore Haiti's democratically-elected government, it continued to encourage the very forces that were preventing the restoration of that government.

The Clinton Administration's support for Constant and FRAPH seemed to contradict its ostensible dedication to the return of Haiti's democratically-elected government. Some were puzzled by "a contradictory U.S. policy that publicly supports Aristide as "the people's choice" while privately grooming those who ardently oppose him."[630] After all, Clinton went so far as to invade Haiti in order to restore Aristide to power, so wasn't covert support for the right-wing opposition somewhere between pointless and disastrous?

It was not. As Emmanuel Constant himself explained, the U.S. asked him to "balance" Aristide's leftist movement, a task he took to with violent enthusiasm.[631] By supporting the FRAPH, the U.S. increased its bargaining power in negotiations with Aristide. Returning Aristide to power was conditional on his agreeing to an austerity and privatization program, and through ensuring that Haiti remained divided between competing factions, the Clinton Administration was able to ensure that Aristide would be compliant while in office, and not attempt to implement the radical redistributionist economic policies that the IMF and United States feared he might enact.

As a means of ensuring U.S. control, this was an intelligent policy. As a moral act, it was hideous. After all, what the Clinton Administration did was intentionally foment discord (in the form of murder) in order to ensure that Aristide would remain compliant upon his return to power. But the plan did work. Aristide was returned to office, but agreed to an austerity program that prevented him from taking Haiti in a social democratic direction.

That program had terrible consequences of its own. The economic aspects of Clinton's Haiti policy would cause the country to starve.

RICE IS A CRITICAL COMPONENT OF THE HAITIAN DIET. The UN's Food and Agricultural Organization (FAO) reports that 23% of Haitians' average total daily calories comes from rice.[632] Traditionally, domestic rice growers had been an important part of the Haitian economy.

But in 1995, as part of the IMF/World Bank "structural adjustment program" that Aristide was required to adopt, Haiti dropped its import tariffs on rice from 50% to 3%. At the same time, United States farm subsidies were giving hundreds of millions of dollars to American rice farmers, keeping prices artificially low. The moment Haiti eliminated its tariffs, it was flooded with cheap rice from the United States; Haiti soon became the fifth-largest importer of rice in the world, despite having a population of only 10 million.

The American farm subsidies destroyed the Haitian rice industry. Even though rice farming was one of the most important industries in Haiti, domestic rice growers had no way to compete with subsidized U.S. rice. As a result, an entire major Haitian industry all but disappeared, with rice sales benefitting American companies rather then poor Haitian farmers.

Interestingly enough, the companies that benefitted were highly concentrated in Arkansas, which is home to several of the U.S.'s major rice producers. The two largest are Producers Rice Mill and Riceland Foods, the latter being the largest rice exporter in the world.[633] After the Clinton-imposed trade liberalization, Haiti became "a critical market for farmers in Arkansas,"[634] due to the extremely high volume of its rice importation. Indeed, Clinton himself admitted the policies had been "good for some of my farmers in Arkansas."[635] Arkansas rice companies had been looking forward to Clinton's presidency precisely because they believed Clinton would open up new markets and increase subsidies. In 1992, shortly after Clinton's election, the *Chicago Tribune* ran a story under the headline "Clinton Gives Rice Trade Home-state Advantage," which quoted Arkansas rice executives saying of Clinton: "I feel like he's going to be the best president we've ever had for agriculture... We always feel the president will take care of his state." Indeed he did. Riceland Foods and Producers Rice Mill received over $868 million in federal farm subsidies over a fifteen-year period beginning in 1995, making them largest recipients of federal farm subsidies in all of Arkansas.[636] (Predictably, the CEOs of Producers Rice Mill and Riceland Foods were both donors to Clinton's presidential campaigns.[637])

One might have expected cheaper rice to be beneficial, but the generous subsidies to Arkansas agribusiness have ultimately made the subsidies "devastating to Haiti's rice production and made it harder for the country to feed itself."[638] The free-market Cato Institute concluded that rice subsidies to American businesses "perpetuate poverty and hardship for millions of rice farmers in developing countries."[639] As *Foreign Policy* reports, development experts have noted that "while U.S. exports may feed people cheaply in the short run, they have exacerbated poverty and food insecurity over time, and subsidies are largely to blame."[640] As an official with the Haitian American Chamber of Commerce noted, "You have a country which is 70 percent farmers and you're importing 60 to 70 percent of your food." While lower rice prices make rice more affordable, in a farming-based economy, they also keep Haiti from becoming globally competitive as a producer. So while Haiti became the least trade-restrictive country in the Caribbean,[641] it experienced little economic growth, and remains the poorest country in the area.

It's also the case that where "cheap rice" is controlled by small cartels, both producers *and* consumers may see their well-being diminish. As an Oxfam report on the global rice trade explained, "increased imports do not always translate into lower retail prices. When a few large importers control the market... the gains may well not be passed on, leaving both farmers and consumers worse off."[642] That's precisely the case in Haiti, where "a handful of figures, some of whom have longstanding business relationships with mills in Arkansas," dominate the rice business. In Haiti, "a mere six importers control 70 percent of the import market and often exhibit rent-seeking behavior—seeking profits without creating new wealth—that can further exacerbate food insecurity in the country."[643]

The situation remains difficult to fix. Disruptions to the supply chain could make matters worse. Yet at present, whenever rice prices get a bump worldwide, import-dependent Haitians are liable to starve. In 2008, when the cost of rice suddenly jumped 141%, the country experienced "immense hardship" and mass child malnutrition.[644] (The CEO of Riceland had proudly boasted to shareholders that "friendly" rice prices would mean healthy profits from Haiti that year.[645])

Haiti had little choice in accepting this flood of Arkansas rice. According to the Haitian Finance Minister "It was a must. If you don't have an agreement with the IMF, you're dead in the water. You can't do anything."[646] With the Clinton Administration willing to go to extraordinary lengths to ensure liberalization (such as the maintenance of instability using FRAPH), it was almost a certainty that Aristide would not take power again without an arrangement to benefit Arkansas.

The rice trade policies were a shameful part of Clinton's Haiti policy, as Clinton himself was ultimately forced to admit after leaving office. As *Foreign Policy* puts it, Clinton-era policies were good at "keeping Arkansas rice growers fat on the farm and starving millions of Haitians."[647] Jesse Jackson summarized the situation simply: the Clinton administration "allowed the Riceland rice company to drop rice on Haiti, drive Haiti farmers out of business, and then raise the price of rice"[648] (*CNN* fact-checked Jackson's statement, and to their evident surprise could find nothing to dispute.[649]) While Haitians struggled to subsist, and frequently resorted to eating mud,[650] Bill Clinton continued to impose an economic regime that benefitted his Arkansas campaign donors, without regard to its consequences for black lives.

BILL AND HILLARY CLINTON HAD LONG SHARED A PERSONAL interest in Haiti, dating back to the time of their honeymoon, part of which was spent in Port-au-Prince. In his autobiography, Bill says that his understanding of God and human nature were profoundly transformed when they witnessed a voodoo ceremony in which a woman bit the head off a live chicken.[651] Hillary Clinton says the two of them "fell in love" with Haiti and they had developed a "deep connection" to the country.[652]

So when Hillary Clinton became Secretary of State in 2009, she consciously made the redevelopment of Haiti one of her top priorities. The country, she announced, would be a laboratory where the United States could "road-test new approaches to development," taking advantage of what she termed "the power of proximity."[653] She intended to "make Haiti the proving ground for her vision of American power."[654] Hillary Clinton selected her own chief of staff, Cheryl Mills, to run the Haiti project. Mills would be joined by Bill Clinton, who had been deputized by the U.N. as a "special envoy" to Haiti. Bill's role was not well-defined, and Haitians were curious about what was in store. Mills wrote in an email to Hillary Clinton that Haitians saw Bill's appointment as "a step toward putting

Haiti in a protectorate or trusteeship status."[655] Soon, "joking that he must be coming back to lead a new colonial regime," the Haitian media "dubbed him *Le Gouverneur.*"[656]

The project was heavily focused on increasing Haiti's appeal to foreign corporations. As *Politico* reported, Clinton's experiment "had business at its center: Aid would be replaced by investment, the growth of which would in turn benefit the United States."[657] One of the first acts in the new "business-centered" Haiti policy involved suppressing Haiti's minimum wage. A 2009 Haitian law raised the minimum wage to 61 cents an hour, from 24 cents an hour previously. Haitian garment manufacturers, including contractors for Hanes and Levi Strauss, were furious, insisting that they were only willing to agree to a seven-cent increase. The manufacturers approached the U.S. State Department, who brought intense pressure to bear against Haitian President René Préval, working to "aggressively block" the 37-cent increase.[658] The U.S. Deputy Mission Chief said a minimum-wage increase "did not take economic reality into account" and simply "appealed to the unemployed and underpaid masses."[659]

But as Ryan Chittum of the *Columbia Journalism Review* explained, the proposed wage increase would have been only the most trivial additional expense for the American garment manufacturers:

> *As of last year Hanes had 3,200 Haitians making t-shirts for it. Paying each of them two bucks a day more would cost it about $1.6 million a year. Hanesbrands Incorporated made $211 million on $4.3 billion in sales last year, and presumably it would pass on at least some of its higher labor costs to consumers. Or better yet, Hanesbrands CEO Richard Noll could forego some of his rich compensation package. He could pay for the raises for those 3,200 t-shirt makers with just one-sixth of the $10 million in salary and bonus he raked in last year.[660]*

The truth of the "economic reality" was that the Haitian undergarment sector was hardly likely to become wildly less competitive as a result of the increase.

The effort to suppress the minimum wage was not solely a Clinton project. It was also a "concerted effort on the part of Haitian elites, factory owners, free trade proponents, U.S. politicians, economists, and American companies."[661] But it was in keeping with the State Department's priorities under Clinton, which prioritized creating a favorable business climate. It was that same familiar Clinton move "from aid to trade." Bill Clinton's program for Haitian development, designed by Oxford University economist Paul Collier, "had garment exports at its center."[662] Collier wrote that because of "propitious" factors like "poverty and [a] relatively unregulated labor market, Haiti has labor costs that are fully competitive with China."[663]

But the Clintons' role in Haiti would soon expand even further. In 2010, the country was struck by the worst earthquake in its history. The disaster killed 160,000 people and displaced over 1.5 million more. (The consequences of the earthquake were exacerbated by the ruined state of the Haitian food economy, plus the concentration of unemployed Haitian farmers in Port-au-Prince.)

Bill Clinton was soon put in charge of the U.S.-led recovery effort. He was appointed to head the Interim Haiti Recovery Commission (IHRC), which would oversee a wide range of rebuilding projects. At President Obama's request, Clinton and George W. Bush created the "Clinton-Bush Haiti Fund," and began aggressively fundraising around the world to support Haiti in the earthquake's aftermath. (With Hillary Clinton as Secretary of State overseeing the efforts of USAID, the Clintons' importance to the recovery could not be overstated; Bill's appointment meant that "at every stage of Haiti's reconstruction—fundraising, oversight and allocation—a Clinton was now involved."[664])

Despite appearances, the Clinton-Bush fund was not focused on providing traditional relief. As they wrote, "[w]hile other organizations in Haiti are using their resources to deliver immediate humanitarian aid, we are using our resources to focus on long-term development."[665] While the fund would advertise that "100% of donations go directly to relief efforts,"[666] Clinton and Bush adopted an expansive definition of "relief" efforts, treating luring foreign investment and jobs as a crucial part of earthquake recovery. On their website, they spoke proudly of what the *New York Daily News* characterized as a program of "supporting long-term programs to develop Haiti's business class."[667]

The strategy was an odd one. Port-au-Prince had been reduced to ruin, and Haitians were crowded into filthy tent cities, where many were dying of a cholera outbreak (which had itself been caused by the negligence of the United Nations).[668] Whatever value building new garment factories may have had as a long-term economic plan, Haitians were faced with somewhat more pressing concerns like the basic provision of shelter and medicine, as well as the clearing of the thousands of tons of rubble that filled their streets.

THE CLINTON-LED RECOVERY WAS A DISASTER. A YEAR AFTER the earthquake, a stinging report from Oxfam singled out Clinton's IHRC as creating a "quagmire of indecision and delay" that had made little progress toward successful earthquake recovery.[669] Oxfam found that "less than half of the reconstruction aid promised by international donors has been disbursed. And while some of that money has been put toward temporary housing, almost none of the funds have been used for rubble removal."[670]

Instead, the Clinton Foundation, IHRC, and State Department created what a *Wall Street Journal* writer called "a mishmash of low quality, poorly thought-out development experiments and half-finished projects."[671] A Haitian IHRC members lamented that the commission had produced "a disparate bunch of approved projects. . . [that] do not address as a whole either the emergency situation or the recovery, let alone the development, of Haiti."[672] A 2013 investigation by the Government Accountability Office found that most money for the recovery was not being dispersed, and that the projects that *were* being worked on were plagued by delays and cost overruns.[673]

Many Clinton projects were extravagant public relations affairs that quickly fizzled. For example, *The Washington Post* reported that "[a] 2011 housing expo that cost more than $2 million, including $500,000 from the Clinton Foundation, was supposed to be a model for thousands of new units but instead has resulted in little more than a few dozen abandoned model homes occupied by squatters."[674]

Other Clinton ventures were seen as "disconnected from the realities of most people in the poorest country in the Western Hemisphere."[675] *Politico* reported that many Clinton projects "have primarily benefited wealthy foreigners and the island's ruling elite, who needed little help to begin with."[676] For example, "the Clinton Bush Haiti Fund invested more than $2 million in the Royal Oasis Hotel, where a sleek suite with hardwood floors costs more than $200 a night and the shops sell $150 designer purses and $120 men's dress shirts." Predictably, the Royal Oasis didn't do an especially roaring trade; *The Washington Post* reported that "[o]ne recent afternoon, the hotel appeared largely empty, and with tourism hardly booming five years after the quake, locals fear it may be failing."[677] In a country with a 30-cent minimum wage, investing recovery dollars in a luxury hotel was not just offensive, but economically daft.

Sometimes the recovery projects were accused not only of being pointless, but of being downright harmful. For instance, Bill Clinton had proudly announced that the Clinton Founda-

tion would be funding the "construction of emergency storm
shelters in Léogâne."[678] But when *The Nation* investigated the
shelters that the Foundation had actually built, it found they
were "shoddy and dangerous" and full of toxic mold.[679] *The
Nation* discovered, among other things, that the temperature
in the shelters reached over 100 degrees, causing children to
experience headaches and eye irritations (which may have
been compounded by the mold), and that the trailers showed
high levels of carcinogenic formaldehyde, linked to asthma
and other lung diseases. The Clinton Foundation had subcon-
tracted the building of the shelters to Clayton Homes, a firm
that had already been sued in the United States by the Federal
Emergency Management Administration (FEMA) for "having
provided formaldehyde-laced trailers to Hurricane Katrina
victims."[680] (Clayton Homes was owned by Warren Buffett's
Berkshire Hathaway, and Buffett had been a longstanding
major donor to the Clinton Foundation.[681])

The Nation's investigation reported on children whose classes
were being held in Clinton Foundation trailers. Their semester
had just been cut short, and the students sent home, because the
temperature in the classrooms had grown unbearable. The mis-
ery of the students in the Clinton trailers was described:

> *Judith Seide, a student in Lubert's sixth-grade class
> [explained that] she and her classmates regularly
> suffer from painful headaches in their new Clinton
> Foundation classroom. Every day, she said, her "head
> hurts and I feel it spinning and have to stop moving,
> otherwise I'd fall." Her vision goes dark, as is the case
> with her classmate Judel, who sometimes can't open
> his eyes because, said Seide, "he's allergic to the heat."
> Their teacher regularly relocates the class outside into
> the shade of the trailer because the swelter inside is*

insufferable. Sitting in the sixth-grade classroom, student Mondialie Cineas, who dreams of becoming a nurse, said that three times a week the teacher gives her and her classmates painkillers so that they can make it through the school day. "At noon, the class gets so hot, kids get headaches," the 12-year-old said, wiping beads of sweat from her brow. She is worried because "the kids feel sick, can't work, can't advance to succeed."[682]

The most notorious post-earthquake development project, however, was the Caracol industrial park. The park was pitched as a major job creator, part of the goal of helping Haiti "build back better" than it was before. The State Department touted the prospect of 100,000 new jobs for Haitians, with Hillary Clinton promising 65,000 jobs within five years. The industrial park followed the Clintons' preexisting development model for Haiti: public/private partnerships with a heavy emphasis on the garment industry. Even though there were still hundreds of thousands of evacuees living in tents, the project was based on "the more expansive view that, in a desperately poor country where traditional foreign aid has chronically failed, fostering economic development is as important as replacing what fell down."[683] Much of the planning was focused on trying to lure a South Korean clothing manufacturer to set up shop there, by plying them with U.S. taxpayer funding. The Caracol project was "the centerpiece" of the U.S.'s recovery effort. A gala celebrating its opening featured the Clintons and Sean Penn, and it was treated as the emblem of the new, "better" Haiti, that would demonstrate the country's commitment to being "open for business."[684] In order to build the park, hundreds of poor farmers were evicted from their land, so that millions of dollars could be spent transforming it.[685]

But the project was a terrible disappointment. After four years, it was only operating at 10% capacity,[686] and the jobs had failed to materialize:

> *Far from 100,000 jobs—or even the 60,000 promised within five years of the park's opening— Caracol currently employs just 5,479 people full time. That comes out to roughly $55,000 in investment per job created so far; or, to put it another way, about 30 times more per job than the average [Caracol] worker makes per year. The park, built on the site of a former U.S. Marine-run slave labor camp during the 1915-1934 U.S. occupation, has the best-paved roads and manicured sidewalks in the country, but most of the land remains vacant.[687]*

Most of the seized farmland went unused, then, and even for the remaining farmers, "surges of wastewater have caused floods and spoiled crops."[688] Huge queues of unemployed Haitians stood daily in front of the factory, awaiting jobs that did not exist. *The Washington Post* described the scene:

> *Each morning, crowds line up outside the park's big front gate, which is guarded by four men in crisp khaki uniforms carrying shotguns. They wait in a sliver of shade next to a cinder-block wall, many holding résumés in envelopes. Most said they have been coming every day for months, waiting for jobs that pay about $5 a day. From his envelope, Jean Mito Palvetus, 27, pulled out a diploma attesting that he had completed 200 hours of training with the U.S. Agency for International Development on an industrial sewing machine. "I have three kids and a wife, and I can't support them," he said, sweating*

in the hot morning sun. "I have a diploma, but I still can't get a job here. I still have nothing." [689]

For some, the Caracol project perfectly symbolized the Clinton approach: big promises, an emphasis on sweatshops, incompetent management, and little concern for the actual impact on Haitians. "Caracol is a prime example of bad help," as one Haiti scholar put it. "The interests of the market, the interest of foreigners are prioritized over the majority of people who are impoverished in Haiti."[690]

But, failure as it may have been, the Caracol factory was among the more successful of the projects, insofar as it actually came into existence. A large amount of the money raised by Bill Clinton after the earthquake, and pledged by the U.S. under Hillary Clinton, simply disappeared without a trace, its whereabouts unknown. As *Politico* explained:

> *Even Bill's U.N. Office of the Special Envoy couldn't track where all of [it] went—and the truth is that still today no one really knows how much money was spent "rebuilding" Haiti. Many initial pledges never materialized. A whopping $465 million of the relief money went through the Pentagon, which spent it on deployment of U.S. troops—20,000 at the high water mark, many of whom never set foot on Haitian soil. That money included fuel for ships and planes, helicopter repairs and inscrutables such as an $18,000 contract for a jungle gym... Huge contracts were doled out to the usual array of major contractors, including a $16.7 million logistics contract whose partners included Agility Public Warehousing KSC, a Kuwaiti firm that was supposed to have been blacklisted from doing business with Washington after a 2009 indictment alleging a conspiracy to defraud the U.S. government during the Iraq War.* [691]

The recovery under the Clintons became notorious for its mismanagement. The Clinton Foundation earned particular criticism in Haiti for its management approach; Foundation staffers "had no idea what Haiti was like and had no sensitivity to the Haitians."[692] They were reportedly rude and condescending toward Haitians, even refusing to admit Haitian government ministers to meetings about recovery plans.[693] While the Clintons called in high-profile consulting firms like McKinsey to draw up plans (at great expense), they had little interest in listening to Haitians themselves. The former Haitian prime minister spoke of a "weak" American staff who were "more interested in supporting Clinton than helping Haiti."[694]

One of those shocked by the failure of the recovery effort was Chelsea Clinton, who wrote a detailed email to her parents in which she said that while Haitians were trying to help themselves, every part of the international aid effort, both governmental and nongovernmental, was falling short. "The incompetence is mind numbing," she wrote. Chelsea produced a detailed memorandum recommending drastic steps that needed to be taken in order to get the recovery on track.[695] But the memo was kept within the Clinton family, released only later under a Freedom of Information Act disclosure of Hillary's State Department correspondence. If it had come out at the time, as Haiti journalist Jonathan Katz writes, it "would have obliterated the public narrative of helpful outsiders saving grateful earthquake survivors that her mother's State Department was working so hard to promote."[696]

The Clintons' Haiti recovery ended with a whimper. The Clinton-Bush Haiti Fund distributed the last of its funds in 2012 and disbanded, without any attempt at further fundraising. The IHRC "quietly closed their doors" in October of 2011, even though little progress had been made.[697] As the *Boston Review*'s Jake Johnston explained, though hundreds of thousands remained displaced, the IHRC wiped its hands of the housing situation:

> *[L]ittle remained of the grand plans to build thousands of new homes. Instead, those left homeless would be given a small, one-time rental subsidy of about $500. These subsidies, funded by a number of different aid agencies, were meant to give private companies the incentive to invest in building houses. As efforts to rebuild whole neighborhoods faltered, the rental subsidies turned Haitians into consumers, and the housing problem was handed over to the private sector.*[698]

The Clintons themselves simply stopped speaking about Haiti. After the first two years, they were "nowhere to be seen" there, despite Hillary's having promised that her commitment to Haiti would long outlast her tenure as Secretary of State. Haiti has been given little attention during Hillary Clinton's presidential campaign, even though the Haiti project was ostensibly one of great pride for both Clintons.

The widespread consensus among observers is that the Haiti recovery, which *TIME* called the U.S.'s "compassionate invasion,"[699] was a catastrophically mismanaged disappointment. Jonathan Katz writes that "it's hard to find anyone these days who looks back on the U.S.-led response to the January 12, 2010, Haiti earthquake as a success."[700] While plenty of money was channeled into the country, it largely went to what were "little more than small pilot projects—a new set of basketball hoops and a model elementary school here, a functioning factory there."[701]

The end result has been that little has changed for Haiti. "Haitians find themselves in a social and economic situation that is worse than before the earthquake," reports a Belgian photojournalist who has spent 10 years in Haiti. "Everyone says that they're living in worse conditions than before… When you look at the history of humanitarian relief, there's never been a situation when such a small country has been the target of such a massive influx of money and assistance in such a short span of time… On paper, with that much money in a territory the size of Haiti, we should have witnessed miracles; there should have been results."[702] "If anything, they appear worse off," says *Foreign Policy* of Haiti's farmers.[703] "I really cannot understand how you could raise so much money, put a former U.S. president in charge, and get this outcome," said one Haitian official.[704] Indeed, the money donated and invested was extraordinary. But nobody seems to know where it has gone.

Haitians direct much of the blame toward the Clintons. As a former Haitian government official who worked on the recovery said, "[t]here is a lot of resentment about Clinton here. People have not seen results. … They say that Clinton used Haiti."[705] Haitians "increasingly complain that Clinton-backed projects have often helped the country's elite and international business investors more than they have helped poor 'Haitians."[706] There is a "suspicion that their motives are more to make a profit in Haiti than to help it."[707] And that while "striking a populist pose, in practice they were attracted to power in Haiti."[708]

BUT PERHAPS WE SHOULD BE MORE FORGIVING OF THE Clintons' conduct during the Haitian recovery, compared to the other cases. After all, instead of doing true harm, the Clintons simply failed to do much good. And perhaps it's better to have a luxury hotel than not to have one, better to have a few jobs than none at all. Thanks to Bill Clinton, there's a gleaming new industrial park, albeit one operating at 10% capacity.

Yet it's a mistake to measure Clinton against what would have happened if the United States had done nothing at all for Haiti. The question is what would have happened if a capable, non-famous administrator, rather than a globetrotting narcissist, had been placed in charge. Tens of millions of dollars were donated toward the Haiti recovery by people across the world; it was an incredible outpouring of generosity. The squandering of that money on half-baked development schemes (many led by cronies), and the ignoring of Haitians' own demands, mean that Clinton may have caused considerable harm through his failure. Plenty of people died in tent cities that *would not have died* if the world's donations had been used effectively. Haitians were unfortunate to have been given Bill Clinton as a recovery chief; it was destined to be the case that he, of all people, would be totally uninterested in putting in the work necessary to create actual improvements to their lives rather than the mere appearance of improvement.

The Clintons' efforts in Haiti are therefore perfectly emblematic of their general approach to black lives: it's not that Bill Clinton does *nothing* to help others, it is that whatever he does to help others is a function of how much pleasure, recognition, or political success it will bring. So while in the immediate aftermath of the earthquake, the Clintons swooped in bearing cash, they didn't follow through with anything, and as soon as the cameras were off, they disappeared. Why? Again, motivations are impossible things to discern absolutely. But since the evidence is that the Clintons stopped helping Haiti when Haiti stopped helping them, it is reasonable to conclude that their actions were never about Haiti to begin with.

Rickey Ray Rector.
Note enormous scar from having shot 1/3 of his brain away.

CHAPTER SIX
The Death of Rickey Ray Rector

Rickey Ray Rector grew up in Conway, Arkansas, just an hour's drive from Bill Clinton's own hometown of Hot Springs.[709] From the very earliest days of his life, Rickey was considered different and strange. He had few friends, and while other children were out running around, Rickey sat under a tree playing alone with sticks. Those who saw him said he was dreamy and detached, "as if he were locked into some private daze of withdrawal." He was slow and inept as a student, with what was later described as an undiagnosed serious learning disability. As time went on, he became even more lost, as well as paranoid, and by junior high he "floundered ever more hopelessly in his classwork, still able only to print in the laboring hand of a third grader." And though unable to understand much of what was going on around him, Rickey was beaten mercilessly by his father.

As he grew up, Rickey became trouble. He would act out, he couldn't focus. Others became unsettled by his presence, and would leave a room whenever he arrived. There was something about him that simply wasn't normal. Soon, as an adolescent, still not having been given mental health treatment, Rickey lapsed into violence and delinquency. He was arrested frequently for petty crimes. He could not maintain a stable job. He was angry. He spiraled into "a kind of slowly accelerating berserkness."

In 1981, Rickey Ray Rector killed a man. After an argument outside a dance hall over a $3 cover charge, Rector removed a gun and started shooting randomly. Two people were wounded, while a third, Arthur Criswell, received a fatal bullet to the head.

Rector fled, but he didn't go very far. Mostly he ducked in and out of various houses in and around Conway, running in circles, unsure where to go. Eventually, he found his way back to his mother and sister. After speaking with them for some time, he decided to turn himself in.

Rector's mother called Officer Bob Martin, a family friend who knew Rector and whom Rector trusted. Martin was known as an affable and kind policeman, who walked the beat and got to know everyone in Conway. Rector was considered dangerous, but if there was one person who could safely bring him in, it was Martin.

Martin arrived at Mrs. Rector's home, and they waited for Rickey to arrive, chatting politely in the living room. But Martin did not get a chance to persuade Rector to surrender. Sneaking in from the rear of the house, Rector approached Martin from behind. When Martin turned around to greet Rector, Rector shot him in the head and ran from the house. Seconds after exiting the front door, Rector put the gun to his own head and pulled the trigger, collapsing into the street.

OFFICER BOB MARTIN DID NOT SURVIVE RECTOR'S GUNSHOT. But Rector himself did survive, albeit only in the most limited sense. In order to save Rector's life, doctors had to remove about one-third of his brain, much of which had been destroyed when Rector shot himself.

The surgery left Rector effectively lobotomized. He had never been particularly mentally sound, but after having so much of his brain removed, Rector could barely function. A psychologist reported that he had "a near-total inability to conceptualize beyond a response to immediate sensations or provocations" and "seemed unable to grasp either the concept of past or future. It was "a classic prefrontal lobotomy" that had left Rector "totally incompetent." After realizing the extent to which Rector's capacity had been destroyed, Rector's sister simply assumed that Rector would be institutionalized for life. His mental functioning was that of a very young child.

But the people of Conway wanted justice. Bob Martin had been a beloved member of the community, and prosecutors wanted nothing less than to make sure Rector was executed for the crime. An expert for the state insisted Rector was competent to assist his own defense, and Rector was put on trial and sentenced to death. When Rector heard the judge read his sentence—death by electrocution—"he stood for a few moments as spectators began leaving the courtroom and the judge and jury also departed, and then turned… and muttered, 'Does this mean I'll get a television in my cell now?'"

Rector's fellow death row inmates immediately knew there was something very wrong with him. One said that "no one can pass his cell without answering a long repertoire of questions that he has about dogs. . . . In the middle of the night, his light goes out, he'll start screaming. He's afraid of the dark… And everybody is up because Rector has woke everybody up." Inmates even began supplying him with their own medications in the hope that it would help him to calm down.

The prison chaplain recalls meeting Rector for the first time: "He was gripping the bars, howling, jumping like an ape. There were Indians, he thought, in the corner of his cell, who he was busy hunting. In between, he would speak to me." The chaplain, Dennis Pigman, said he "thought the guy was completely crazy." Rector was "hollering," "dancing," then "jumping over and shooting at where he had been dancing. Pigman says that "it was obvious [Rector] had the mentality of about a six- or seven-year-old..." For three weeks, Rector cowered in his cell, "like a child cringing in his bunk," and refused to come to the chapel "because he was afraid someone would kill him." Chaplain Pigman conducted his service alone with Rector in his cell, as Rector "hulked" in the corner of the room.

The prison staff's notes read: "Smiles continuously... Occasionally noted to scream and yell without apparent reason... Laughing without apparent reason." There were "intermittent bursts of barking, baying, then blaring laughter and little gleeful shuffles of dancing, fingers snapping."

When Rector's sister Stella visited him, he told her "about serpents slithering across his bunk, alligators and chickens set loose by the guards, and people shining spotlights into his cell." She remembers that "he was afraid of everything that moved. He was afraid to go outside in the yard, because he thought somebody would hurt him, do something to him." Rector believed his guards were releasing loose alligators and chickens into his cell. At one point, Stella visited Rector to let him know that his brother had just died. "He asked only a few questions," she said, "and then all of a sudden he asked, 'You see all that monkey smoke in here?' And began to pace like a wild animal."

Rector's reaction to his mother's death was similarly bizarre. "Rickey and my mother had always had this sort of special bond between them," Stella recalled. But when one of his attorneys told Rector that his mother was dead, "there was absolutely no reaction... [he] only said, 'She is?' And then, 'When's dinner?'" When his sister took him to the funeral home to see his mother's body, "he started laughing when he saw her... said, 'Yeah, that's her all right, she's dead.'"

After a few visits, Stella concluded that "[t]he person you see here and the person that I see, it looks like Rickey. He talks like Rickey, he has some characteristics of Rickey. But the real Rickey Ray Rector was destroyed when he shot himself with the gun. This person is just not my brother."

It was clear that Rector had become deeply disturbed. A psychologist described his linguistic capacity as operating at a "very, very primitive type of level" and his motor skills as negligible ("he fumbles, he has trouble picking up coins.") Rector's functioning was so obviously impaired, according to the psychologist, that there was "no possibility that Rector was shamming his pitiable performances in their examinations" (one of the state's own specialists reported that Rector was "trying to do the best he could on those tests").

Rickey Ray Rector had been set for an execution date several times, but his case had been winding through the appellate process. Finally, his appeals exhausted (the state had insisted he was perfectly normal), Rector was set to be executed in January of 1992. At that point, without any legal remedies left, his only hope for reprieve was to be granted clemency by Governor Bill Clinton.

IT WAS AN INCONVENIENT MOMENT FOR RICKEY RAY RECTOR'S life to depend on Bill Clinton's mercy. As Rector's execution date approached in 1992, Clinton was "fighting for his political life." The New Hampshire Democratic primary was about to be held, and Clinton was facing a scandal that threatened to derail his presidential candidacy. An Arkansas woman named Gennifer Flowers had come forward to allege that she and the Governor had engaged in a twelve-year affair, and that she had audio tapes to prove it. In a close race against Massachusetts senator Paul Tsongas, Clinton was unsure whether he could withstand the heat from the Flowers allegations, and felt he could not afford to take political risks.

Clinton had also spent a great deal of energy trying to position himself as a "tough on crime" Democrat, in order to distinguish himself from previous generations of soft-hearted liberals. Clinton's crime stance had been consciously cultivated back in Arkansas. Earlier in his political career, Clinton had lost a race against a "law and order" candidate, and those around him said he was determined not to make the same mistake twice. There was a sharp difference between Clinton's attitude during his first term as governor from 1978-1980 (when he lost reelection), and that of his four subsequent terms from 1982 to 1992.

As one observer noted, "one almost metaphysical lesson [the loss] provided him was never to range, whatever his own impulses, too far beyond the standing disposition of the general populace." So when Clinton returned to the governor's mansion, he rid himself of any merciful inclinations he may have had toward convicted criminals. While in his first term, Clinton had commuted 70 prison sentences, in his ten subsequent years in office he would commute a total of only 7, a small fraction of those that had been approved for commutation by the state Pardon Board. That Clinton had gotten tougher was not just the impression of observers. A Clinton spokesman confirmed that the governor "had indeed changed some of his policies toward prison inmates."*

---

*Clinton was, however, generous enough to allow inmates from Arkansas prisons to work as unpaid servants in the Governor's Mansion. In *It Takes a Village*, Hillary Clinton writes that the residence was staffed with "African-American men in their thirties," since "using prison labor at the governor's mansion was a longstanding tradition, which kept down costs."[710] It is unclear just *how* longstanding the tradition of having chained black laborers brought to work as maids and gardeners had been. But one has no doubt that as the white residents of a mansion staffed with unpaid blacks, the Clintons were continuing a certain historic Southern practice. (Hillary Clinton did note, however, that she and Bill were sure not to show undue lenience to the sla...servants, writing that "[w]e enforced rules strictly and sent back to prison any inmate who broke a rule."[711])

As Rector's attorney explained, the new Clinton "would set new execution dates at just about every stage, every tick in the process of a case, though the parties were nowhere near exhausting their remedies." By 1992, Clinton had set seventy execution dates for twenty different inmates, including four for Rickey Ray Rector alone. Even though many of these were stayed by the courts, setting them, according to Rector's lawyer, "[enabled Clinton to say] 'Look, see how many executions I've ordered.'"

Thus as the New Hampshire primary approached, Clinton was not oblivious to the fact that, as *The New York Times* reported, "many political experts feel a record of favoring the death penalty is a major plus for a Democratic Presidential candidate."[712]

As Rector's execution approached, Jeff Rosenzweig, Rector's attorney and an old friend of Clinton's, was desperately trying to get in touch with Clinton. Rosenzweig was convinced that Clinton must simply not have understood what Rector was actually like, and believed that if he could just speak to Clinton, he would be able to clear up the misunderstanding. As Rosenzweig explained:

> *I doubted deeply if he had actually talked with anyone who really knew Rector and the actual condition he was in. He needed to hear an affirmation from somebody who actually knew Rector and whom he knew, hear it himself ear to ear, plainly, that this guy was indeed truly zombied out, seriously, seriously mentally deficient, just no doubt about it.*

In this judgment, Rosenzweig was seconded by one of Rector's fellow death row inmates, a white man named William Frank Parker, who said at one of Rector's final hearings:

> *I seen you attacking a retarded child, I'm going to get in it. Rector is not normal... He has no foothold on reality. He doesn't know what's going on most of*

the time. . . I don't care what all these psychiatrists
and psychologists say… it doesn't take a licensed – A
garbage truck guy, or anybody, could tell you that
Rector is not normal.

Jeff Rosenzweig also wanted to tell Clinton that "the politics of
it he should be aware of as well – that Rector had been convicted
by an all-white jury, and this was something that just might
come to waylay him down the road."

But Rosenzweig's repeated calls to the Governor's Mansion were
going unanswered. In the meantime, the records of the prison
"death log" note Rector's activity during the countdown to his
execution: "6.46am: Inmate Rector began howling. 6.59am:
Inmate Rector began dancing in his cell." Soon after, Rector told a
guard that "If you eat grass, lethal injection won't kill you."

Jeff Rosenzweig wasn't alone in his desperate attempt to reach the
governor. Other old Clinton friends were frantically begging Clinton to give Rector clemency. As *The Guardian* reported in 1993:

Others, close to Clinton, were making their own
appeals to him. Mrs. Freddie Nixon, wife of
the pastor who had married the Clintons, had
even written to Rickey on Death Row, and was
particularly distraught. Dr. Douglas Brown, the
psychiatrist, faxed the governor to say the case had
been a "travesty" – far from being "competent,"
Rector was the least competent individual he had
ever evaluated. He got no reply. Some of Clinton's
staunchest admirers, aware of his compassion and
warmth, confidently expected him to intervene.
"Nobody could believe that he would go through
with it," says one. "After all, the guy was berserk.
You might as well execute a child."

Even Jesse Jackson stepped in. "Now, Bill, just on a moral, humanitarian basis," Jackson said to Clinton in a phone call, the execution should be stopped. Clinton responded by telling Jackson that "he'd been researching various ways to get around it, but it just couldn't be done, there were doctors who'd said he was competent." Jackson recalled that Clinton "said he'd be praying about it, though."

Of course, Clinton was lying to Jackson when he said it "couldn't be done" and that he was trying to find ways to get around it. In fact, Clinton had the full power to commute Rector's sentence from death to life imprisonment. He had simply thus far chosen not to exercise his power to do so.

As Rector's execution time drew closer, even the prison warden had become uncomfortable with the idea of executing Rector, with one observer saying the warden "seemed to be coming apart the closer the execution got."

Finally, after explaining on live television that Clinton was not answering his calls, Rosenzweig received a call from Bill Clinton. Rosenzweig explained to Clinton that it was all a horrible misunderstanding, Rector was "crazy, a zombie — it couldn't, it shouldn't be done. He's a child. It's like killing a child." Rosenzweig begged Clinton not to allow the execution to proceed "His execution," Rosenzweig said, "would be remembered as a disgrace to the state."[713] After listening patiently to what Rosenzweig had to say, Clinton "hung up with a non-committal pleasantry."

Still, Rosenzweig believed Clinton couldn't execute Rector, now that he had the facts. "I thought he just might not want to be seen as merciless," Rosenzweig recollected.

CLINTON REFUSED TO GRANT CLEMENCY. RECTOR WAS EXECUTED on January 24, 1992. It is unlikely he had any idea what was about to happen. When he had his last meal, Rector set the dessert aside for later, even though there wouldn't be a later. And in a pitiful and poignant detail, the night before his execution, watching Clinton on television, Rector said that he planned to vote for him in November.

Clinton's plan to appear "tough on crime" had worked. In the following months, the political value of Rector's execution became abundantly clear. It knocked the law-and-order issue out of the campaign. One commentator said it showed Clinton was "a different sort of Democrat."[714] As another put it, "he had someone put to death who only had half a brain. You don't find them any tougher than that."[715] Or, as former prosecutor and Arkansas ACLU director Jay Jacobson said, "You can't law-and-order Clinton... If you can kill Rector, you can kill anybody." In the general election, the National Association of Police Organizations endorsed Clinton over Bush, and so did a law enforcement group in Bush's home state of Texas.[716] (In 1996, the Fraternal Order of Police would endorse Clinton's reelection, with the group's president saying that police officers "have never had a better friend in the White House than Bill Clinton."[717])

The Rector execution would send a strong message of what it meant to be a "different sort" of Democrat. That Clinton was willing to allow this execution to proceed, despite the widespread pleas coming in from across the nation, was a notice about the direction in which he would take the Democratic Party and the nation in the years to come.

But Rector's would not be the only execution that Clinton carried out that year. In May, as Clinton's primary campaign wrapped up successfully, he would similarly refuse clemency in the case of Steven Douglas Hill, the youngest of Arkansas' 35 death row inmates. Hill had been just 18 when he committed the crime for which he was sentenced to death. He and another, much older, inmate named Michael Cox had broken out of a correctional facility, and when the police arrived at their hiding place, they shot an officer. Hill initially confessed that he had been the one who pulled the trigger. Later, however, Cox admitted that he had been the one who fired the shotgun. Cox was nevertheless granted a plea deal and sentenced to 80 years, while Hill took his chances at trial and received a death sentence. Despite Hill's youth, and Cox's confession, Bill Clinton did not grant clemency, and Hill died by lethal injection on May 7, 1992, a few days after the North Carolina and Indiana primaries. (Eventually, after Hill was executed, Cox was released, only to commit three further murders, further substantiating the theory that the older accomplice Cox, and not the teenaged Hill, had done the killing for which Hill was put to death.)[718]

The Hill case was quickly forgotten, though Amnesty International was quoted at the time saying of Clinton that "[h]e's not dying to be President, but he is killing to be President." The case of Rickey Ray Rector, by contrast, did become a moderately infamous chapter in Clinton political history, and is mentioned from time to time as a "controversial" act.

Its facts, however, are rarely given full appreciation. For Clinton did not just execute Rector quietly, but was active in using Rector's death politically, flying back to Arkansas just so he could be there for the execution. As *The Guardian* reported:

> *The same week, Gennifer Flowers came forward with her story of a 12-year affair with the candidate. Beset by crisis, Governor Clinton broke off his campaign in New Hampshire to return to Little Rock for Rector's execution. There was no legal obligation on him to do so; as the Houston Chronicle remarked, "never— or at least not in the recent history of presidential campaigns—has a contender for the nation's highest elective office stepped off the campaign trail to ensure the killing of a prisoner."*

It's important, then, to be clear about just what Clinton did here. He deliberately had a hallucinating disabled man killed, in an execution so callous it made even the warden queasy. He personally ensured the execution of a someone who was mentally a small child, just so as not to appear weak. As Derrick Jackson wrote in the *Boston Globe*: "The killing of human vegetables is an exercise for brutes."[719]

As Daryl Carter writes, the Rector case is a window through which Clinton can be understood.[720] The late Christopher Hitchens believed Rector's execution offered a "defining insight into [Clinton's] character," because it displayed "creepily sadistic attitude and a willingness to bid for the racist subconscious in the electorate, to say 'don't call *me* soft, I can snuff this black guy who doesn't know what the charge against him is.'"[721] Hitchens suggested that liberals' silence on the Rector execution, given how unthinkably monstrous it was, was a display of rank partisanship that demonstrated just how successfully Clinton had eliminated the Democratic Party's commitment to progressive principle: "[i]f an ambitious Republican governor trying to be president had, in the course of a tough primary, returned to his home state and supervised the execution of a mentally disabled black man, the name of that man would be very well known." Paul Greenberg suggested that if Bush had done the same thing, it would have been *the* defining issue of the 1992 election.

Clinton correctly guessed that executing Rector would help rather than hurt his chances politically. The Rector killing therefore offers a telling insight into Clinton's treatment of black lives. If one is willing to lethally inject a hallucinating human vegetable, purely to win the news cycle during the presidential primary, then there are no limits to what one will do to get elected. Norman Mailer reportedly said of Clinton that "there is nothing you could say, that he will not do" to advance himself.[722] On the surface, this doesn't seem like an especially damning assessment;

plenty of politicians will "do anything to get elected." But the Rector case shows that Clinton is one of the few politicians for whom this is true in a literal sense, for whom there are *actually* no limits. Clinton was, after all, faced with a scenario in which his chances of becoming President would be slightly helped if he was seen to kill a mental patient. He did not flinch. If the death of Rickey Ray Rector was politically useful, then Rickey Ray Rector needed to die. For Clinton to ignore friends' desperate pleas for him not to kill a child, for him to wave off all appeals to his humanity in an act that made even the warden sick, this shows a stunning capacity for calculating brutality. It is hard to think of a political figure who has more conclusively demonstrated that they truly have no conscience, no empathy.

Bill Clinton connects with Black America.

CHAPTER SEVEN

The First Black President

B ILL CLINTON SOMETIMES SAID THAT THE ONLY PRINCIPLE on which he would never compromise was racial equality.[723] "I don't have to defend myself on civil rights," he insisted. [724] Clinton was confident that even given a checkered and dubious political résumé, this was the one area in which he was, so to speak, unimpeachable.

It was plainly false that Clinton never compromised on racial equality; he did it routinely, almost reflexively. Yet he wasn't wrong to note that he didn't have to defend himself on civil rights. Nobody ever really asked him to. For Bill Clinton exercised a strange kind of magic when it came to black public opinion, of a kind no white politician before or since has possessed. No matter what he did, African Americans never became *cynical* about him. Most felt that, however *disappointing* he may have been (and he was very disappointing indeed), he meant what he said, and his heart was good and true. Dewayne Wickham's *Bill Clinton and Black America* features scores of black journalists, clergy members, and politicians vouching for Clinton's bona fides. Bill Clinton, they testify, was different because he "took our calls"[725]

and they were "just happy someone was finally paying attention."[726] Johnnie Cochran explained that Clinton "would listen
to what we had to say"[727] and BET's Bob Johnson called Clinton
"engaging" and "easygoing."[728]

There's some evidence that parts of these warm feelings were based
on misperception. Melissa Harris-Lacewell examined survey data
revealing that black Americans overestimated the extent to which they
were benefitting from the Clinton economy,[729] affecting their evaluation of him. She argued that "[t]he hypnotic racial dance of cultural
authenticity that Bill Clinton performed in office lulled many blacks
into a perceptual fog."[730] Under this theory, the cultural concessions
were not just valued for their own sake, but fed into an erroneous
assessment of African Americans' material conditions.

But one also shouldn't get carried away here, and risk over-
looking black dissent. In both 1992 and 1996, Clinton received
a smaller percentage of the black vote than Dukakis and Mon-
dale had.[731] Plenty of leading black figures did not hesitate to tell
Clinton precisely what they thought he was. Despite supporting
Clinton during the impeachment, Jesse Jackson was a persistent
and blunt critic of the president's policies. Journalist George Curry
insisted that "I never bought into this garbage about Bill Clinton
being a black president."[732] George Mason University professor
and civil rights veteran Roger Wilkins observed:

> Look at this man's record... When he wanted to
> establish himself as a different kind of Democrat . . .
> in 1992, he broke off campaigning to go preside over
> the execution of this self-lobotomized black inmate.
> When he was low in the polls a year ago, he came to
> Washington and took a swack at Sister Souljah and
> Jesse Jackson... And I can't tell you that, as I look at the
> Lani Guinier episode, that my mind does not run back
> to all of those other things. That is his record.[733]

An editorial in *The Crisis* was similarly unsparing, suggesting that those entranced by Clinton seemed to have lost their minds:

> *How many more 'snow jobs' will the disenfranchised,*
> *the working class folks of color, and others who are*
> *oppressed, have to see and hear before they come*
> *to the conclusion that many Americans truly cast*
> *their votes for a Slick Willie?* [734]

And yet none of this resulted in true mass revulsion. Melissa Harris-Lacewell was correct to note that there was something strangely "hypnotic" going on in Clinton's relationship with African Americans. Black America did not even cringe when Toni Morrison made her unfortunate remark that Bill Clinton was the country's "first black president."[735]* It's truly extraordinary how excessive praise for this "soul brother" became

---

*Morrison's comment was quickly twisted beyond its original intended meaning; she was attempting to draw a parallel between Clinton's persecution during the Lewinsky years and the kind of kangaroo justice experienced by black Americans. Morrison herself later attempted to correct the record: "People misunderstood that phrase... I said he was being treated like a black on the street, already guilty, already a perp."[737] But they partially misunderstood it because Morrison also made a cultural comparison. Clinton, she said, "displays almost every trope of blackness: single-parent household, born poor, working-class, saxophone-playing, McDonald's-and-junk-food-loving boy from Arkansas." Such a remark had the effect, albeit inadvertently, of reaffirming those very stereotypical tropes, and making Clinton seem blacker than he actually is. Why Morrison felt this comparison was helpful to begin with, God only knows. She suggested that Clinton was being "persecuted for his sexuality" the way black men were. But when black men were persecuted for their sexuality, they were lynched. The treatment of Clinton by Newt Gingrich and the congressional Republicans, however nasty, had absolutely nothing in common with the deranged and bloody injustices meted out to black Americans. To even mention the Lewinsky affair and perjury fiasco in the same breath as white supremacy is at best absurd, and at worst perverse. It's no wonder people forgot the quote's original intended meaning; that meaning made no sense. But the fact that Morrison could even think of comparing Bill Clinton's interaction with Republicans to Jim Crow justice, and the fact that black Americans didn't disgustedly repudiate her remark, demonstrates the incredibly intoxicating power of the Clinton spell.

among certain African American elites; as Kevin Gray wrote, "[n]o other president in United States history has managed to get so much black support for giving so little."[736]

The fact that much of the praise *did* come from elites is important. Contrary to the popularly received impression, black opinion on Clinton was never monolithic and uniform. Some of that divide can be attributed to age and class. As political analyst Farai Chideya observed at the time, "[w]ealthier blacks are happier; poorer blacks are not so happy. The civil rights generation is happier; younger people are not so happy."[738]

Those particular demographic fractures make intuitive sense, given the nature of Clintonian race politics. The steps Clinton took that benefited African Americans most (cabinet appointments, a voice in policymaking, etc.) were of most importance to people of higher socioeconomic status. Those things he did that were most harmful (Drug War, welfare, Rwanda) hurt the poor and marginal. Clinton took black people's calls, yes, but these were the calls of Vernon Jordan and Johnnie Cochran and Carol Moseley-Braun, not the calls of single mothers in Milwaukee and inmates at the Louisiana State Penitentiary.

Bill Clinton reveled in the "black president" moniker. With a big smile on his face, Clinton gave a speech as the Black Caucus dinner saying that Chris Tucker couldn't be the first black president, because the country already had one. "He exploited the whole Toni Morrison thing," said Deborah Mathis.[739] Mary Frances Berry recalls how "he went around telling everybody he was the first black president."[740] By all accounts, Clinton loved the adulation he got in African American circles. It made him feel very hip indeed.

Yet when it came to his actions, Clinton did not show signs of being a particularly "black" president at all. In fact, Clinton explicitly tried to distance himself from the Democratic Party's perceived sympathies with black causes. Clinton adjusted his rhetoric to remove all traditional liberal concern with the lives of the disadvantaged and dispossessed. As Alexander Cockburn observed after watching the 1992 Presidential Debates:

> *Never once, in three debates, did Clinton permit the word justice to pass his lips. Never once, in my hearing, did he disturb the airwaves with expressions of concern about the poor, the hungry, the homeless, the nonwhite and—for 99% of his allotted time— the non-male.*[741]

The political logic of this was obvious: since liberals could be relied on to vote Democratic, one should attempt to peel off as many Republican voters as possible by being as right-wing as it was possible to be within the Democratic Party. In the 1996 election, the Republicans found this so baffling that Clinton was labeled the "me-too" president.[742] "[Bob Dole]'s looking for ways to draw contrasts, and every time they think they have a way, the President buys into it, at least rhetorically," said political analyst Stuart Rothenberg.[743] Dole would accuse Clinton of "trying to lift" Dole's issues, such as welfare reform.[744] During the 1996 election, a frustrated Republican source told the *New York Times* that Clinton kept responding to Dole's tough talk on crime by simply adopting it for himself: "We say [limit] habeas corpus, they say sure… We say prisons; they say sure."[745]

As conservative journalist David Frum explained, the strategy was quite simple:

> *Clinton has offered the Democratic party a devilish bargain: Accept and defend policies you hate (welfare reform, the Defense of Marriage Act), condone and excuse crimes (perjury, campaign finance abuses) and I'll deliver you the executive*

branch of government... Clinton has survived and even thrived by deftly balancing between right and left. He has assuaged the Left by continually proposing bold new programs—the expansion of Medicare to 55 year-olds, a national day-care program, the reversal of welfare reform, the hooking up to the Internet of every classroom, and now the socialization of the means of production via Social Security. And he has placated the Right by dropping every one of these programs as soon as he proposed it. Clinton makes speeches, Rubin and Greenspan make policy; the Left gets words, the Right gets deeds; and everybody is content.[746]

(It is perhaps worth noting once again that even the "right-wing" Rubin found welfare reform too much to stomach.)

Under Clinton's theory, when it came to race, there was simply no political gain to be had in supporting civil rights. But to prevent a full-scale revolt of the Democratic base, Clinton continued to use racially progressive language. His speeches included numerous rhetorical tributes to traditional liberal values, while making sure white conservatives knew he could be relied on not to act on those values. As far as black voters went, Clinton held their support by working hard to incorporate black Americans *culturally,* so that he would not be called upon to give them anything *politically* (and thereby risk alienating his conservative white constituency). As Michelle Alexander explained:

Clinton mastered the art of sending mixed cultural messages, appealing to African Americans by belting out "Lift Every Voice and Sing" in black churches, while at the same time signaling to poor and working-class whites that he was willing to be tougher on black communities than Republicans had been.[747]

Hence Stone Mountain: Clinton would attend a Congressional Black Caucus luncheon on one day, then visit the birthplace of the Klan on another. CBC members would be too flabbergasted that a white politician cared enough to come to their events to muster any real objection when Clinton aggressively pursued the votes of Southern racists.

But as much as Clinton made a show of publicly embracing black culture, part of his political strategy also involved intentionally repudiating traditionally "black" issues and castigating black behavior, so that white voters would feel at ease in the Democratic Party. At a 1992 event, Clinton made a show of denouncing minor hip-hop artist Sister Souljah, who had sardonically suggested that America take a week off from killing black people to kill white people instead. Clinton compared Souljah to David Duke, in what was widely seen as a calculated effort to publicly demonstrate his willingness to chastise black behavior. It would not be the only time that Clinton would publicly lecture the black community on their moral standards. In a 1993 speech in front of 5,000 African Americans at the Church of God in Christ, Clinton explained that if Martin Luther King were still alive, he would be extremely disappointed in them:

> *If Martin Luther King... were to re-appear by my side today and give us a report card on the last 25 years, what would he say? You did a good job, he would say, voting and electing people who formerly were not electable because of the color of their skin... You did a good job creating a Black middle class of people who really are doing well, and the middle class is growing more among African Americans than among non-African Americans. You did a good job in opening opportunity. But he would say, I did not live and die to see the American family destroyed...*

I fought for freedom, he would say, but not for the freedom of people to kill each other with reckless abandonment, not for the freedom of children to have children and the fathers of the children to walk away from them and abandon them, as if they don't amount to anything... This is not what I lived and died for. My fellow Americans, he would say, I fought to stop white people from being so filled with hate that they would wreak violence on black people. I did not fight for the right of black people to murder other black people with reckless abandonment.[748]

By making an issue of "black on black crime" and the perceived decline of black fatherhood, Clinton echoed conservative rhetoric about the dysfunctions of black life, attributing problems in the black community to the failure of blacks themselves to exercise personal responsibility. It was a similar approach to the one Bill Cosby would take in his infamous "pound cake" speech (in which "I wanted the pound cake, but I didn't take it" was used to illustrate responsibility).[749] Cosby, however, did not go so far as to give a monologue in Martin Luther King's voice about how black men were bad fathers and destroying the American family.

Clinton almost seems to have *known* just how much he needed to concede to African Americans in order to be able to turn his back on them. As Donna Brazile observed, "I haven't seen any other white politicians master the black vote and the black community as well as Bill Clinton."[750] (Brazile's use of the m-word is either unfortunate or telling, depending on one's level of cynicism.) At every point, Clinton carefully weighed whether one of his conservative policies was so abhorrent to black voters that they would finally reject him. Usually, he decided that so long as he continued to remember the birthdays of black journalists' children, and attend a few church picnics, he did not need to worry about being abandoned. But occasionally the decision went the other way. When Jesse Jackson threatened to run against Clinton in 1996, Clinton was forced to reconsider his decision to publicly reject government affirmative action policies.[751] The process by which Clinton arrived at his opinion was, by all accounts, agonizing; he simply was not sure which way to come out on the issue. Ultimately, Clinton decided that condemning affirmative action would be asking too much of black voters, and gave a speech on the importance of remedying discrimination, saying that while affirmative action needed "mending," it should not be dropped entirely.

The affirmative action case illustrates Clinton's entire approach to politics. He did not have a *personal* principle to fight for; instead, his public position was the product of a careful balancing of the relevant interests, and a determination of how they would affect him. Black lives could matter to Clinton, *if they had something to offer.*

One may simply see this as smart politics. Some commentators, puzzled by those who loathe Clinton's compromises, suggest that it's absurd to reject Clinton's pragmatism and dubious ethics. David Milne writes that it is simply "among the accepted truths of modern living" that "politicians don't always tell the truth, that election pledges often fail to materialize, that secret deals and questionable compromises disrupt democracy and that presidents ain't always angels."[752]

The argument has an extraordinary intuitive appeal. But it is far too cynical. Not all compromises are equal, and not all motives for compromise are alike. Lyndon B. Johnson was the sort of hard-nosed, deal-brokering scoundrel that one might associate with the "dirty hands" school of political thinking. But Johnson made compromises in the pursuit of political ends. It was worth knocking a few heads, or sitting down with some racists, if it meant one got a Civil Rights Act passed. Johnsonian politics is ugly, and it is possibly indefensible. But it is distinct from Clinton's politics of triangulation. Triangulation operates on a fundamentally different first principle: instead of compromising certain values in order to achieve the political power necessary to act on other values, it simply sees values as an impediment to political power. Instead of asking "What do we need to do in order to achieve racial justice?" and coming up with an ethically disquieting answer, it asks "What do I need to do in order to become president?" and instantly responds that one should start by forgetting about racial justice. Randall Kennedy describes Clinton's "hard-nosed political calculation" in abandoning Lani Guinier as follows: "he believed that he stood to lose less by abandoning than supporting her."[753] Note that such a calculation excludes "the right thing to do" even as a *minor* factor; politics is simply increasing one's gains, decreasing one's losses, *rather than* increasing the amount of good and decreasing the amount of bad. In this way, Clintonian triangulation makes politics something hollow; instead of weighing the right thing against the expedient thing, and trying to balance the two, one simply does the expedient thing regardless. The ends of politics disappear; it becomes a game of gains and losses for their own sake. As the *Arkansas Democrat-Gazette* observed of Clinton, "[i]t is not the compromises he has made that trouble so much as the unavoidable suspicion that he has no great principles to compromise."[754] Even George Stephanopoulos, who served as one of Clinton's chief attack dogs in his 1992 campaign war room, wondered in his memoir whether Clinton ultimately aimed to *do* anything at all, besides get elected: "Is it about power's potential?" Stephanopoulos asked. "Or just power?[755]"

That distinction, between seeking power because of its potential, and seeking power for its own sake, is the difference between the pragmatist and the narcissist. In practice, it can be difficult to tell these two character types apart, because the narcissist and the pragmatist will often end up making the same decisions, and justifying them with similar reasoning. Since political power is necessary for the enacting of a program, those who seek nothing but power and those who seek power for the sake of a program will look somewhat alike.

How could we tell the difference between the Clinton who is a well-intentioned pragmatist stymied by right-wingers, and the Clinton who is calculating, unprincipled, and entirely self-serving? Both will be charming and intelligent. Both will make strong rhetorical commitments to certain values, then apparently abandon those values. And both will then say that they were forced to abandon those values out of necessity, but that they still hold those values dear. It's especially difficult to tell them apart because every compromise made for self-advancement can be defended as a compromise made for the sake of one's policy goals; if killing a disabled man helps one get to office, and getting to office lets one help more disabled people, well, you may not like it, but there's a trail of broken eggs leading to every omelet.

Was Clinton a utilitarian or a psychopath, then? The two often look identical, so how do we tell them apart? One of the clearest ways is to examine the points at which Clinton did things that pursued *no* objective except his own political gain, and over which he had complete discretion. We want to look at the moments when Clinton did not make a political compromise because it served the greater human good, but because it served Bill Clinton's own ambition, and the compromise was not forced, but was unquestionably the product of his own free choice.

The record contains countless examples of such decisions. Clinton did not, for example, have to make welfare reform a major campaign issue in 1992 (in fact, advisor Bruce Reed was shocked that Clinton did so, since it wasn't the sort of thing Democrats did). Clinton didn't have to dangle the promise of a drug crime amnesty, before pardoning a series of felonious campaign donors and family cronies instead. He didn't have to direct HUD to permanently kick families out of public housing over first-time criminal infractions. He didn't have to single out Sistah Souljah for a nasty public rebuke. He didn't have to propose drug testing every single mother before they could receive a benefit check, or every teenager before they could take a driving test. He didn't have to pressure the United Nations to let the Rwandan genocide carry on unimpeded, or order his administration to downplay the atrocity in order to avoid the Genocide Convention. He didn't have to dump Haitian HIV patients in Guantánamo, forcing them to spend the last months of their lives in a filthy tent jail. He didn't have to threaten South Africa with sanctions over its desperate attempt to create cheaper AIDS drugs. He didn't have to squander Haitian relief money on building a disused, pointless sweatshop. He didn't have to go to Stone Mountain to pose in front of black prisoners with Cooter from the *Dukes of Hazzard*. Ultimately, nobody forced him to sign the Personal Responsibility and Work Opportunity Reconciliation Act, the Violent Crime Control and Law Enforcement Act, or the Anti-Terrorism and Effective Death Penalty Act. He *certainly* didn't have to travel specially to Arkansas to execute a severely mentally disabled man, with people desperately pleading with him not to go through with it.

None of these acts makes sense on a theory that Clinton was good-hearted but simply bound by political constraints. In fact, he took repeated deliberate and voluntarily acts that had terrible consequences for black people, even when it was totally unnecessary to do so. It was not that he took these steps when there was intense political demand for him to take them, it was that he took them whenever there was *any political advantage whatsoever* to be gained from them. This is one of the key errors that proponents of the "Republicans made him do it" theory make when assessing the facts. They treat "believed there was no conceivable way out" and "believed there was some trivial piece of political capital to be gained" as the same scenario.

In fact, Clinton is somewhat notorious for his efforts to blame impossible political constraints for his own actions. In Dick Morris' examination of Clinton's memoirs, Morris documents Clinton's constant attempts to portray himself as being buffeted about helplessly by circumstance, a blameless victim of fate's cruel vicissitudes:

> *The man who held the most powerful post on the planet spends page after page lamenting his inability to take action. The word 'can't' looms around every corner; obstacles seem to leave him helpless to carve out his own direction or even policies. Yet most of these inhibitions were fictions, intended to cover Clinton's real motivations or pumped up into major obstacles to protect his inactivity from criticism.*[756]

As always, words from Morris should be consumed alongside liberal helpings of salt. But the description rings true. One of Clinton's most noticeable traits is the tendency to refuse to admit that his choices were his freely made by himself. Instead, he blames other people, or a lack of information. We can see this in every one of the examined historical cases. He told Jesse Jackson that there was "nothing he could do" to save Rickey Ray Rector's life, even though it was quite obvious what he could do.

CLINTON WAS WILLING TO SACRIFICE ANY AMOUNT OF BLACK people's well-being for *any amount* of political gain. No matter how small the political risk was, if a risk existed *at all,* Clinton would not take an act regardless of its impact on black lives. This means that black lives were simply assigned a value of 0 in Clinton's calculus. Even in a case such as Rwanda, where Clinton knew from the newspapers that *hundreds of thousands* of black lives would be lost if he did not act, a minutely small cost to his own interests meant he did not intervene.

Another example of similar reasoning (with Hispanic lives instead) occurred during Clinton's tenure as Arkansas governor. In 1980, Fidel Castro had allowed 125,000 Cubans to depart the country in what became known as the "Mariel boatlift." As thousands of Cuban refugees began streaming onto American shores, President Jimmy Carter needed someplace to put them. He decided to use Fort Chaffee, a military installation in northwest Arkansas, to temporarily house 20,000 refugees. Governor Clinton was livid; bringing thousands of Cuban undesirables to Arkansas created a tense political issue in the state. (Clinton suggested that Carter house the refugees at Guantánamo instead, but Carter refused.) Soon, a thousand Cuban refugees escaped from Fort Chaffee, turning Clinton's political headache into a catastrophe. The military refused to round up the Cubans on the grounds that it had no authority. Clinton feared that the escaped Cubans would soon encounter armed Arkansans and violence would ensue. So Clinton dispatched the state police and the National Guard. But Clinton was insistent that the primary objective was to avoid further political fallout; he was terrified about how the refugee crisis would affect his reelection chances. As part of his orders, Clinton gave the troopers a chilling instruction: "If somebody has to die, it'd better be a Cuban... Do I make myself clear?"[757]

Ultimately, the troopers successfully corralled the Cubans without any unpleasantness. But Clinton's words demonstrate how he thinks about the lives of others: purely in terms of their political value. Clinton was scared that an Arkansan would be injured or killed after picking a fight with a Cuban, and that this would reflect badly on him as governor. If he had to *kill Cubans* in order to avoid this outcome, he would do it. The rules of engagement, justice, racial equality, all disappeared instantly in the face of a crisis affecting Clinton's political fortunes. It didn't matter whether the Cubans were in the right or in the wrong; what mattered was that nothing occur that could damage Clinton politically. In a situation where someone was going to die, regardless of whether the Cuban attacked an Arkansan or an Arkansan attacked a Cuban, *it needed to be the Cuban that died.*

Again, this is not because Clinton has a personal animus toward Cubans. Clinton has no animus toward anyone at all. It is simply that Clinton's values reflect those of the people around him, because the values of those around him are going to determine Clinton's political success. And so if Clinton governs a state that would care little if a score of Cubans died, but would throw the governor out of office if even one Arkansan got a black eye from a refugee, Clinton will carefully ensure that the Cuban life is given its due political weight: none at all. And in a society that values black and Hispanic lives less than white ones, and rewards politicians accordingly, Clinton will value black and Hispanic lives less as well.

Of course, a calculus like this does not mean that the result will not occasionally coincide, like a stopped clock, with something faintly resembling justice. But this will always be pure happenstance. For if one could achieve *perfect, universal justice*, but at the cost of *a tiny risk to Bill Clinton's popularity or political career,* justice will be out of luck. The only hope is that one can arrange matters so that the interests of Bill Clinton and the interests of the moral good coincide rather than conflict.

This is why the difference between pragmatism and narcissism matters so much. Even though both might spend their time performing roughly the same acts (selling out the values of their core constituencies), the narcissist is capable of *monstrous evil* in a society where evil is rewarded, while the pragmatist will at least be making an attempt to resist as much of that evil as possible. The two calculi may look similar at first. In the case of the Rwandan genocide, on the first day the pragmatist may decide that saving a few thousand Rwandan lives is not worth the risk. But as the number of lives at stake ticks up into the tens and then hundreds of thousands, the pragmatist will change her mind. The political costs of action are now dwarfed by the human consequences of inaction. There is, therefore, hope that the pragmatist will do the decent thing. But for someone like Bill Clinton, there is no such hope. Even at 800,000 lives, it did not matter. The calculus never changes; the lives affected are immaterial, no matter the quantity. "If someone dies, it had better be a Cuban." *No matter what.*

B UT THOSE DISAPPOINTED AND BETRAYED BY CLINTON HAVE long been tortured by the question: "How could someone do something so terrible yet seem so genuinely friendly?" If he's truly a wolf, then he is one in exquisitely-tailored sheep's clothing. Clinton is, after all, *a charmer.* We are used to having evil announce its presence a bit more clearly (e.g. Ted Cruz).

The disjunction between Clinton's demeanor and behavior has long led his admirers to call him "complex." One oral history of Clinton is called *A Complicated Man.*[758] What has confused Clinton's friends and admirers for so long is that Clinton always seems to have a smile on his face and want to make people happy, but then everything he does is self-serving and two-faced. *How can this be?*

Yet the fact that people have such a hard time disliking Clinton says more about human beings' charitable nature than it does about any complexity on Clinton's part. For, no matter how much they may affirm cynicism in theory, most people simply have a hard time believing that people who seem kind and well-intentioned are not, in fact, kind and well-intentioned. It's strange that this should be so difficult to accept, that it should be hard to truly believe a "charming" individual is capable of monstrous things. But this is the nature of predators generally. They're the nicest guys you'll ever know. Until they're not.

It is interesting that so many who know him call Clinton "complicated" or "paradoxical." For it is rare that a person who is genuinely well-intentioned but flawed is called "complicated." Usually, when someone is complicated, when we have a hard time understanding what could possibly be going on inside them, it is because most of the time they are kind, but then occasionally they commit unbelievably atrocious acts that *a person who was truly kind would not be capable of committing.* The abusive are often "complicated." They can seem warm and effervescent one moment, and then suddenly they will turn dark, angry, and terrifying. Another second and it's over, and they're back to normal again. If you point out what they did, they'll be sweet and apologetic. "Baby, I didn't mean it, you know I'm not like that." And because most of the time they're *not* like that, it's tempting to accept the apology. (As one advice-website explained to women: "A guy who acts like a total piece of crap towards you isn't 'complicated'... he's a total piece of crap!"[759])

One should not doubt that Clinton can be ruthless and angry. He has a legendary temper, and any signs of the cuddly Clinton hastily dissipate as soon as he feels wronged. In George Stephanopoulos' memoir, he describes Clinton's "tornadoes" of fury, the volcanic torrents of blame and bile that regularly erupted from Clinton.[760] When the situation in Somalia began to go awry, Clinton began shouting:

> *We're not inflicting pain on these fuckers... When people kill us, they should be killed in greater numbers... I believe in killing people who try to hurt you, and I can't believe we're being pushed around by these two-bit pricks.*[761]

Of course, soon enough he was back to being Bubba again, and he would apologize profusely to those whom he had hurt during his rage. In fact, Clinton's apologies are one of his more disturbing tendencies. Clinton cannot stop apologizing. He apologizes for everything. He apologized for the crime bill. He apologized for ignoring Rwanda. He apologized for starving Haiti. But the apologies always turn out to be either manipulative or insincere. In the case of the crime bill apology, Clinton immediately reversed himself and began defending the policy again when Black Lives Matter protesters were getting the better of him over it. In the case of Rwanda, he used the opportunity of his apology to rewrite the historical record in order to suggest his inaction was due to a lack of knowledge. John Ryle, writing during Clinton's 1998 "apology tour" of Africa, noted how curiously promiscuous Clinton was with his apologies, which were "not exactly insincere but they were clearly subordinate to political interests."[762]

The same observation was made when Clinton released his autobiography, *My Life*. Robert McCrum, the reviewer for *The Guardian*, wrote that Clinton's book was "utterly self-serving." "For every line of contrition," McCrum wrote, "there are two of self-justification. For every attempt at atonement, there is yet another display of self-aggrandisement.[763] Thus Clinton's ostensible attempt to right his past wrongs was actually aimed at convincing people that he had done no wrong at all. It's no secret that Clinton's primary motivation in life is to be liked, and when someone feels mistreated by one's cruel actions, the easiest way to regain their favor is to issue a profuse and abject apology. But when one apologizes not out of any true remorse, but because one wants to be liked again, the apology is worse than nothing at all. It is just yet another act of manipulation.

False apologies are just one of the lawyerly tricks in the Clinton rhetorical repertoire. More notorious is the delicate massaging of language to disguise true meaning (which reached its absurd apotheosis in "it depends what the meaning of 'is' is.") As one person who knew him said, "You've got to listen to everything he says. Because you can walk away thinking you've convinced him and he's going to do something. And he can look you square in the eye later on and say 'I didn't promise that.'"[764] So Clinton promised that he would never turn away a Haitian political refugee, and refugee advocates cheered, but upon taking office he looked them square in the eye and said "I promised I'd never turn away a *political* refugee. Weren't you listening?" And Clinton repeatedly told people the crack-powder sentencing disparity pained him, and that he wanted to see it ended. But if people pointed out that he had rejected a chance to end the disparity, Clinton's reply was essentially akin to: "I said I wanted to end the disparity, not lower crack sentences. What I really want to do is raise the powder sentences to match the crack sentences." In this way, as Arkansas columnist Paul Greenberg explained, "the governor is seldom if ever caught in a lie, yet he can deceive without blinking."[765]

This may seem terribly clever, but it's actually a cruel form of rhetorical gaslighting: work as hard as possible to give someone the impression you mean one thing, while leaving open the tiniest possible door to meaning another thing, then when the person receives the impression you intentionally gave them, say "I can't believe you misinterpreted me." It is using a lawyer's skills to abuse and betray people, and then to cast their feelings of betrayal as being their own fault, even though they are the direct product of a conscious strategy on the part of the betrayer.

When it comes to issues of race, this kind of slipperiness has moral consequences. Paul Greenberg says Clinton excels at "being all things to all men, women, children and ethnic groups" and that what [he thinks] about an issue may depend on where you catch him in his career trajectory, and what constituency he's courting at the moment."[766]

Because Clinton literally wishes to court *all* voters (Greenberg says Clinton will take any political act, so long as it doesn't alienate a single interest group or voting bloc), he ends up pandering to white supremacists. For Clinton's gubernatorial inauguration in 1979, he invited his disgraced predecessor, Orville Faubus, to attend the ceremony. Faubus had long been considered toxic in Arkansas politics. He was the segregationist governor who had refused to follow *Brown v. Board of Education*'s order to integrate the schools. It was Faubus who had deployed the Arkansas National Guard to prevent the Little Rock Nine from attending school. Yet at the inauguration ceremony, Clinton hugged Faubus and praised him as "a man of considerable ability."[767]

Clinton also praised another segregationist, J. William Fulbright, who had voted against the 1964 Civil Rights Act and signed the Southern Manifesto calling for organized resistance to the *Brown* decision.[768] Clinton called Fulbright "my mentor, a visionary, a humanitarian" and awarded Fulbright the Presidential Medal of Freedom. Clinton said of Fulbright that "[t]he American political system produced this remarkable man, and my state did, and I'm real proud of it."[769] (Note that when Republican Trent Lott similarly praised the segregationist Strom Thurmond, Democrats successfully hounded him out of office.)

The *National Review* (of all places) pointed out that while Clinton was governor, he issued birthday proclamations honoring Jefferson Davis and Robert E. Lee, signed an act to "commemorate the Confederate States of America," and said nothing about the state practice of observing an annual Confederate Flag Day.[770] Civil rights attorney Dayna Cunningham never trusted Clinton again after watching him give a speech in the 1980s to a white audience in which he "irresponsibly pandered to the backwards feeling of the white constituency" on race. After the speech was over, Clinton approached Cunningham and suddenly "became all sweetness, seductively ambiguous in his charm. He turned to me, touched me to make certain I heard, and said 'I love the [NAACP] Legal Defense Fund. I love Lani Guinier.'"[771]

Such sudden switches were a Clinton commonplace. One day, he would stand in front of black prisoners at Stone Mountain alongside segregationists and Confederate sympathizers. The next day, he would be singing "Lift Every Voice" in a black church. One day, Clinton would go golfing at a segregated country club.[772] The next day, he would apologize for it and insist he valued the NAACP. Clinton would be praised for his warm demeanor and lack of condecension in dealing with African Americans. But in private, he bitterly ranted to Ted Kennedy about Barack Obama that "a few years ago, this guy would have been carrying our bags."[773] The warmth disappeared when black lives posed political obstacles.

In Alexander Cockburn's words, "everything is negotiable" for Clinton,[774] and if there is nothing Clinton will stand firm on, then pandering to white supremacists becomes acceptable. Clinton wants to be liked by everyone, and the logical consequence of that is giving Orville Faubus a great big hug and telling him how wonderful he is. But as Christopher Hitchens has noted, if you can charm *everyone*, it means you don't actually care about anyone.

Believing that segregation is a moral evil means *not praising and befriending segregationists*. If one *does* praise segregationists, if one is willing to pin a medal on them without even mentioning their hateful and racist deeds, then one doesn't believe segregation is a moral evil at all. It's fair to say, then, that Bill

Clinton doesn't oppose segregation; this is simply a corollary of the observation that Bill Clinton doesn't oppose *anything*.

None of this is news. From the very beginning of Clinton's appearance on the political scene, observers were characterizing him as a cold-hearted and predacious operative. He was consistently described as "opportunistic, poll driven, and primarily concerned with electoral victories, not principled positions."[775] Historian Martin Jay called him "a master of self-serving prevarication, reckless irresponsibility and spineless disloyalty."[776]

But the implications of Clinton's extreme amorality are rarely drawn out. It is easy to call him names and observe that he is the least trustworthy figure in the history of American politics. But since politics have actual high stakes, removing principle from the enterprise costs lives. A narcissism-fueled political philosophy isn't some forgivable character flaw. It hurts and destroys people; Paul Rusesabagina, Rickey Rector, and blind Al Shifa survivor Fadil Reheima have all experienced the human consequences wrought by Bill Clinton's politics of limitless ego.

At Stone Mountain.
Left to right: Rep. Ben Jones, Pres. Bill Clinton,
Gov. Zell Miller, Sen. Sam Nunn.

Stone Mountain, Race, and "When Jim Crow Goes to Yale"

ILL CLINTON HAD A BETTER RELATIONSHIP WITH BLACK Americans than any President before him. And yet this was a man who would execute a black mental patient if it meant getting a two-point bump in New Hampshire. A man whose administration conspired to deny a genocide, because saving black lives didn't play well among swing voters. A man who deliberately made a campaign issue out of gutting the social safety net, and putting black single mothers to work. A man whose most courageous black appointees were unceremoniously dumped the moment the right-wing press made a stink. A man who sent HIV-positive refugees to slowly die in Guantánamo. A man who destroyed the death penalty appeal process, reaffirmed the racist crack/powder disparity, sapped prisoners' ability to protest unlawful conditions, and oversaw the largest expansion in the prison population in all of American history. Far from being the first black president, Clinton seems like exactly what happens when, as Jesse Jackson said, "Jim Crow goes to Yale." Measures that would have been vigorously resisted had Ronald

Reagan introduced them were disguised beneath respectable euphemism and implemented without complaint.

Jesse Jackson's explanation is a potent description of many of Clinton's actions. Yet it does not explain how the same president that intensified the War on Drugs and denied a genocide could also sign the Family and Medical Leave Act and expand the Earned Income Tax Credit. These things helped working families, many of whom were African American. What kind of Jim Crow president would do such a thing? If he was deliberately trying to destroy black lives, he certainly seems only half-heartedly committed to it.

The explanation of Clinton as motivated by racial *hatred* does not fit the facts. From the accounts of everyone who knows him, Clinton likes black people and wants them to like him. That he amassed a résumé befitting of George Wallace seems, initially, to be in puzzling tension with his personal disposition. But it is Clinton's very desire to be liked that is the problem. To desire to be liked, rather than to do good, is to be driven by ego. *Doing the right thing requires being willing to be unpopular.* It requires not viewing everything through the prism of how much people like you. If one's sole motivation is to become popular, then one will be willing to inflict terrible injustices if doing so brings reward. Far from being respectable, wanting to be liked can motivate callous and selfish deeds.

This is what is most important to understand about Clinton: his political philosophy is not to deliberately hurt African Americans, but to advance his interests and satisfy his ego, *even if this means hurting African Americans.* This is a crucial distinction, because without it, many of Clinton's more positive policies make little sense. So Clinton will proudly display Lillie Harden to the world as a mother who has gone from welfare to work, but as her life later unravels and she becomes ineligible for benefits, Clinton will be nowhere to be seen. Clinton will beamingly cut the ribbon in front of a Haitian clothing factory, but when the factory becomes an empty husk with little economic benefit, Clinton will simply avoid mentioning Haiti in his speeches ever again. There's nothing Clinton loves more than black lives, until they become politically inconvenient.

Others have tried to understand the mixture of horrendous crimes with historic appointments by calling Clinton "complicated." Because there was good to go along with the bad, he must have been a sincere person doing his best under conditions of constraint. But the evidence can't support that theory. At moments of clear discretion, Clinton *still* rejected the moral course of action when it came with no political or personal gain to himself. And the most reprehensible acts, such as genocide denial and killing the disabled, are *so* reprehensible that they could not be performed by anyone in possession of a conscience.

Instead, the facts suggest something different, something far simpler and more logical: Clinton treated black interests with total mercenary cynicism. If cultivating their support helped him, Clinton would go to every length to connect with black voters. But the moment he faced a difficult choice between the politically expedient thing to do and the racially just thing to do, there was quite literally no harm he was unwilling to inflict upon black people in order to secure even minor political victories.

A ND SO WE RETURN TO STONE MOUNTAIN. THAT SINGLE image could serve as an iconic representation of Clinton's entire legacy on race. It belies all of his claims to have stumbled innocently into the creation of mass incarceration, to be a person who would never compromise on matters of race. Instead, he voluntarily and intentionally made a campaign issue out of his willingness to lock up as many black people as it took to secure his own political success.

If black lives have ever mattered to Bill Clinton, then, it is solely to the extent that they conferred black political support. One could say that Bill Clinton has made a career of throwing black people under the bus, but what Bill Clinton actually did was throw black people under the bus, drive over them, back up, drive over them again, then get out, pull them from underneath, dust them off and ask them if they were okay and if he could get them a glass of water, then throw them under the bus again.

Bill Clinton's defense of the "superpredator" idea was therefore just the latest instance of a career-long repetition of the same tropes. At every turn, he has pulled the same maneuver: rhetorically claim to be acting in the interests of black lives, but being willing to abandon this commitment the moment it gets in the way of a political goal. Even as he totally dismissed Black Lives Matter's concerns over the crime bill, Clinton still insisted he was looking out for the interests of the black community. As always, his words insist he serves black people, while his deeds pitilessly betray them.

It is a matter of historical fact that Bill Clinton used black people in the most despicable way possible, doing everything he could to convince them he cared while doing nothing but using their lives to advance himself politically. They trusted him, and he threw them in jail by the millions. As Michael Eric Dyson has explained, Clinton "exploited black sentiment because he knew the rituals of black culture," then "exploited us like no president before him."[777] Nobody in the history of American race relations from slavery to the present has ever so cruelly manipulated the aspirations of the black population, has ever so heartlessly tormented them with empty promises while happily destroying their lives.

Thanks to Clinton's cultivated charm and savvy rhetoric, people have still not quite appreciated just how amoral Clinton's treatment of race has been. Perhaps, now that his angry attack on Black Lives Matter has provided such a revealing illustration of Clinton's tactics, the understanding will shift. Perhaps we will finally realize that Bill Clinton's legacy on race is precisely what the Stone Mountain photograph shows: a man for whom black Americans have always been a prop, to be praised, disparaged, championed, taunted, freed, imprisoned, and sometimes killed, depending on the particular daily political needs of Bill Clinton. A man who will tell any fib (or offer any apology) necessary to exonerate himself. A man with no conscience, no empathy... A superpredator.

Acknowledgments

I OWE MY DEEPEST THANKS TO A NUMBER OF PEOPLE WHO HELPED me through the process of writing this book. Oren Nimni contributed a good deal of tireless research, and I am grateful to him for causing the book to be much more in-depth and thorough than it otherwise could have been. My parents, Peter and Rosemary Robinson, were endlessly supportive as usual, and I would like to thank my mother for carefully reviewing and giving comments on several drafts of the book.

I also owe thanks to my many encouraging and patient friends. Several in particular were especially kind and generous during the preparation of this book, including Sarah Hailey, Howie Lempel, Ben Saucier, Jessica Elliott, Tyler Rosebush, Zach Wehrwein, Heather Gillman, Robert Manduca, and Sparky Abraham.

Thanks also to everyone who supports and reads *Current Affairs*, and to our dedicated writers, like Yasmin Nair and Amber Frost, whose talents have made it a success.

Daryl Carter's book *Brother Bill* proved an invaluable asset during the research process. Thanks to the University of Arkansas Press for arranging to let *Current Affairs* see an advance copy. Matthew Lutz of the Associated Press was incredibly helpful in arranging the license for the cover photo. Without the research support of the Harvard University Sociology Department and my advisor, Lawrence Bobo, I would have been unable to write this book.

Supredator relies heavily on the research of numerous journalists and historians. I would not have discovered the Haiti material without Doug Henwood's writing on the subject. Michelle Alexander's work also guided my thinking. Thanks go to the hundreds of people whose work is cited or drawn from.

Sources

1   Allan Smith, "Bill Clinton unleashes blistering rebuttal to Black Lives Matter protesters," *Business Insider* (April 7,2016).

2   Julia Zorthian, "Black Lives Matter Activist Confronts Clinton at Fundraiser," *TIME* (Feb. 25, 2016).

3   Charles M. Blow, "I'm Not A Superpredator," *The New York Times* (Feb. 29, 2016).

4   The actual date was 1996.

5   Tim Hains, "'Black Lives Matter' Activist Interrupts Clinton Event: 'Apologize For Mass Incarceration... I Am Not A Super-Predator,'" *Real Clear Politics* (Feb. 24, 2016).

6   Jonathan Capehart, "Hillary Clinton on 'superpredator' remarks: 'I shouldn't have used those words'," *The Washington Post* (Feb. 25, 2016).

7   Quoted in Goldie Taylor, "Bill Clinton's Ugly Defense Of His Crime Bill That Harmed Black Communities," *The Daily Beast* (April 9, 2016).

8   Peter Baker, "Bill Clinton Concedes His Crime Law Jailed Too Many for Too Long," *The New York Times* (July 16, 2015).

9   Charles P. Pierce, "Bill Clinton Doesn't Understand What Black Lives Matter Is All About," *Esquire*, (April 8, 2016).

10   Steven W. Thrasher, "How dare Bill Clinton shout over Black Lives Matter protesters?" *The Guardian* (April 8, 2016).

11   Michelle Goldberg, "Fire Bill Clinton," *Slate* (April 7, 2016).

12   John J. DiIulio, "Prisons Are a Bargain By Any Measure," *The New York Times* (Jan 16, 1996).

13   William J. Bennett, John J. DiIulio, Jr., and John P. Walters, *Body Count: Moral Poverty...And How To Win America's War Against Crime and Drugs* (Simon & Schuster, 1996), p. 27.

14   *Id.*

15   *Id.*

16   John J. DiIulio, Jr., "Moral Poverty The Coming Of The Super-predators Should Scare Us Into Wanting To Get To The Root Causes Of Crime A Lot Faster," *The Chicago Tribune* (Dec. 15, 1995).

17   See Bernard E. Harcourt, *Illusion of Order: The False Promise of Broken Windows Policing* (Harvard University Press, 2005).

18   George L. Kelling and James Q. Wilson, "Broken Windows: The police and neighborhood safety," *The Atlantic* (March, 1982).

19   James Q. Wilson, "Crime and Public Policy," in *Crime*, James Q. Wilson and Joan Petersilia, eds. (Institute for Contemporary Studies Press, 1995), p. 507

20   *Id.*

21   James C. Howell, *Preventing and Reducing Juvenile Delinquency: A Comprehensive Framework* (SAGE Publications, 2003), p. 3.

22   John DiIulio, Jr., *How to Stop the Coming Crime* Wave (Manhattan Institute, 1996), p. 1.

23   "Community-oriented policing was prelude to zero-tolerance plan," *Milwaukee Journal-Sentinel* (March 12, 1996).

24   "The Superpredator Myth: 20 Years Later," Equal Justice Initiative (April 7, 2014).

25   Michelle Alexander, "Why Hillary Clinton Doesn't Deserve the Black Vote, *The Nation* (Feb. 10, 2016).

26   John DiIulio, Jr. "Moral Poverty, The Coming Of The Super-predators Should Scare Us Into Wanting To Get To The Root Causes Of Crime A Lot Faster," Dec. 15, 1995, h

27   *Id.*

28   *Id.*

29   Brief of Jeffrey Fagan, et al., *Miller v. Alabama,* No. 10-9646, 63 So. 3d 676.

30   *Id.*

31   Mark Kleiman, "The Current Crime Debate Isn't Doing Hillary Justice," *Washington Monthly* (Feb. 17, 2016).

32   Fagan, *supra.*

33   P. Atkinson, "Superpredators," *The Sunday Mail* (Jan. 21, 1996).

34   "Interim report of the Special Rapporteur of the Human Rights Council on torture and other cruel, inhuman or degrading treatment or punishment," United Nations Special Rapporteur (Aug. 5, 2011).

35   Michael Schwirtz and Michael Winerip, "Kalief Browder, Held at Rikers Island for 3 Years Without Trial, Commits Suicide," *The New York Times* (June 8, 2015).

36   *Growing Up Locked Down: Youth in Solitary Confinement in Jails and Prisons Across the United States,* American Civil Liberties Union/Human Rights Watch (2012), p. 24.

37   Vincent Schiraldi and Jason Zeidenberg, *The Risks Juveniles Face When They Are Incarcerated With Adults,* Juvenile Policy Institute (1997).

38   See *Jailing Juveniles: The Dangers of Incarcerating Youth in Adult Jails in America,* Campaign for Youth Justice (Nov., 2007).

39   T.J. Parsell, "Unsafe Behind Bars," *The New York Times* (Sept. 18, 2005).

40   Natasha Vargas-Cooper, "Twilight of the Superpredators," *The Baffler* (Feb. 2, 2016).

41   Lori Montgomery, "Debating the links between guns and teen violence," *The Toronto Star* (June 9, 1996).

42   *Id.*

43   *Id.*

44   *Id.*

45   John DiIulio, Jr., "The Coming of the Super Predators," *The Weekly Standard* (Nov. 27, 1995).

46   Jonathan Capehart, "Hillary Clinton on 'superpredator' remarks: 'I shouldn't have used those words,'" *The Washington Post* (Feb. 25, 2016).

47   Dewayne Wickham, *Bill Clinton and Black America* (One World/Ballantine, 2002), p. 130.

48   *Id.,* at 101.

49   *Id.,* at 116.

50   For an overview of financial deregulation during the Clinton Administration, see Timothy A. Canova, "The Legacy of the Clinton Bubble," *Dissent* (Summer 2008). For a description of the lasting effects of the financial crisis on the economic prospects of African Americans, see Yian Q. Mui, "For black Americans, financial damage from subprime implosion is likely to last," *The Washington Post* (July 8, 2012). And for a dissection of Bill Clinton's excuses for his deregulatory policies, see Ryan Chittum, "Bill Clinton on deregulation: 'The Republicans made me do it!'; The ex-president seriously mischaracterizes his record," *Columbia Journalism Review* (Oct. 1, 2013).

51   Alexander, *supra.*

52   Christopher Brian Booker, "The Paradoxical Presidency of Bill Clinton," *African Americans and the Presidency.* http://www.blacksandpresidency.com

53   *Id.*

54   "Clinton Inducted into Arkansas Black Hall of Fame," *FOX News* (Oct. 17, 2002).

55   "Clinton Inducted into Arkansas Black Hall of Fame," *Jet* (Nov. 11, 2002).

56   Quoted in Wickham, *supra*, at 94.

57   Id., at 115.

58   Charles O. Jackson, "William J. Simmons: A Career in Ku Kluxism," *The Georgia Historical Quarterly*, Vol. 50, No. 4 (December, 1966), pp. 351-365.

59   Donald E. Wilkes, Jr., "Steve Oney's List of the Leo Frank Lynchers," *Flagpole* (May 5, 2004).

60   Ed Kilgore, "Confederacy and Neo-Confederacy on Stone Mountain," *Washington Monthly* (July 14, 2015).

61   Albert Boime, "Patriarchy Fixed in Stone: Gutzon Borglum's "Mount Rushmore,'" *American Art*, Vol. 5, No. 1/2. (Winter-Spring, 1991), pp. 142-167, at 165.

62   Christopher Petrella, "On Stone Mountain: White Supremacy and the Birth of the Modern Democratic Party," *Boston Review* (March 30, 2016).

63   Duane D. Stanford, "Stone Mountain Park: Is rebel image cut too deep?" *The Atlanta Journal-Constitution* (April 17, 1994).

64   *Id.*

65   Tony Allen-Mills, "Black mayor triumphs in lair of the Ku Klux Klan dragon," *The Sunday Times* (Nov. 23, 1997).

66   Shirley L. Smith, "A 'Freedom' ride to the mountaintop King Week begins with train journey," *The Atlanta Journal-Constitution* (January 10, 1993).

67   Allen-Mills, *supra*.

68   Peter Applebome, "Atlanta in Contrast: Civil Rights and Racial Hate," *The New York Times* (Dec. 22, 1989).

69   D. Thompson, "America the Hateful," *The Courier-Mail* (Nov. 14, 1987).

70   *Id.*

71   Tony Allen-Mills, "Black mayor triumphs in lair of the Ku Klux Klan dragon," *The Sunday Times* (Nov. 23, 1997).

72   *Id.*

73   "Stone Mountain, Georgia: Everybody's Mad," *The Orlando Sentinel,* (Aug. 4, 1988).

74   For more information on beautiful Lake Venable, see "Stone Mountain Guide: Lakes" http://www.stonemountainguide.com/Lakes.html

75   Rev. Dr. Martin Luther King, Jr., "I Have a Dream," in *A Testament of Hope: The Essential Writings and Speeches of Martin Luther King, Jr.*, James M. Washington, ed. (HarperOne, 2003), p. 217.

76   Alexander, *supra*.

77   See Roger Simon, "How A Murderer And Rapist Became The Bush Campaign's Most Valuable Player," *The Baltimore Sun* (Nov. 11, 1990).

78   Michael Kramer, "The Political Interest: Frying Them Isn't The Answer," (*TIME*, Mar. 14, 1994).

79   "Georgia Prisons," Georgia State Advisory Committee to the U.S. Commission on Civil Rights (1976), available at http://files.eric.ed.gov/fulltext/ED178671.pdf

80   "FY 1989 Annual Report," Georgia Department of Corrections (1989), available at https://www.ncjrs.gov/pdffiles1/Digitization/141118NCJRS.pdf

81   Jim Galloway, Greg Bluestein, and Daniel Malloy, "Barney Frank says he's the reason Sam Nunn never became secretary of state," *The Atlanta Journal-Constitution* (May 4, 2015).

82   Jones now runs "Cooter's Place," a shop selling *Dukes of Hazzard* novelty items and Confederate memorabilia. http://cootersplace.com/

83   Tierny McAffee, "Dukes of Hazzard Actor Defends Confederate Flag: It Represents 'Courage and Family and Good Times,'" *People* (June 24, 2015). Jones does not mention which "good times" he is referring to, but we can speculate that they may roughly coincide with the years from the antebellum period to about 1956.

84   Petrella, *supra*.

85   Sonni Efron and Paul Richter, "Two Clinton Rivals Level a Double-Barreled Attack: Tsongas and Harkin use terms like 'cynical' and 'insensitive' on eve of South Carolina primary," *The Los Angeles Times* (March 7, 1992). http://articles.latimes.com/1992-03-07/news/mn-3576_1_south-carolina-primary

86   Joan Didion, "Eye on the Prize," *The New York Review of Books* (Sept. 24, 1992,

87   Efron and Richter, *supra* note 50.

88   *Id.*

89   Kevin Sack, "Birthplace of Klan Chooses a Black Mayor," *The New York Times* (Nov. 19, 1997).

90   Didion, *supra.*

91   *Id.*

92   Paul Starr and Robert Kuttner, "What We Know Now," *The American Prospect* (April 27, 2015).

93   Stanley B. Greenberg, "From Crisis to Working Majority," *The American Prospect* (Fall 1991).

94   Jon F. Hale, "The Making of the New Democrats," *Political Science Quarterly* Vol. 110, No. 2 (Summer, 1995), pp. 207-232, 207.

95   Corey Robin, "The Clintons' Cynical Race Game: No One Will Say It, but the Clintons' Rise Was Premised on Repudiating Black Voters," *Salon* (Jan. 31ˢᵗ, 2016).

96   *Id.*

97   *Id.*

98   Daniel B. Wood, "U.S. Crime Rate At Lowest Point In Decades," *The Christian Science Monitor* (Jan. 9, 2012).

99   Richard M. Nixon, "Address Accepting the Presidential Nomination at the Republican National Convention in Miami Beach, Florida," (August 8, 1968).

100   *Id.*

101   Daryl A. Carter, *Brother Bill: Bill Clinton and the Politics of Race and Class* (University of Arkansas Press, 2016), p. 102.

102   Timothy J. McNulty, "'Outrageous' Debate Question Angers Kitty Dukakis," *The Chicago Tribune* (Oct. 15, 1988).

103   M. J. Stephy, "Dukakis' Deadly Response," *TIME* (undated).

104   Carter, *supra,* at 99.

105   "Debate '92," *Saturday Night Live*, available at: http://snltranscripts.jt.org/92/92cdebate.phtml

106   Carter, *supra,* at 101.

107   Angie Cannon, "While Crime Has Declined, The Campaign Rhetoric Hasn't," *The Philadelphia Inquirer,* (Oct. 20, 1996).

108   Quoted in Carter, *supra,* at 103

109   Michael Fortner, "The Clintons Aren't the Only Ones to Blame for the Crime Bill," *The Marshall Project* (Oct. 7, 2016).

110   Goldie Taylor, "Bill Clinton's Ugly Defense Of His Crime Bill That Harmed Black Communities," *The Daily Beast* (April 9, 2016).

111   "Fact Sheet: Violent Crime Control and Law Enforcement Act of 1994," United States Department of Justice.

112   David Johnston and Steven A. Holmes, "Experts Doubt Effectiveness Of Crime Bill," *The New York Times* (Sept. 14, 1994).

113   Robert Farley, "Bill Clinton and the 1994 Crime Bill," *FactCheck.org*, The Annenberg Public Policy Center (April 12, 2016).

114   "Ending Mass Incarceration: The Need for Federal Incentives," Equal Justice Initiative (Jan. 29, 2016).

115   *Id.*

116   George F. Will, "Peanut's Prison Tale," *The Washington Post* (January 30, 1994).

117   Colman McCarthy, "Better 100,000 More Teachers Than 100,000 More Police," *The Washington Post* (Jan. 29, 1994).

118   Statement of Claiborne Pell, Congressional Record (Feb. 9, 1994).

119   Glenn Walker Moomau, "Cutting prison Pell Grants would be a crime," *The Baltimore Sun* (June 24, 1994).

120   Michelle Munn, "Inmates Get Second Chance at Education," *The Los Angeles Times* (Feb. 12, 2003)

121   "Education and Vocational Training in Prisons Reduces Recidivism, Improves Job Outlook," RAND Corporation (Aug. 22, 2013)

122   Jeff Smith, *Mr. Smith Goes to Prison: What My Year Behind Bars Taught Me About America's Prison Crisis,* (St. Martin's, 2015), p. 129.

123   Martin Walker, "Clinton Gives Sermon on Crime Reform," *The Guardian* (Aug. 15, 1994).

124   William J. Clinton, "Remarks on Signing the Violent Crime Control and Law Enforcement Act of 1994" (Sept. 13, 1994), in *Public Papers of the Presidents of the United States, William J. Clinton* (Government Printing Office), p. 1540.

125   Vargas-Cooper, *supra.*

126   Goldberg, *supra.*

127   Joe Palazzolo, "Racial Gap in Men's Sentencing," *The Wall Street Journal* (Feb. 14, 2013).

128   Nsenga Burton, "More Black Men in Prison Today Than Enslaved in 1850," *The Root*, (March 30, 2011). Note that, contrary to the headline, it is *not* the case that there are more black men in *prison* than were enslaved in 1850.

Instead, there are more black men *under correctional control* than were enslaved in 1850. Correctional control includes probation and parole. There were 870,000 black men enslaved in 1850, whereas there are 1.7 million under correctional control. See Max Ehrenfreund, "There's a disturbing truth to John Legend's Oscar statement about prisons and slavery," *The Washington Post* (Feb 23, 2015).

129   Ezra Klein, "70% of black high-school dropouts born in 1975 have been to prison," *Vox,* (May 5, 2014).

130   Bruce Western and Becky Pettit, "Incarceration and Social Inequality," *Daedalus* (Summer 2010).

131   *Id.*

132   "Rev. Jesse Jackson Sr. Speaks Loudly Against Clinton Crime Bill," available on YouTube https://www.youtube.com/watch?v=7pQfKeHtsfo

133   See, for example, Kleiman, *supra*; Bill Scher, Don't Punish Clinton, Sanders for 1994 Crime Bill, *Real Clear Politics* (Feb. 22, 2016); Jamelle Bouie, "The Messy, Very Human Politics of Bill Clinton's Crime Bill," *Slate* (April 11, 2016).

134   Angie Cannon, "While Crime Has Declined, The Campaign Rhetoric Hasn't," *The Philadelphia Inquirer* (Oct. 20, 1996).

135   Wolf Blitzer, "Clinton Supports Curfews to Curb Youth Crime," *CNN* (May 30, 1996).

136   See 20 U.S. Code § 7151, "Gun-free requirements."

137   Hillary Rodham Clinton, *Living History* (Simon and Schuster, 2003).

138   Cannon, *supra.*

139   Pierre Thomas and Ann Devroy, "President Clinton to Order Drug Testing for All Arrested on Federal Charges," *The Washington Post* (Dec. 15, 1995).

140   *Id.*

141   John F. Harris, "Clinton Would Link Prison Construction Aid to State Inmate Drug Testing," *The Washington Post* (Sept. 12, 1996).

142   Alison Mitchell, "Clinton Proposes Drug-Testing Plan for Young People," *The New York Times* (Oct. 20, 1996).

143   *Id.*

144   *Id.*

145   "Racially Disproportionate Drug Arrests," *Human Rights Watch* (2000).

146 Ann Devroy, "Clinton Retains Tough Law on Crack Cocaine; Panel's Call to End Disparity In Drug Sentencing Is Rejected," *The Washington Post* (October 31, 1995).

147 Jefferson Morley, "Crack in Black and White: Politics, Profits and Punishment In America's Drug Economy," *The Washington Post* (Nov. 19, 1995).

148 Lyle Denniston, "New law puts heat on crack dealers Clinton signs measure to fight cocaine use," *The Baltimore Sun* (Oct. 31, 1995).

149 Thomas Frank, "Bill Clinton's crime bill destroyed lives, and there's no point denying it," *The Guardian* (April 15, 2016).

150 David G. Savage and Paul Richter, "Clinton to Sign Bill Preserving Stiff Penalties for Crack: It would block a move to treat powdered cocaine violations equally," *The Los Angeles Times* (Oct. 17, 1995).

151 Denniston, *supra*.

152 Savage and Richter, *supra*.

153 William J. Clinton, "Remarks at the University of Texas at Austin" (Oct. 16, 1995).

154 Savage and Richter, *supra*.

155 "Clinton and Crack," *The Washington Post* (Nov. 2, 1995).

156 Wickham, *supra*, at 213.

157 William J. Clinton, "Statement on Signing Legislation Rejecting U.S. Sentencing Commission Recommendations" (Oct. 30, 1995).

158 Wickham, *supra*, at 171.

159 Jefferson Morley, "Crack in Black and White: Politics, Profits and Punishment In America's Drug Economy," *The Washington Post* (Nov. 19, 1995).

160 Steven A. Holmes, "Black Lawmakers Criticize Clinton Over Cocaine Sentencing," *The New York Times* (July 24, 1997).

161 "Bill Clinton Loses His Cool in *Democracy Now!* Interview on Everything But Monica: Leonard Peltier, Racial Profiling, Iraqi Sanctions, Ralph Nader, the Death Penalty and Israel-Palestine," *Democracy Now!* (June 22, 2004).

162 Wickham, *supra*, at 161.

163 Lincoln Caplan, "The Destruction of Defendants' Rights," *The New Yorker* (June 21, 2015).

164   Stephen R. Reinhardt, "The Demise of Habeas Corpus and the Rise of Qualified Immunity: The Court's Ever Increasing Limitations on the Development and Enforcement of Constitutional Rights and Some Particularly Unfortunate Consequences," *Michigan Law Review*, Vol. 113, pp. 1219-1254, 1220 (2015).

165   Emily Bazelon, "The Law That Keeps People on Death Row Despite Flawed Trials," *The New York Times* (July 17, 2015).

166   *Id.*

167   Quoted in Liliana Segura, "Gutting Habeas Corpus: The Inside Story of How Bill Clinton Sacrificed Prisoners' Rights for Political Gain," *The Intercept* (May 4, 2016).

168   Alex Kozinski, "Criminal Law 2.0," *Georgetown Law Journal Annual Review of Criminal Procedure* (2015), p. iii.

169   Quoted in Segura, *supra.*

170   James S. Liebman, Jeffrey Fagan, and Valerie West, "A Broken System: Error Rates in Capital Cases, 1973-1995" (2000), p. i.

171   *Id.*

172   Caplan, *supra.*

173   Ian Head, "Another Clinton-Era Law that Needs to Be Repealed," *The New Republic* (April 18, 2016).

174   "Combating Prisoner Abuse," *The New York Times* (Dec. 20, 2009).

175   James Ridgeway, "Two Clinton-Era Laws That Allow Cruel and Unusual Punishment," *Mother Jones* (Nov. 19, 2010).

176   Amy Howe, "Argument preview: Filing fees and payments under the Prison Litigation Reform Act," *SCOTUSBlog* (Nov. 3, 2015).

177   Catherine Bowman, "Son's Troubles May Cost Woman Her Apartment / She fights "one-strike' policy at S.F. housing projects," *The San Francisco Chronicle* (July 16, 1996).

178   "One Strike Eviction Rule To Be Enforced In Public Housing," *TIME* (March 28, 1996).

179   "Clinton Orders 1-Strike Rule in Public Housing," *The Los Angeles Times* (March 29, 1996).

180   William J. Clinton, "Remarks Announcing the "One Strike and You're Out" Initiative in Public Housing" (March 28, 1996).

181   "Federal 'One-Strike' Legislation," Human Rights Watch (2004).

182   Bowman, *supra*.

183   Wendy J. Kaplan and David Rossman, "Called 'Out' At Home: The One-Strike Eviction Policy and Juvenile Court," *Duke Forum for Law and Social Change,* (Vol. 3, 2011), p. 135.

184   *Id.*

185   *Id.*

186   *HUD v. Rucker*, 535 U.S. 125 (2002)

187   *Rucker v. Davis*, 237 F.3d 1113,1124 (9th Cir. 2001) at 1121.

188   *HUD v. Rucker, supra.*

189   *Id.*

190   Kaplan and Rossman, at 110.

191   *Id.*

192   Timothy Lynch, "Dereliction Of Duty: The Constitutional Record of President Clinton," Cato Policy Analysis No. 271, The Cato Institute (March 31, 1997).

193   "Gun Sweeps: No Model for Cities," *The New York Times* (April 20, 1994).

194   Charles Ogletree and Abbe Smith, "Clinton's Plan Is Misguided," *The New York Times* (May 7, 1994).

195   Leon Neyfakh, "The Clintons Aren't to Blame for Mass Incarceration," *Slate* (Feb. 11, 2016).

196   Chauncey Devega, "Racist then, racist now: The real story of Bill Clinton's crime bill," *Salon* (April 16, 2016).

197   Erik Eckholm, "Prison Rate Was Rising Years Before 1994 Bill," *The New York Times* (April 10, 2016).

198   "Too Little Too Late: President Clinton's Prison Legacy," Center on Juvenile and Criminal Justice (February 2001).

199   Greg Krikorian, "Federal and State Prison Populations Soared Under Clinton, Report Finds," *The Los Angeles Times,* (Feb 19, 2001).

200   *Id.*

201   John Pfaff, "The War on Drugs and Prison Growth: Limited Importance, and Limited Legislative Options," *Harvard Journal on Legislation,* Vol. 52 (2015), pp. 198-200.

202   "Fewer Federal Drug Prosecutions, More Convictions Under Clinton Administration," National Drug Strategy Network (Dec. 1996).

203   "Too Little, Too Late: President Clinton's Prison Legacy," Justice Policy Institute (Feb. 2001).

204 U.S. Constitution, Article II, Section 2.

205 "Pardon Power," The Heritage Guide to the Constitution, The Heritage Foundation.

206 "Thomas Jefferson: Domestic Affairs," Miller Center of Public Affairs, University of Virginia.

207 Leon Neyfakh, "The untapped power of presidential pardons," *The Boston Globe* (March 17, 2013).

208 Margaret Colgate Love, "Twilight of the Pardon Power," 100 J. Crim. L. & Criminology 1169 (2010), at 1178.

209 Neyfakh, *supra* note 191.

210 Josh Gerstein, "Clinton pardon records offer fuel for Hillary's foes," *Politico* (Jan. 28, 2016).

211 *Id.*

212 Dennis Cauchon, "Clinton examines clemency cases Groups seek release of low-level drug offenders," *USA Today* (Dec. 22, 2000).

213 *Id.*

214 Gerstein, *supra.*

215 *Id.*

216 Sonya Ross, "Clinton Pardons More Than 100," *The Washington Post* (Jan 20, 2001).

217 Gerstein, *supra.*

218 Kevin Sack, "Pardoned Couple Say Access Has Served Them Well," *The New York Times* (March 10, 2001).

219 Marc Lacey and Don van Natta, Jr., "Second Clinton In-Law Says He Helped to Obtain Pardon," *The New York Times* (March 3, 2001).

220 Neyfakh, *supra* note 191.

221 "An Indefensible Pardon," *The New York Times* (Jan. 24, 2001).

222 Quoted in Patrick J. Maney, *Bill Clinton: New Gilded Age President* (University Press of Kansas, 2016), p. 261.

223 E.J. Dionne, Jr., "And the Gifts that Keep on Giving," *The Washington Post* (Feb. 6, 2001).

224 *Id.*

225 *Id.*

226 Peter Schweizer, "Bill Clinton's pardon of fugitive Marc Rich continues to pay big," *The New York Post* (Jan 17, 2016).

227   William Jefferson Clinton, "My Reasons for the Pardons,
       The New York Times (Feb. 18, 2001). The day after print-
       ing Clinton's defense of the pardons, *New York Times* was
       compelled to add the following editor's note clarifying that
       Clinton was engaging in some dubious fudging: *An Op-Ed
       article by former President Bill Clinton yesterday about the par-
       dons of Marc Rich and Pincus Green stated erroneously in some
       editions that "the applications were reviewed and advocated" by
       three prominent lawyers, Leonard Garment, William Bradford
       Reynolds and Lewis Libby. Mr. Clinton's office and the lawyers
       are in agreement that none of the three men, former lawyers for
       Mr. Rich, reviewed the pardon applications or advocated for the
       pardons. During the press run, Mr. Clinton's office asked that
       the reference to "applications" be changed to "the case for the
       pardons" to try to clarify Mr. Clinton's point. Even the revised
       wording, however, could be read as leaving the impression that
       the lawyers were involved in the pardon process, which Mr.
       Clinton's spokesmen said was not the intended meaning.*

228   Schweizer, *supra.*

229   Michelle Mark, "Here's what everyone is getting wrong
       about Bill Clinton's 1994 crime reforms," *Business Insider*
       (April 10, 2016).

230   Nathan J. Russell, "An Introduction to the Overton Win-
       dow of Political Possibilities," The Mackinac Center for
       Public Policy, Jan. 4, 2006.

231   Kevin Drum, "Take It Easy on Hillary Clinton and the 1994
       Crime Bill," *Mother Jones* (Jan. 25, 2016).

232   Quoted in Elizabeth Hinton, Julilly Kohler-Hausmann,
       and Vesla M. Weaver, "Did Blacks Really Endorse the 1994
       Crime Bill?" *The New York Times* (April 13, 2016).

233   *Id.*

234   *Id.*

235   "Justice in Focus: The Crime Bill at 20," The Vera Institute.

236   Kweisi Mfume, *No Free Ride: From the Mean Streets to the
       Mainstream* (Random House, 1996), p. 336.

237   Karen Hosler, "Black Caucus yields on crime bill," *The Bal-
       timore Sun* (Aug. 18, 1994).

238   *Id.*

239   Charles P. Pierce, "The Clintons Can Have Their Own
       Opinions, But They Can't Have Their Own History,"
       Esquire (April 13, 2016).

240   Lynne Duke, "Black Leaders Press Action on Crime, Youth,"
       The Washington Post (Jan. 9, 1994).

241 Anthony Lewis and Robert Reno, "Bars put on academic aims," *The Guardian* (Sept. 22, 1994).

242 David C. Baldus, Charles Pulaski, and George Woodworth, "Comparative Review of Death Sentences: An Empirical Study of the Georgia Experience," *Journal of Criminal Law and Criminology*, Vol. 74, No. 3 (Fall 1983), pp. 662-731.

243 *Id.* For summary of the Baldus study, see "Race and the Death Penalty," Capital Punishment in Context, available at http://www.capitalpunishmentincontext.org/issues/race For more detail on race and the death penalty more broadly, see Richard C. Dieter, *The Death Penalty in Black and White*, Death Penalty Information Center (1998).

244 *Id.*

245 David C. Baldus, George Woodworth, David Zuckerman, Neil Alan Weiner& Barbara Broffitt, "Racial Discrimination and the Death Penalty in the Post-*Furman* Era: An Empirical and Legal Overview, With Recent Findings From Philadelphia," *Cornell Law Review*, Vol. 83 (1998), pp. 1643-1770.

246 Maura Dolan, "Study Finds Death Penalty Unevenly Applied," *The Los Angeles Times* (June 4, 1998).

247 *McCleskey v. Kemp*, 481 U.S. 279 (1987), at 315.

248 *Id.*, at 313.

249 David G. Savage, "Supreme Court Report: How Did They Get It So Wrong?" *A.B.A Journal* (Jan. 2009).

250 Quoted in Adam Liptak, "New Look at Death Sentences and Race," *The New York Times* (April 29, 2008).

251 *Id.*

252 *McCleskey, supra,* at 319.

253 Carter, *supra,* at 108.

254 "The Silent White House," *The New York Times,* (July 15, 1994).

255 *Id.*

256 *Id.*

257 Steven A. Holmes, "Blacks Relent on Crime Bill, But Not Without Bitterness," *The New York Times* (Aug. 18, 1994).

258 Alexander, *supra.*

259 Marc Mauer, "Bill Clinton, 'Black Lives' and the Myths of the 1994 Crime Bill," *The Marshall Project* (April 11, 2008).

260 Steven A. Holmes, "Prominent Blacks Meet to Search For an Answer to Mounting Crime," *The New York Times* (Jan. 8, 1994).

261   *Id.*

262   Hinton et. al., *supra.*

263   *Id.*

264   Peter Beinart, "Hillary Clinton and the Tragic Politics of Crime," *The Atlantic* (May 1, 2015).

265   Scher, *supra.*

266   Beinart, *supra.*

267   Kleiman, *supra.*

268   "Teen-age drug use a top campaign issue," *USA Today* (Oct. 25, 1996).

269   Patrick Cockburn, "Crime bill win may not be enough to put Clinton back on top," *The Independent* (Aug. 26, 1994).

270   Quoted in Farley, *supra.*

271   See Jeremy Travis, Bruce Western, and Steve Redburn, eds., *The Growth of Incarceration in the United States: Exploring Causes and Consequences,* Committee on Causes and Consequences of High Rates of Incarceration (National Academies Press, 2014).

272   Segura, *supra.*

273   John L. Worrall and Tomislav V. Kovandzic, "COPS Grants and Crime Revisited," *Criminology,* Vol. 45, Issue 1 (Feb. 2007), pp. 159–190.

274   Quoted in Segura, *supra.*

275   Oliver Roeder, Lauren-Brooke Eisen, and Julia Bowling, "What Caused the Crime Decline?" Brennan Center for Justice (2014).

276   Quoted in "The Crime Bill at 20," Vera Institute.

277   *Id.*

278   Quoted in David Johnston and Tim Weiner, "Seizing the Crime Issue, Clinton Blurs Party Lines," *The New York Times* (Aug. 1, 1996).

279   "Crime Bill at 20," *supra.*

280   David Johnston and Steven A. Holmes, "Experts Doubt Effectiveness Of Crime Bill," *The New York Times* (Sept. 14, 1994).

281   *Id.*

282   Bouie, *supra.*

283   "Teen-age drug use a top campaign issue," *USA Today* (Oct. 25, 1996).

284 Greg Krikorian, "Federal and State Prison Populations Soared Under Clinton, Report Finds," *The Los Angeles Times* (Feb 19, 2001).

285 Thomas Frank, "Bill Clinton's crime bill destroyed lives, and there's no point denying it" (April 15, 2016).

286 Note: One may be dubious that so many facilities can be located in areas such as the Florida Panhandle, which are relatively sparsely populated. But the Florida Department of Corrections confirms on its website that it operates 30 facilities in the northernmost part of Florida alone. See "Information on Florida Prison Facilities," Region 1 and Region 2, http://www.dc.state.fl.us/

287 Quoted in Alexander, *supra.*

288 Jason DeParle, *American Dream: Three Women, Ten Kids, and a Nation's Drive to End Welfare* (Penguin, 2005), p. 3.

289 "Announcement Speech," Bill Clinton for President campaign, Old State House, Little Rock, Arkansas, (October 3, 1991), available at http://www.4president.org/speeches/billclinton1992announcement.htm

290 Brendon O'Connor, *A Political History of the American Welfare System: When Ideas Have Consequences* (Rowman and Littlefield, 2003), p 191.

291 *Id.*, at 195.

292 William J. Clinton, "How We Ended Welfare, Together," *The New York Times* (Aug. 22, 2006).

293 Carter, *supra,* at 171.

294 *Id.*

295 Howard Fineman, Mark Miller, and Joe Klein, "Hillary Clinton, First Lady: The 1993 Newsweek Cover Story," *Newsweek* (April 11, 2015).

296 *Id.*

297 Josh Levin, "The Welfare Queen," *Slate* (Dec. 19, 2013).

298 Carter, *supra,* at 170.

299 Donna Murch, "The Clintons' War on Drugs: When Black Lives Didn't Matter," *The New Republic* (Feb. 9, 2016).

300 *Id.*

301 *Id.*

302 Quoted in Joshua Holland, "How Bill Clinton's Welfare "Reform" Created a System Rife With Racial Biases," *Moyers & Company* (May 12, 2014).

303   *Id.*

304   *Id.*

305   Kenneth J. Neubeck and Noel A. Cazenave, *Welfare Racism: Playing the Race Card against America's Poor* (Routledge, 2001), p. *v.*

306   Thomas Byrne Edsall and Mary D. Edsall, *Chain Reaction: The Impact of Race, Rights, and Taxes on American Politics* (W. W. Norton & Company, 1991), p. 192.

307   "Homeless Families With Children," National Coalition for the Homeless (Aug. 2007).

308   *The Negro Family: The Case For National Action*, Office of Policy Planning and Research, United States Department of Labor (March, 1965).

309   Eduardo Porter, "The Myth of Welfare's Corrupting Influence on the Poor," *The New York Times* (Oct. 20, 2015).

310   Daniel Patrick Moynihan, *Miles to Go: A Personal History of Social Policy* (Harvard University Press, 1996), p. 230.

311   Quoted in Holland, *supra.*

312   *Id.*

313   "Mothers Who Receive AFDC Payments: Fertility and Socioeconomic Characteristics, Economics and Statistics Administration, U.S. Department of Commerce (March, 1995).

314   Hillary Rodham Clinton, *Living History, supra,* at 368.

315   Congressional Record, March 21, 1995.

316   Ben Norton, "John Lewis staunchly opposed the Clintons' gutting of welfare in 1996, yet now endorses Hillary and slams Sanders," *Salon* (Feb. 22, 2016).

317   Conference Report On H.R. 3734, Personal Responsibility And Work Opportunity Reconciliation Act Of 1996.

318   Senate Conference Report Personal Responsibility And Work Opportunity Reconciliation Act (1996).

319   House report, *supra* note 292.

320   Robert A. Moffitt, "The Temporary Assistance for Needy Families Program," in Means-Tested Transfer Programs in the United States (University of Chicago Press, 2003).

321   Francis X. Clines, "Clinton Signs Bill Cutting Welfare; States in New Role," *The New York Times* (Aug. 23, 1996).

322   Robert Reich, "Clinton's Leap in the Dark," *Times Literary Supplement* (Jan. 22, 1999).

323   Marchevsky and Theoharis, *supra.*

324   Peter Edelman, The Worst Thing Bill Clinton Has Done, *The Atlantic* (March 1997).

325   Teddy Davis, "Obama Shifts on Welfare Reform," *ABC News* (July 2, 2008).

326   "Clinton Signs Welfare Reform Bill, Angers Liberals," *CNN* (Aug. 22, 1996).

327   Quoted in Clines, *supra.*

328   Clyde Haberman, "20 Years Later, Welfare Overhaul Resonates for Families and Candidates," *The New York Times* (May 1, 2016).

329   "Impacts of Welfare Reform on Recipients of Housing Assistance: Evidence From Indiana and Delaware," United States Department of Housing and Urban Development (Feb. 2003).

330   "Data Show Welfare Reform Has Been Overwhelmingly Successful," House Ways and Means Committee (July 17, 2012).

331   Christine Kim and Robert Rector, "Welfare Reform Turns Ten: Evidence Shows Reduced Dependence, Poverty," The Heritage Foundation (Aug. 1, 2006.

332   Heather Mac Donald, "Don't Mess With Welfare Reform's Success," *City Journal* (Winter, 2002).

333   Quoted in Alejandra Marchevsky and Jeanne Theoharis, "Why It Matters That Hillary Clinton Championed Welfare Reform," *The Nation* (March 1, 2016).

334   Dylan Matthews, "Welfare reform took people off the rolls. It might have also shortened their lives." *The Washington Post* (June 18, 2013).

335   Haberman, *supra.*

336   "Wellstone Challenges White House Assertion of Welfare Reform 'Success Story'; Cites Disturbing Evidence of Childhood Poverty and Hunger, Dearth of Information on Former Recipients," Press Release, Office of Sen. Paul Wellstone (Aug. 3, 1999).

337   Reich, *supra.*

338   Ife Floyd, Ladonna Pavetti, and Liz Schott, "TANF Continues to Weaken as a Safety Net," Center on Budget and Policy Priorities (Oct. 27, 2015).

339   *Id.*

340   Marchevsky and Theoharis, *supra.*

341 Marianne Bertrand Sendhil Mullainathan, "Are Emily and Greg More Employable than Lakisha and Jamal? A Field Experiment on Labor Market Discrimination" National Bureau of Economic Research Working Paper Series (2003).

342 Diana Spatz, "The End of Welfare as I Knew It," *The Nation* (Dec. 14, 2011).

343 Yonatan Ben-Shalom, Robert Moffitt, and John Karl Scholz, "An Assessment of the Effectiveness of Anti-Poverty Programs in the United States," Institute for Research on Poverty Discussion Paper no. 1392-11 (2010).

344 See Kathryn Edin and Luke Schaefer, *$2.00 a Day: Living on Almost Nothing in America* (Houghton Mifflin Harcourt, 2015).

345 Melinda Henneberger, "Will Hillary Clinton Run Against Her Husband's Welfare Legacy," *Bloomberg News* (May 26, 2015).

346 Amanda Freeman, "Single Moms and Welfare Woes: A Higher-Education Dilemma," *The Atlantic* (Aug. 18, 2015).

347 Floyd et al., *supra.*

348 Marchevsky and Theoharis, *supra.*

349 Eric Levitz, "Bill Clinton Accuses Black Lives Matter Protesters of Defending Murderous Drug Dealers," *New York* (April 7, 2016).

350 *Id.*

351 Quoted in Peter S. Goodman, "From Welfare Shift in '96, a Reminder for Clinton," *The New York Times* (April 11, 2008).

352 "Dole Says Clinton Stole Ideas on Welfare," *St. Louis Post-Dispatch* (May 21, 1996).

353 William J. Clinton, "How We Ended Welfare, Together," *The New York Times* (Aug. 22, 2006).

354 Neubeck and Casavere, *supra,* at *vii.*

355 Quoted in Zaid Jilani, "John Kasich and the Clintons Collaborated on Law That Helped Double Extreme Poverty," *The Intercept* (Feb. 13, 2016).

356 Marchevsky and Theoharis, *supra.*

357 DeParle, *supra,* at 325.

358 *Id.*

359   Quoted in Jilani, *supra.*

360   Joycelyn Elders, *Joycelyn Elders, M.D.: From Sharecropper's Daughter to Surgeon General of the United States of America,* (Thorndike, 1997), p. 90. All basic facts of Elders' life are sourced from her autobiography.

361   *Id.,* at 5.

362   *Id.,* at 54.

363   *Id.,* at 90.

364   *Id.,* at 92.

365   *Id.*

366   *Id.,* at 93.

367   *Id.*

368   *Id.,* at 96-7.

369   "Dr. Joycelyn Elders," Who We Are: Board Members, National Center for Health Housing.

370   Mimi Hall, "Surgeon General nominee 'has that magic power,'" *USA Today* (April 6, 1993).

371   Elders, *supra,* at 223.

372   Paul Hendrickson, "Dr. Elders' Prescription for Battle; Outspoken and Upfront, Here's Clinton's Pick for Surgeon General," *The Washington Post* (Feb. 16, 1993).

373   *Id.*

374   Helen Dewar, "Elders Is Confirmed As Surgeon General; GOP Conservatives Fail to Derail Nomination, *The Washington Post* (Sept. 8, 1993).

375   Hendrickson, *supra.*

376   Dewar, *supra.*

377   Mike Stobbe, *Surgeon General's Warning: How Politics Crippled the Nation's Doctor* (University of California Press, 2014), p. 201

378   *Id.*

379   John Schwartz and Pierre Thomas, "Surgeon General's Son Faces Drug Charges," *The Washington Post* (Dec. 21, 1993).

380   "A Surgeon General's Untimely Candor," *The New York Times* (Dec. 10, 1994).

381   Stobbe, supra, at 207.

382   Joshua Green, "Former surgeon general Everett Koop: An unsung hero in the fight against AIDS," *The Washington Post* (February 27, 2013).

383   Stobbe, *supra,* at 207.

384   *Id.*

385   Fiona Morgan, "Dr. Joycelyn Elders, former U.S. Surgeon General," *IndyWeek* (June 24, 2008).

386   Angie Cannon, Vanessa Gallman and Steven Thomma, "Surgeon General Is Fired: Joycelyn Elders Has Been Controversial. Her Remark On Masturbation Was The Last Straw," *The Philadelphia Inquirer* (Dec. 10, 1994).

387   Claudia Dreifus, "Joycelyn Elders," *The New York Times* (Jan. 30, 1994).

388   Joycelyn Elders, Speech to the 142nd Meeting of the American Public Health Association (2014), available at https://www.youtube.com/watch?v=bzORS85svqE

389   Cannon et al., *supra.*

390   Quoted in "Wisdom Watch: Dr. Joycelyn Elders," *NPR* (May 30, 2007).

391   Stobbe, *supra,* at 207.

392   Hendrickson, *supra.*

393   Cannon et al., *supra.*

394   Elders, *supra,* at 335.

395   "Genii Guinier, 91, Civil Rights Champion," *Vineyard Gazette,* Aug. 27, 2009,

396   *Id.*

397   *Id.*

398   Carter, *supra,* at 68.

399   Clint Bolick, "Clinton's Quota Queens," *The Wall Street Journal* (April 30, 1993).

400   Carter, *supra,* at 77.

401   Lani Guinier, "Second Proms and Second Primaries: The Limits of Majority Rule," *Boston Review* (Sept./Oct. 1992).

402   Lani Guinier, *Lift Every Voice: Turning a Civil Rights Setback into a New Vision of Social Justice* (Simon and Schuster, 2003), p. 28.

403   William T. Coleman Jr., "Three's Company: Guinier, Reagan, Bush," *The New York Times* (June 4, 1993).

404   "The Lani Guinier Mess," *The New York Times* (June 5, 1993).

405   Michael Isikoff, "Confirmation Battle Looms Over Guinier," *The Washington Post* (May 21, 1993).

406   *Id.*

407   Carter, *supra,* at 89.

408   Guinier, *Lift Every Voice,* at 111.

409   Neil A. Lewis, "Aids Say Clinton Will Drop Nominee For Post On Rights," *The New York Times* (June 3, 1993).

410   Carter, *supra,* at 89.

411   Guinier, *Lift Every Voice,* at 116.

412   Carter, *supra,* at 91.

413   "Transcript of President Clinton's Announcement on the Nomination of Lani Guinier" (June 4, 1993).

414   Quoted in Lewis, *supra.*

415   Guinier, *Lift Every Voice,* at 125.

416   Hanna Rosin, "State of Withdrawal," *The New York Times* (April 12, 1998).

417   Steven A. Holmes, "On Civil Rights, Clinton Steers Bumpy Course Between Right and Left," *The New York Times* (Oct. 20, 1996).

418   Stephen Labaton, "Abandoned By Clinton, She Finds Acceptance," *The New York Times* (July 14, 1993).

419   Randall Kennedy, "Lani Guinier's Constitution," *The American Prospect* (Fall 1993).

420   Michael Kelly, "Ideology Seems to Doom Cabinet Contender," *The New York Times* (Dec. 17, 1992).

421   Kennedy, *supra.*

422   "The Lani Guinier Mess," *supra.*

423   Carter, *supra,* at 91.

424   *Id.,* at 87,

425   Lewis, *supra.*

426   "Interview: General Romeo Dallaire," Ghosts of Rwanda, *Frontline.*

427   The account of Rusesabagina's activities is taken from Philip Gourevitch, *We Wish To Inform You That Tomorrow With Our Families: Stories From Rwanda* (Picador, 1999).

428   Romeo Dallaire, *Shake Hands with the Devil: The Failure of Humanity in Rwanda* (Da Capo, 2004), p. 382.

429   Longman, *supra.*

430   William J. Clinton, Remarks at the Dedication Ceremony of the United States Holocaust Museum (April 22, 1993).

431   Samantha Power, *A Problem From Hell: America and the Age of Genocide* (Basic Books, 2002), *xxi*.

432   Samantha Power, "Bystanders to Genocide," *The Atlantic* (Sept. 2001).

433   "Text of Clinton's Rwanda Speech," Associated Press (1998).

434   For a comprehensive history of the events of the Rwanda, see Alison Des Forges, *Leave None to Tell The Story*, Human Rights Watch (1999).

435   "Text of Clinton's Rwanda Speech," *supra*.

436   Colum Lynch, "Rwanda Revisited," *Foreign Policy* (April 5, 2016).

437   *Id.*

438   "Prime Minister Slain in Rwanda Rampage," *St. Louis Post-Dispatch* (April 8, 1994).

439   "Leaders' Deaths Spark Blood Bath in Rwanda," *Reuters* (April 8, 1994).

440   Thaddee Nsengiyaremye, "Hundreds die as tribal violence sweeps Rwanda," *Reuters* (April 8, 1994).

441   Robert Pear, "U.S. Envoy in Rwanda Decides on Overland Convoy to Evacuate Americans," *The New York Times* (April 10, 1994).

442   William J. Clinton, Presidential Radio Address (April 10, 1994).

443   Allan Thompson, The Media and the Rwanda Genocide (Pluto, 2007), p. 199.

444   Jerry Gray, "Two Nations Joined By Common History of Genocide," *The New York Times* (April 9, 1994).

445   William E. Schmidt, "Refugee Missionaries From Rwanda Speak of their Terror, Grief, and Guilt," *The New York Times* (April 12, 1994).

446   Hugh McCullum, "Shaken Canadians arrive in Nairobi from Rwanda Head of Canadian mission weeps over African colleague's fate in ethnic bloodbath," *The Globe and Mail* (April 12, 1994).

447   Donatella Lorch, "U.N. in Rwanda Says It Is Powerless to Halt the Violence," *The New York Times* (April 15, 1994).

448   Irwin Block, "Don't abandon us, Rwandan exile pleads," *The Gazette* (April 16, 1994).

449   "So That The World Does Not Forget Rwanda," *The Washington Post* (April 24, 1994).

450   Jennifer Parmelee, "Fade to Blood," *The Washington Post* (April 24, 1994).

451   "Massacre in Rwanda; where's the outrage?" *USA Today* (May 2, 1994).

452   Des Forges, *supra,* at 970.

453   Quoted in Michael Takiff, *A Complicated Man: The Life of Bill Clinton as Told by Those Who Know Him* (Yale University Press, 2011).

454   Quoted in "The Triumph of Evil," *PBS Frontline* (Jan. 26, 1999).

455   *Id.*

456   *Id.*

457   Rory Carroll, "U.S. chose to ignore Rwanda genocide," *The Guardian* (March 31, 2004).

458   *Id.*

459   *Id.*

460   Lynch, *supra.*

461   Jared Cohen, *One Hundred Days of Silence: America and the Rwanda Genocide* (Rowman and Littlefield, 2006), p. 136.

462   Triumph of Evil, *supra.*

463   *Id.*

464   *Id.*

465   *Id.*

466   Carroll, *supra.*

467   Power, "Bystanders," *supra.*

468   Takiff, *supra,* at 206.

469   Lynch, *supra.*

470   Paul Lewis, "U.N. Backs Troops for Rwanda But Terms Bar Any Action Soon" *The New York Times* (May 17, 1994).

471   "1994 Rwanda Pullout Driven by Clinton White House, U.N. Equivocation," National Security Archive Electronic Briefing Book No. 511, National Security Archive at George Washington University (April 16, 2015).

472   Tim Weiner, "Clinton in Africa: The Blood Bath; Critics Say U.S. Ignored C.I.A. Warnings of Genocide in Rwanda," *The New York Times* (March 26, 1998).

473   *Id.*

474   Triumph of Evil, *supra.*

475   Pear, *supra.*

476   William J. Clinton, Remarks at the United States Naval Academy Commencement Ceremony in Annapolis, Maryland (May 25, 1994).

477   Dick Morris and Eileen McGann, *Because He Could* (Harper, 2005), p. 64.

478   Power, "Bystanders," *supra.*

479   Longman, *supra.*

480   Power, "Bystanders," *supra.*

481   Dana Hughes, "Bill Clinton Regrets Rwanda Now (Not So Much in 1994)," *ABC News* (Feb. 28, 2014).

482   Alice Gatabuke and Claude Gatabuke, "On This Anniversary of Rwandan Genocide, Bill Clinton's Words Ring Hollow," *The Huffington Post* (April 13, 2016).

483   "Triumph of Evil," *supra.*

484   *Id.*

485   Quoted in *Humo,* no. 3365 (March 1, 2005).

486   "Estimated and Projected Deaths Due to AIDS by Region, 1980-2030," in John Bongaarts, François Pelletier, and Patrick Gerland, "Global Trends in Aids Morality," Population Council Working Paper No. 16 (2009), p. 16.

487   William W. Fisher III and Cyrill P. Rigamonti, "The South Africa AIDS Controversy: A Case Study in Patent Law and Policy," Harvard Law School case study (Feb. 10, 2005), p. 3.

488   *Id.*

489   Craig Timberg, "Mandela Says AIDS Led to Death of Son," *The Washington Post* (Jan. 7, 2005).

490   Donald G. McNeil, Jr., "South Africa's Bitter Pill for World's Drug Makers," *The New York Times* (March 29, 1998).

491   Ian Murphy, "The 9 Most Loathsome Lobbyists," *The Progressive* (July 12, 2012).

492   "Podesta Group," OpenSecrets.org, Center for Responsive Politics.

493   Pieter Fourie, *Turning Dread into Capital: South Africa's AIDS Diplomacy,* Center for Strategic and International Studies (June, 2012), p. 12.

494   Marcia Angell, *The Truth About the Drug Companies: How They Deceive Us and What to Do About It* (Random House, 2005), p. 206.

495   Simon Barber, "U.S. Withholds Benefits Over Zuma's Bill," *Africa News* (July 15, 1998).

496   Reginald Dale, "Super 301: A Trade 'Monster' It Isn't," *The New York Times* (April 9, 1993).

497   "Drugs for AIDS in Africa," *The New York Times* (August 23, 1999).

498   Ed Vulliamy, "How drug giants let millions die," *The Observer* (Dec. 19, 1999).

499   *Id.*

500   "Drugs for AIDS in Africa," *supra.*

501   Julian Borger, "Gore accused of working against cheap drugs," *The Guardian* (Aug. 10, 1999).

502   Angell, *supra,* at 206.

503   "Clinton Aims to Get Africa More AIDS-Drugs Access," *Wall Street Journal* (May 11, 2000).

504   J. Stephen Morrison and Jennifer G. Cooke, *Africa Policy in the Clinton Years: Critical Choices for the Bush Administration,* Center for Strategic and International Studies (2001).

505   Ethan Wallison, "Clinton Backs Bill For Giving Africa Trade Preferences," *The Chicago Tribune* (June 18, 1998).

506   William J. Clinton, Opening Remarks at the National Summit on Africa, Washington Convention Center, Washington, D.C., (February 17, 2000).

507   Shepard Forman and Stewart Patrick, eds., *Good Intentions: Pledges of Aid for Postconflict Recovery* (Center on International Cooperation Studies in Multilateralism, 2000), p. 302.

508   Alison Mitchell, "Clinton Proposes Incentives for Free Market in Africa," *The New York Times* (June 18, 1997).

509   *Id.*

510   Mimi Hall, "'Trade, not aid' in Africa; To executives, trip is business—and more," *USA Today* (March 30, 1998).

511   Mary Dejevsky Washinthon, "Clinton to offer Africa a new deal," *The Independent* (June 18, 1997).

512   Alec Russell, "A cool reception awaits Clinton in South Africa: President Nelson Mandela is determined to show that he can't be pushed around," *The Vancouver Sun* (March 26, 1998).

513 Steven Greenhouse, "Administration Is Faulted Over Conference on Africa," *The New York Times* (June 27, 1994).

514 Alec Russell, "South Africans cool on Clinton," *Hamilton Spectator* (March 26, 1998).

515 Eric Pianin, "Gates Gives Clinton Administration a Low Grade on Foreign Aid," *The Fiscal Times* (March 13, 2014).

516 "Mandela off U.S. terrorism watch list," *CNN* (July 2, 2008).

517 "U.S. shamed by Mandela terror link," *BBC News* (April 10, 2008).

518 Eugene Robinson, "George W. Bush's greatest legacy—his battle against AIDS," *The Washington Post* (July 26, 2012).

519 *Id.*

520 *Id.*

521 Quoted in Celia W. Dugger, "Clinton revels in post-presidential life," *The New York Times* (Aug. 28, 2006).

522 *El-Shifa Pharmaceutical Industries Co. v. United States*, 607 F.3d 836 (D.C. Cir. 2010).

523 Scott Peterson, "Sudanese factory destroyed by US now a shrine," *The Christian Science Monitor* (Aug. 7, 2012).

524 *Id.*

525 Timothy Noah, "Khartoum Revisited, Part 2," *Slate* (March 31, 2004).

526 *Id.*

527 Richard Bernstein and *The New York Times* staff, *Out of the Blue: A Narrative of September 11, 2001* (Times Books, 2002), p. 119.

528 James Risen, "To Bomb Sudan Plant, or Not: A Year Later, Debates Rankle," *The New York Times* (Oct. 27, 1999).

529 *Id.*

530 James Astill, "Strike One," *The Guardian* (Oct. 2, 2001).

531 Noah, *supra.*

532 "Letter to President Clinton Urges Sudan Factory Inspection," Human Rights Watch (Sept. 15, 1998).

533 *Id.*

534 Risen, *supra.*

535 *El-Shifa Pharm. Indus. Co. v. United States*, 55 Fed. Cl. 751, 774 (2003).

536 Astill, *supra.*

537 Werner Daum, "Universalism and the West: An Agenda for Understanding," *Harvard International Review* (Summer 2001).

538 Jonathan Belke, "Year later, U.S. attack on factory still hurts Sudan," *The Boston Globe* (Aug. 22, 1999).

539 Risen, *supra.*

540 "'Disbelief' at Patrick Karegeya death in South Africa," *BBC News* (Jan 17. 2014), clip available at https://www.youtube.com/watch?v=PHRW7z2-ej8

541 David Smith, "Rwanda's former spy chief 'murdered' in South Africa," *The Guardian* (Jan. 2, 2014).

542 Rob Walker, "Rwanda government denies link to assassinations," *BBC News* (Aug. 5, 2010).

543 Nicholas Bariyo, "President Kagame Says Rwandan Dissidents Will 'Pay the Price,'" *The Wall Street Journal* (Jan. 13, 2014).

544 "Rwandan Ambassador to UK on murder of Karegeya," *BBC* (2014), clip available at https://www.youtube.com/watch?v=DL7s22dtByI

545 Aislinn Laing, "Rwanda's president Paul Kagame 'wishes' he had ordered death of exiled spy chief," *The Telegraph* (Jan. 24, 2014).

546 Ambassador interview, *supra.*

547 Marian Tupy, "Bill Clinton's 'New Generation' of African Leaders Mostly Still Around in 2016," *Reason* (Feb. 2, 2016).

548 "The Rwandan Patriotic Front," in Des Forges, *supra.*

549 "Democratic Republic of the Congo 1993-2003," Report of the United Nations Human Rights Commissioner (2010), p. 14.

550 "Rwanda: Allow Human Rights Watch to Work," Human Rights Watch (April 23, 2010).

551 Ian Birrell, Darling of the West, terror to his opponents: Meet Rwanda's new scourge - Paul Kagame," *The Independent* (Jan. 3, 2014).

552 Howard W. French, "The Case Against Rwanda's President Paul Kagame," *Newsweek* (Jan. 14, 2013).

553 Haroon Siddique, "Rwandan exiles warned of assassination threat by London police," *The Guardian* (May 20, 2011).

554   Kevin Sack and Sheri Fink, "Rwanda Aid Shows Reach and Limits of Clinton Foundation," *The New York Times* (Oct. 18, 2015).

555   *Id.*

556   Filip Reyntjens, Political Governance in Post-Genocide Rwanda (Cambridge University Press, 2015), p. 98.

557   "20 minutes with Bill Clinton - up against 'big poppa,'" *BBC News* (Aug. 12, 2013).

558   Dana Goldstein, "Bill Clinton's Rwanda Guilt," *The Daily Beast* (Sept. 23, 2010).

559   *Id.*

560   Sack and Fink, *supra.*

561   "20 minutes with Bill Clinton," *supra.*

562   Sack and Fink, *supra.*

563   *Id.*

564   Xan Rice, "Rwandan opposition leader found dead," *The Guardian* (July 14, 2010).

565   Birrell, *supra.*

566   David Smith, "Paul Kagame's Rwanda: African success story or authoritarian state?," *The Guardian* (Oct. 10, 2012).

567   Paul Rusesabagina, "Hotel Rwanda's Rusesabagina cautions President Clinton regarding Rwanda," *San Francisco Bay-View* (July 31, 2012).

568   Peter Baker, "Bush a Fond Presence in Africa for Work During and Since His Presidency," *The New York Times* (July 2, 2013).

569   Carol Felsenthal, *Clinton in Exile: A President Out of the White House* (Harper, 2008), p. 295.

570   *Id.,* at 278.

571   *Id.,* at 163.

572   Sack and Fink, *supra.*

573   *Id.*

574   Jonathan Rauch, "This is Not Charity," *The Atlantic* (Oct., 2007).

575   *Id.*

576   Nicholas Confessore and Amy Chozick, "Unease at Clinton Foundation Over Finances and Ambitions," *The New York Times* (Aug. 13, 2013).

577   Rauch, *supra*.

578   Quoted in Isabel Vincent, "Charity watchdog: Clinton Foundation a 'slush fund,'" *The New York Post* (April 26, 2015).

579   Jonathan Rauch, "This is Not Charity," *The Atlantic* (Oct., 2007).

580   Vincent, *supra*.

581   Louis Jacobson, "Rush Limbaugh says Clinton Foundation spends just 15 percent on charity, 85 percent on overhead," *PunditFact* (April 29, 2015).

582   "Clinton Health Access Initiative (CHAI)," GiveWell Charity Research (Nov. 2012).

583   "Clinton Foundation: Standards Not Met," Better Business Bureau Wise Giving Alliance (May 2016).

584   Maggie Haberman, "Clinton Foundation reports spike in travel expenses," *Politico* (Nov. 19, 2014); Evan Halper, "Behind a Bill Clinton speaking engagement: A $1,400 hotel phone bill and $700 dinner for two," *The Los Angeles Times* (July 11, 2016).

585   Confessore and Chozick, *supra*.

586   Cameron Joseph, "Bill Clinton received $500K 'quid pro quo' donation to Clinton Foundation by speaking at 2014 Happy Hearts charity gala," *The New York Daily News* (May 30, 2015).

587   Takiff, *supra*, at 409.

588   Ann M. Simmons, "Haiti's troubled succession of leaders: 'They don't really want to work for the Haitian people,'" *The Los Angeles Times* (Feb. 18, 2016).

589   "Haiti 1991-1994: Death Squads and State Violence Under the Military Regime," Center for Justice and Accountability.

590   David W. Haines, *Refugees in America in the 1990s: A Reference Handbook* (Greenwood, 1996) p. 182.

591   See Barry Sautman, "The Meaning of "Well-Founded Fear of Persecution" in United States Asylum Law and in International Law, *Fordham Law Journal*, Vol. 9, Issue 3 (1985), pp. 483-589.

592   "Bush Orders Coast Guard to Intercept Haitian Boats," *Associated Press* (May 25, 1992).

593   "U.S. Processing of Haitian Asylum Seekers," United States General Accounting Office, GA 1.5/2 T-NSIAD 92-25 (Apr. 1992).

594   Marc A. Thiessen, "The Clinton solution for refugees: Guantanamo," *The Washington Post* (Nov. 23, 2015).

595   Elaine Sciolino, "Clinton Says U.S. Will Continue Ban on Haitian Exodus," *The New York Times* (Jan. 15, 1993).

596   *Id.*

597   Christopher Marquis and Robert A. Rankin, "Clinton Extends Bush Policy On Haitians Refugees Are To Be Turned Back. In The Campaign, Clinton Pledged To Lift Bush's Order Immediately." *The Philadelphia Inquirer* (Jan 15, 1993).

598   *Id.*

599   Mfume, *supra,* at 321.

600   *Id.*

601   Sciolino, *supra.*

602   Michael Ratner, "How We Closed the Guantanamo HIV Camp: The Intersection of Politics and Litigation," *Harvard Human Rights Journal,* Vol. 11 (1998), p. 195.

603   Brandt Goldstein, "Clinton's Guantanamo: How the Democratic president set the stage for a land without law," *Slate* (Dec. 21, 2005).

604   Paul Farmer, *The Uses of Haiti* (Common Courage, 3rd edition, 2005), p. 233.

605   Lizzy Ratner, "The Legacy of Guantánamo," *The Nation* (July 21, 2003).

606   *Id.*

607   Farmer, *supra,* at 229.

608   *Id.,* at 233.

609   *Id.,* at 230.

610   Quoted in Ratner, "The Legacy of Guantánamo," *supra.*

611   Quoted in Philip J. Hilts, "U.S. Denies Appeal for 4 Ill Haitians," *The New York Times* (Dec. 13, 1992).

612   Quoted in Ratner, "The Legacy of Guantánamo," *supra.*

613   *Id.*

614   *Id.*

615   Good Advice For Haitian Refugees: Go Home And Help Rebuild Nation," *The Miami Sun-Sentinel* (Dec. 31, 1994).

616   Goldstein, *supra.*

617   Allan Nairn, "Haiti Under the Gun," *The Nation* (Jan. 8/15, 1996).

618   William I. Robinson, *Promoting Polyarchy: Globalization, US Intervention, and Hegemony,* p. 304.

619 Anne-Christine D'Adesky, "As Tensions Swirl in Haiti, Just What is the U.S. Role," *The Los Angeles Times* (Oct. 9, 1994).

620 *Id.*

621 "U.S. Urged to Return Seized Haitian Documents," Human Rights Watch (Nov. 3, 1999).

622 *Id.*

623 Juan Gonzalez, "Bill Sits on Hot Haiti Files," *The New York Daily News* (May 3, 1996).

624 "U.S. Urged to Return Seized Haitian Documents," *supra.*

625 Christopher S. Wren, "U.S. Soldiers Agree to Return Documents Confiscated in Haiti," *The New York Times* (Dec. 7, 1995).

626 Colum Lynch, "U.S. Pressured to Surrender Secret Files of Haitian Militia," *The Washington Post* (Nov. 6, 1999).

627 Wren, *supra.*

628 "Haiti: Different Coup, Same Paramilitary Leaders," *Democracy Now!* (Feb. 26, 2004).

629 *Id.*

630 D'Adesky, *supra.*

631 Allan Nairn, "Our Man in FRAPH," *The Nation* (Oct. 24, 1994).

632 Nancy Cochrane, Nathan Childs, and Stacey Rosen, "Haiti's U.S. Rice Imports," United States Department of Agriculture Economic Research Service (Feb. 2016).

633 "Riceland Foods," *The Encyclopedia of Arkansas History and Culture* (April 7, 2016).

634 Maura R. O'Connor, "Subsidizing Starvation: How American tax dollars are keeping Arkansas rice growers fat on the farm and starving millions of Haitians," *Foreign Policy* (Jan. 11, 2013).

635 *Id.*

636 *Id.*

637 *Id.*

638 Sullivan and Heldeman, *supra.*

639 Daniel Griswold, "Grain Drain: The Hidden Cost of U.S. Rice Subsidies," The Cato Institute, Trade Briefing Paper No. 25 (Nov. 16, 2006).

640 O'Connor, *supra.*

641   "Haiti: Selected Issues," International Monetary Fund, IMF Staff Country Report No. 01/04 (Jan. 2001).

642   "Kicking down the door: How upcoming WTO talks threaten farmers in poor countries," Oxfam International Briefing Paper (2005), p. 3.

643   O'Connor, *supra*.

644   Leonard Doyle, "Starving Haitians riot as food prices soar," *The Independent* (April 9, 2008).

645   Forrest Laws, "Riceland: 'Friendlier' rice prices in 2007-08," *Delta Farm Press* (Nov. 21, 2007).

646   J. Regan, "Some areas really miss tariffs," *Miami Herald* (October 3, 2003).

647   O'Connor, *supra*.

648   Jim Dexter, "Fact Check: Do U.S. food policies contribute to Haiti's poverty?" *CNN* (Jan. 27, 2010).

649   *Id.*

650   "Haiti's poor resort to eating mud as prices rise," *NBC News* (Jan. 29, 2008).

651   Bill Clinton, *My Life*, p. 313.

652   Dana Hughes, "Bill and Hillary Share Romantic Moment In Haiti," *ABC News* (Oct. 23, 2012).

653   Jonathan M. Katz, "The King and Queen of Haiti," *Politico* (May 4, 2015).

654   Karen Attiah, Hillary Clinton needs to answer for her actions in Honduras and Haiti," *The Washington Post* (March 10, 2016).

655   "Many Haitians See Bill Clinton Appointment as Setting Up Protectorate," Hillary Clinton Email Archive, *WikiLeaks,* (June 4, 2009).

656   Katz, *supra*.

657   *Id.*

658   "WikiLeaks Haiti: The Nation Partners With Haïti Liberté on Release of Secret Haiti Cables," *The Nation* (June 1, 2011).

659   Linda Qiu, "Did Hillary Clinton's State Department help suppress the minimum wage in Haiti?" *PolitiFact* (April 17, 2016).

660   Ryan Chittum, "A Pulled Scoop Shows U.S. Fought to Keep Haitian Wages Down," *The Columbia Journalism Review* (June 3, 2011).

661   Brooke Binkowski, "Haitian Wages," *Snopes* (April 5, 2016).

662   Katz, *supra.*

663   Paul Collier, "Haiti: From Natural Catastrophe to Economic Security, A Report for the Secretary-General of the United Nations" (January 2009).

664   Katz, *supra.*

665   Quoted in Ansel Herz, "The Clinton Bush Haiti Fund is Lying to You," *The Huffington Post* (May 25, 2011).

666   *Id.*

667   Ansel Herz, "Insult to injury: Cholera has Haiti reeling, and Bill Clinton & Anderson Cooper haven't done enough," *The New York Daily News* (Nov. 1, 2010).

668   Jonathan M. Katz, "In the Time of Cholera: How the U.N. created an epidemic—then covered it up," *Foreign Policy* (Jan. 10, 2013).

669   "A year of indecision leaves Haiti's recovery at a standstill," Oxfam International (Jan. 6, 2011).

670   Sal Gentile, "Report criticizes Haiti recovery commission led by Bill Clinton," *PBS* (Jan. 7, 2011).

671   Mary Anastasia O'Grady, "Bill, Hillary and the Haiti Debacle," *The Wall Street Journal* (May 18, 2014).

672   Jake Johnston, "Outsourcing Haiti," *Boston Review* (Jan. 16, 2014).

673   "Haiti Reconstruction: USAID Infrastructure Projects Have Had Mixed Results and Face Sustainability Challenges," Report to Congressional Requesters, United States Government Accountability Office (June 2013).

674   Kevin Sullivan and Rosalyn S. Helderman, "How the Clintons' Haiti development plans succeed—and disappoint," *The Washington Post* (March 20, 2015).

675   *Id.*

676   Katz, *supra.*

677   Sullivan and Helderman, *supra.*

678   "Clinton Foundation Accused of Sending Haiti Shoddy Trailers Found Toxic After Katrina," *Democracy Now!* (July 12, 2011).

679   Isabel Macdonald and Isabeau Doucet, "The Shelters That Clinton Built," *The Nation* (July 11, 2011).

680   *Id.*

681   Rick Cohen, "Clinton Foundation Charged with Providing Shoddy and Dangerous Emergency Shelters in Haiti," *Nonprofit Quarterly* (July 20, 2011). In an investigation by the Center for Public Integrity, *The Seattle Times*, and *BuzzFeed*, Buffett's Clayton Homes has also been accused of racially biased predatory lending practices. According to the investigation, Clayton Homes "systematically pursues unwitting minority homebuyers and baits them into costly subprime loans, many of which are doomed to fail." See Mike Baker and Daniel Wagner, "Minorities exploited by Warren Buffett's mobile-home empire," *The Seattle Times* (Jan. 13, 2016) and Mike Baker and Daniel Wagner, "The mobile-home trap: How a Warren Buffett empire preys on the poor," *The Seattle Times* (April 2, 2015).

682   Macdonald and Doucet, *supra.*

683   Deborah Sontag, "Earthquake Relief Where Haiti Wasn't Broken," *The New York Times* (July 5, 2012).

684   Sullivan and Helderman, *supra.*

685   Sontag, *supra.*

686   Andres Schipani, "Haiti's economy held together by polo shirts and blue jeans," *Financial Times* (April 17, 2015).

687   Katz, *supra.*

688   Jonathan M. Katz, "A glittering industrial park in Haiti falls short," *Al Jazeera America* (Sept. 10, 2013).

689   Sullivan and Helderman, *supra.*

690   Nicola Luksic and Tom Powell, "Haiti shows how wealthy countries 'continue to cause disaster,'" *CBC News* (Sept. 15, 2015).

691   Katz, *supra.*

692   Johnston, *supra.*

693   Janet Reitman, "How the World Failed Haiti," *Rolling Stone* (Aug. 4, 2011).

694   *Id.*

695   Allan Smith, "Chelsea Clinton wrote 'Dad' and 'Mom' an email about the incompetence of the Haitian relief effort," *Business Insider* (Sept. 1, 2014).

696   Jonathan M. Katz, "The Clintons' Haiti Screw-Up, As Told By Hillary's Emails," *Politico* (Sept. 2, 2015).

697   Vijaya Ramachandran and Sneha Raghavan, "Haiti Quake: Four Years Later, We Still Don't Know Where the Money Has Gone," Center for Global Development (Jan. 7, 2014).

698   Johnston, *supra*.

699   Mark Thompson, "The U.S. Military in Haiti: A Compassionate Invasion," *TIME* (Jan. 16, 2010).

700   Katz, "King and Queen of Haiti," *supra*.

701   *Id*.

702   Olivier Laurent, "Haiti Earthquake: Five Years After," *TIME* (Jan. 12, 2015).

703   O'Connor, *supra*.

704   O'Grady, *supra*.

705   Sullivan and Helderman, *supra*.

706   Kevin Sullivan and Rosalind S. Helderman, "Role of Hillary Clinton's brother in Haiti gold mine raises eyebrows," *The Washington Post* (March 20, 2015).

707   Sullivan and Helderman, "How the Clintons' Haiti Plans…" *supra*.

708   Katz, "King and Queen of Haiti," *supra*.

709   The factual assertions and quotations in this chapter are collected from several sources. Primarily, they are from Marshall Frady, "Death in Arkansas," *The New Yorker* (Feb. 22, 1993). Frady collects most of the important details about Rector's life and death, and his article is strongly recommended for those seeking more detail on the execution. Several other sources of information were used in preparing this chapter. These were: Peter Applebome, "Arkansas Execution Raises Questions on Governor's Politics," *The New York Times* (Jan. 25, 1992); Christopher Olgiati, "The White House Via Death Row: At a key moment in his presidential campaign, Bill Clinton had to decide whether a convicted murderer with brain damage should live or die. To prove his toughness, the anxious candidate chose death for him," *The Guardian* (Oct. 12, 1993). Rector's name has been listed variously as "Ricky" and "Rickey"; I follow Frady in using "Rickey."

710   Hillary Rodham Clinton, *It Takes a Village* (Simon and Schuster, 2006), p. 52.

711   *Id*.

712   Applebome, *supra*.

713   *Id*.

714   Quoted in Frady, *supra*.

715   Quoted in Olgiati, *supra*.

716   Sharon LaFraniere, "Governor's Camp Feels His Record on Crime Can Stand the Heat," *The Washington Post* (Oct. 5, 1992).

717   "Fraternal Order of Police to Endorse Clinton," *The New York Times* (Sept. 16, 1996).

718   Information about the Hill case taken from the following sources: "Killer Executed After Clinton Denies Clemency," *The New York Times* (May 8, 1992); *Hill v. Lockhart* 927 F.2d 340 (1991); Lt. Dempsie Coffman, *Arkansas State Troopers: A Breed Apart* (Xlibris, 2005), p. 119.

719   Quoted in Linda Diebel, "Admirers say he's 'very bright' the right man for the times. Critics call him 'Slick Willy,' the consummate yuppie. But why, when he's on the verge of becoming U.S. president, are people still wondering: Who is Bill Clinton?" *The Toronto Star* (Oct. 25, 1992).

720   Carter, *supra,* at 96.

721   Christopher Hitchens interviewed by Charlie Rose (April 28, 1999), available at https://www.youtube.com/watch?v=S_RqyXT5bt4

722   *Id.*

723   Guinier, *Lift Every Voice, supra,* at 122.

724   Takiff, *supra,* at 417.

725   Wickham, *supra,* at 64.

726   *Id.,* at 97.

727   *Id.,* at 40.

728   *Id., at* 112.

729   Melissa Harris-Lacewell and Bethany Albertson, "Good Times? Understanding African American Misperceptions of Racial Economic Fortunes," *Journal of Black Studies,* vol. 35 no. 5 (May 2005), pp. 650-683.

730   Melissa Harris-Lacewell, "The Clinton Fallacy: Did blacks really make big economic gains during the 90's," *Slate* (Jan. 24, 2008).

731   "How Groups Voted," The Roper Center for Public Opinion Research, Cornell University.

732   Wickham, *supra,* at 93.

733   Quoted in Bill Nichols, "For some blacks, Guinier case part of a pattern," *USA Today* (June 8, 1993).

734   "'Slick Willie' Rides Again?" *The Crisis* (Aug.-Sept. 1993).

735   Toni Morrison, "Comment," *The New Yorker* (Oct. 5, 1998).

736   Kevin Alexander Gray, "Clinton and Black Americans," in *Dime's Worth of Difference,* Alexander Cockburn and Jeffrey St. Clair, eds. (AK Press, 2004), p 96.

737   This was inaccurate in two ways: (1) because anyone who thinks Clinton was treated like black men are treated does not know how black men are treated, and (2) because as Jesse Jackson, Jr. pointed out, in the strictly Morrisonian sense of being unfairly persecuted by the right, Lincoln was the first black president.

738   Wickham, *supra,* at 128.

739   *Id.* at 96.

740   *Id.* at 111.

741   Alexander Cockburn, "Bill Clinton, Puppy Dog of Neo-liberalism: For those who think the free-trade agreement is disastrous, Perot is the man.," *The Los Angeles Times* (Oct 25, 1992).

742   Fred Barnes, "The Perils of Me-Too-ism," *The Weekly Standard* (June 10, 1996). Barnes described how the "me too" strategy threw off Republicans by so completely abandoning all Democratic principles: *[Clinton] flummoxed Republicans by saying he would agree to sign a bill letting states bar gay marriage. He devilishly upstaged Bob Dole, his GOP rival, by seeming to endorse a conservative welfare reform plan in Wisconsin authored by Republican governor Tommy Thompson. And he surprised even many of his supporters by echoing Republican attacks on a liberal federal judge he had appointed.*

743   Steven Thomma and Vanessa Gallman, "Dole Speech Will Try to Reclaim Welfare as GOP Issue," *The Philadelphia Inquirer* (May 21, 1996).

744   Alison Mitchell, "Clinton Proposes Drug-Testing Plan for Young People," *The New York Times* (Oct. 20, 1996).

745   Johnston and Weiner, *supra.*

746   David Frum, "When the Economy Turns," *The Weekly Standard* (Feb. 1999).

747   Alexander, *supra.*

748   William J. Clinton, "The Freedom to Die" (1993).

749   "Dr. Bill Cosby Speaks at the 50th Anniversary Commemoration of the Brown vs Topeka Board of Education Supreme Court Decision" (2004).

750   Wickham, *supra,* at 49.

751   *Id.*

752   David Milne, "Hitchens dying by his own poison pen," *The Sunday Herald,* May 23, 1999.

753   Kennedy, "Lani Guinier's Constitution," *supra.*

754 Paul Greenberg, *No Surprises: Two Decades of Clinton-Watching* (Brassey's, 1996), p. 136.

755 George Stephanoupolos, *All Too Human* (Back Bay, 2000), p. 66.

756 Morris, *Because He Could, supra,* at 7.

757 Takiff, *supra,* at 59.

758 Takiff, *supra.*

759 Rebecca Mercy, "6 Signs Which Mean That That 'Complicated' Guy Is Actually A Huge Douche-Nozzle," *VixenDaily* (June 22, 2015).

760 Stephanopoulos, *supra,* at 96.

761 *Id.,* at 214.

762 John Ryle, "A sorry apology from Clinton," *The Guardian* (April 13, 1998).

763 Robert McCrum, "Still pressing the flesh," *The Guardian* (June 27, 2004).

764 Takiff, *supra,* at 72.

765 *Id.,* at 71.

766 Greenberg, *supra,* at 17.

767 *Id.,* at 86.

768 Randall Bennett Woods, *J. William Fulbright, Vietnam, and the Search for a Cold War Foreign Policy,* 13.

769 Phil McCombs, "An 88-Candle Salute to Senator Fulbright; On His Birthday, a Presidential Award," *The Washington Post* (May 6, 1993).

770 Deroy Murdock, "Dems Need to Houseclean," *National Review* (Jan. 6, 2003).

771 Guinier, *Lift Every Voice, supra,* at 52.

772 Andrew Rosenthal, "Clinton Says Golfing at All-White Club Was Mistake," *The New York Times* (March 21, 1992).

773 Ryan Lizza, "Let's Be Friends," *The New Yorker* (Sept. 10, 2012).

774 Cockburn, *supra.*

775 Carter, *supra,* at 31.

776 Martin Jay, "Mendacious Flowers," *The London Review of Books* (July 29, 1999).

777 "Professor tells fund-raiser Clinton 'exploited' blacks," *The Washington Times* (April 30, 2002).

INDEX

About *Current Affairs*

C URRENT AFFAIRS IS A BIMONTHLY PRINT MAGAZINE OF
political commentary, journalism, and satire. It's a fresh,
fearless, and independent antidote to contemporary political media. We focus on challenging preconceptions and
undermining orthodoxies. *Current Affairs* showcases some of the
country's best contemporary writers, and is edited by a highly experienced team of professionals with backgrounds in law, litera-
ture, design, technology, and politics. We bring a sharp critical eye
to the absurdities of modern American life, and provide a new and
unique set of perspectives on major political issues.

currentaffairs.org